"Come to My Sunland"

Florida History and Culture Series

Florida History and Culture Series
Series Editors: Gary R. Mormino, Raymond Arsenault

The Florida History and Culture Series comprises important works written to promote an understanding of the state's rich history and diversity. Accessible and attractively designed, the books in this series contribute a historical perspective to studies focusing on the environment, politics, literature, material culture, and cultural studies.

Other books in this series:
Al Burt, Jr., *Al Burt's Florida: Snowbirds, Sand Castles, and Self-Rising Crackers*
Marvin Dunn, *Black Miami in the Twentieth Century*
Glen Simmons and Laura Ogden, *Gladesmen: Gator Hunters, Moonshiners, and Skiffers*

"Come to My Sunland"

Letters of Julia Daniels Moseley
from the Florida Frontier,
1882–1886

Edited by Julia Winifred Moseley
and Betty Powers Crislip

University Press of Florida
Gainesville Tallahassee Tampa Boca Raton
Pensacola Orlando Miami Jacksonville

03 02 01 00 99 98   6 5 4 3 2 1

Figure page i: Bookplate of Julia Daniels Moseley, made by her son
Carl and presented to her on Christmas Day, 1904.
Figure page iii: Photograph of Julia Daniels Moseley,
set in burnt-wood frame she designed.
Figure page vi: Script of Julia Daniels Moseley.

LIBRARY OF CONGRESS CATALOGING-IN-PUBLICATION DATA
Moseley, Julia Daniels, 1849-1917
Come to my sunland: letters of Julia Daniels Moseley from the Florida frontier,
1882-1886 / edited by Julia Winifred Moseley and Betty Powers Crislip.
p. cm. — (Florida history and culture series)
Includes bibliographical references (p.   ) and index.
ISBN 0-8130-1605-3 (cloth: alk. paper)
1. Moseley, Julia Daniels, 1849-1917—Correspondence. 2. Women pioneers—
Florida—Limona—Correspondence. 3. Frontier and pioneer life—Florida—
Limona. 4. Limona (Fla.)—Biography. I. Moseley, Julia Winifred. II. Crislip,
Betty Powers. III. Title. IV. Series.
F319.L56M67 1998
975.9'65—dc21 98-17500

The University Press of Florida is the scholarly publishing agency for the State
University System of Florida, comprising Florida A & M University, Florida
Atlantic University, Florida International University, Florida State University,
University of Central Florida, University of Florida, University of North
Florida, University of South Florida, and University of West Florida.

University Press of Florida
15 Northwest 15th Street
Gainesville, FL 32611
http://nersp.nerdc.ufl.edu/~upf

To the dearest friend of my life, Charles S. Moseley:
"Age cannot wither it."

To be saved for our children, Karl and Hallock.
—Julia Daniels Moseley
(written on first page of book of copied letters)

To Frindy, who saved the letters from the burning log cabin.
—Julia Winifred Moseley

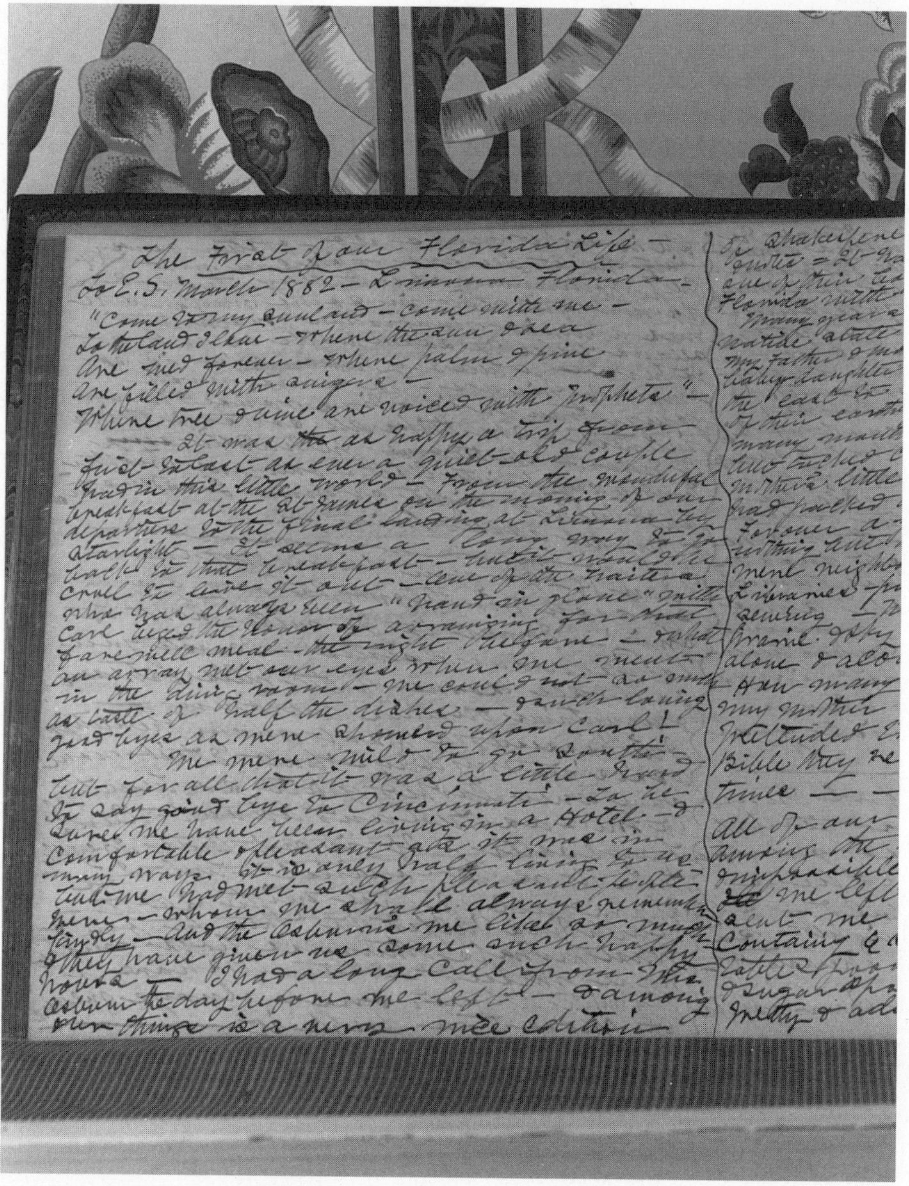

The First of our Florida Life —
to E.S. March 1882 — Lemuna Florida —

"Come to my sunland — come with me —
To the land I love — where the sun & sea
Are wed forever — where palm & pine
Are filled with singers —
Where tree & vine are voiced with prophets" —

It was the as happy a trip from
first to last as ever a quiet old couple
had in this little world — From the wonderful
breakfast at the St James on the morning of our
departure to the final landing at Lemuna by
starlight — It seems a long way to go
back to that breakfast — but it would be
cruel to leave it out — like of the waiter
who was always seen "hand in glove" quite —
Carl used the honor of arranging for their
farewell meal — the night before we started —
an array met our eyes when we went
in the dining room — we could not see one
as little as half the dishes — such loving
good eyes as were showered upon Carl!

We were mild to go south
till for all that it was a little raw —
to say good bye to Cincinnati — In the
surer we have been living in a Hotel — &
comfortable & pleasant as it was in
many ways, it is anything but like to us
but we had met such pleasant people
here — whom we should always remember
fondly — And the Osburns we liked so much
they have given us some such happy
hours — I had a long call from Mrs
Osburn the day before we left — & among
our things is a very nice cushion

[right column, partially cut off]
the Shakespere
notte — & it was
one of their ...
Florida with

Many years
another aunt
my father & mo
really daughter
the care &
of their earth
many month
And those w
in their little
had walked ...
forever a
nothing until
were neighbor
Lemunas fr
sewing — ...
served — D...
alone & alo
How many
my mother
gratitude & G
Bible they ...
times —

All of our
anxious th...
unspeakable
& we left
sent me
containing &
little Fran
& sugar ...
pretty & adv...

Contents

Illustrations

Photographs Following Page 200

During the past half century, Florida's burgeoning population and its increased national and international visibility have sparked a great deal of popular interest in the state's history. As the favorite destination of countless tourists and the new home of millions of retirees and other migrants, modern Florida has become a demographic, political, and cultural bellwether. Unfortunately, however, the volume and quality of literature showcasing Florida's distinctive heritage and character have not kept pace with popular interest in the Sunshine State.

In an effort to remedy this situation—to provide an accessible and attractive format for the publication of Florida-related books—the University Press of Florida has established the Florida History and Culture Series. As coeditors of the series, we are committed to the creation of an eclectic but carefully crafted set of books that will provide a new focus for the field of Florida studies while encouraging Florida researchers and writers to consider the broader implications and context of their work. The series will include monographs, works of synthesis, memoirs, and anthologies. Although its predominant focus will be on books of historical interest, we also encourage authors researching Florida's environment, politics, literature, and popular or material culture to submit manuscripts. We want each book in the series to retain a distinct character and voice; at the same time, we hope to foster a sense of community and collaboration among Florida scholars.

"Come to My Sunland": Letters of Julia Daniels Moseley from the Florida Frontier, 1882–1886 is the fourth volume in the series. The book documents and illustrates the life and adventures of a remarkable woman who migrated to Florida in the late nineteenth century. It begins amid the political climate of March 1882, when the raucous leaders of the Gilded Age—from Chester A. Arthur and James G. Blaine to Andrew Carnegie and John D. Rockefeller—were busy transforming America into an urban, industrial power.

But the hurly-burly of Wall Street and Capitol Hill went almost unnoticed by Julia Daniels Moseley, a young Illinois woman then reporting and recording detailed observations of her new home in Limona, Florida. Her collected letters from the years 1882 to 1886 provide an extraordinary portrait of Florida during a period of profound change and adjustment. From first words to last thoughts, she offers us an intimate view of both her exterior and interior life, a dual biography of a distinctive place and a complex individual.

The Julia Moseley who emerges from these letters was a frontierswoman and a naturalist, a mother and a daughter, a lover and a friend, a writer and an inveterate raconteur. Her first letter conveys the rapturous joy of a traveler in a strange but exciting new land:

> Come to my sunland—come with me—
> To the land I love
> Where the sun and sea are wed forever—
> Where palm and pine are filled with singers—
> Where tree and vine are voiced with prophets.

In 1882 Charles Scott Moseley, an executive with the Elgin Watch Company, moved his family from Elgin, Illinois, to the frontier town of Limona in west central Florida. The Elgin company had purchased a large tract of land in Limona in the 1870s, hoping to create a winter colony adorned with citrus groves. An isolated rural community located ten miles east of the village of Tampa, Limona stood in a sparsely settled hinterland, a rugged but awe-inspiring backwater filled with natural springs, meandering streams, and subtropical wildlife.

When the Moseleys moved to Limona, they left behind a community that was both larger (Elgin's population in 1880 was 10,057) and more sophisticated than any Florida city. But Scott's severe asthmatic condition had compelled him to seek the healing powers of the Florida sun. Stimulated by the favorable accounts of Florida boosters like Sidney Lanier, he arranged to spend as much time as possible in the Sunshine State, despite the demands of a career that frequently took him away from Limona and left his wife and children alone.

The physical and social challenges of nineteenth-century Florida exacted a heavy toll on many pioneers, but Julia Moseley countered the inevitable impositions with vigorous activity, mental acuity, and a spirited temperament. Florida emboldened her, and with the zest of a frontier scout she explored the region's bayous and scrub lands. Classically educated, she embellished her reports of her Florida encounters with literary allusions and musings. She was influenced by writers such as pre-Raphaelite William Morris and naturalist Henry David Thoreau.

Julia shared her experiences in the frequent letters she wrote to Eliza Slade, a lifelong friend who remained in the relative security of "civilized" Elgin. After killing a fox in 1884, Julia triumphantly observed: "Think of it, my girl. While you are in the heart of a town, I'm in the wilderness and rising in the dead of night to help slay wild beasts. . . . Beauty is a power." One can only imagine the bemusement of her Illinois friend after reading Julia's 1883 Christmas letter: "We had our dinner out-of-doors," a proud Julia declared, "with morning glories on the table." On another occasion she reported, in a less celebratory vein, "We have roaches here that if they could be trained are large enough for watch dogs."

Although Limona was sparsely inhabited in the 1880s, the Moseleys enjoyed the camaraderie of an amazing group of neighbors. Fellow pioneers included the enigmatic Frederic Weightnovel, a Russian émigré who practiced medicine, advocated free love, and frequented Tampa's fledgling opera house. "I shouldn't like him often," Julia confessed, "but once in a while I enjoy him very much." She also treasured the companionship of robust Clementine Averill, a "New Hampshire old maid Utopian," who worked with "Northerners who came here half dead with weak lungs or old backs or worn-out chests or softening of the brain." The granddaughter of abolitionists, Julia also offered generally sympathetic commentary on the region's African Americans. With the exception of pioneer neighbors who became friends, she was less charitable to the local white *crackers*, whom she described as "thin, cadaverous looking people."

The Moseleys arrived in Limona at the end of the pioneer era. Indeed, the roar of a "sunset gun" punctuated the stillness of their first night in Limona. Fired at Fort Brooke, the cannon traditionally signaled day's end on the eastern shore of Tampa Bay. But as Julia soon discovered, this quaint custom was coming to an end. In 1882 Fort Brooke was deactivated as an obsolescent relic of the frontier, symbolizing the profound changes that were transforming the region into an aspiring New South metropolis. In the five-year span during which Julia Moseley composed her letters, Henry Plant's railroad linked Tampa to the outside world, entrepreneurs established Port Tampa and the cigar-making community of Ybor City, and wild-cat prospectors began to dredge the mineral-rich Alafia and Peace Rivers for phosphate. In the new Tampa clocks and timetables, not sunset guns or morning glories, marked time.

As the editors of the Florida History and Culture Series, we are grateful to Julia Winifred Moseley and Betty Crislip for their careful transcription of Julia Daniels Moseley's letters. The "lady of Limona" has been found, and the experiences and insights of this talented and observant late-nineteenth-century pioneer deserve our attention and respect.

Raymond Arsenault
Gary R. Mormino
Series Editors

Preface

Julia Daniels Moseley's letters add a welcome and needed richness of detail to our understanding of a portion of 1880s Florida. Moseley tells us exactly how the Tampa Bay region looked, sounded, smelled, and felt to her. Through her words we meet this delightful woman and her family—perhaps, in the process, ridding ourselves of any stereotypical ideas about what pioneer Florida was really like.

Private writings of women continue to add immeasurably to our knowledge of former times, particularly when they have been written by homemakers. However, readers of most of these discovered manuscripts find they must engage themselves with two authors: the diary or journal writer and her editor. Often the editor must try to fill in vital information because portions of the manuscript have been lost or because little is known about the author. Rarely do we have the opportunity to see one of these women whole through only her eyes.

Moseley's letters require no editor because she filled that function herself, selecting and copying from her voluminous correspondence only those letters she wanted to preserve. Her unchanged selection is included here, beginning with her trip down the Mississippi River to Florida.

Moseley's letters differ from the private writings of many of her contemporaries because she celebrates her frontier life and family, whereas letters by other pioneers were often an outlet for dissatisfactions, conflicts, or loneliness. Moseley was fortunate to have had two companions with whom she could share her innermost self—her husband Scott and her lifelong best friend Eliza Slade.

A gregarious woman, Moseley introduces us to her remarkably cosmopolitan and diverse circle of friends. For the Limona community was also home to a Russian exile, a New England Utopian spinster, a university psychology professor turned citrus grower, and several entrepreneurs—as well as to settlers who had arrived earlier from the southern states. Along with the 1954 notes of Julia's daughter Florence, the oral traditions preserved by her granddaughter Julia Winifred Moseley, and the notes by Betty Powers Crislip, also reared on Ten Mile Lake, this book becomes a social history of the Limona community and its neighboring settlements on Florida's west coast.

Although Julia Daniels Moseley copied her selected letters as a memento for her children, she would probably not be offended that her brown-leather journal is being shared with other readers as well. Her letters reveal that she took great delight in reading the collected letters of others and, on reflection, she would probably not want to deny us a similar opportunity. Ironically, on the back of her journal's title page she copied these words: "She carries some small litter in her reticule which she calls her documents." Although always aware of her lack of formal training, she could hardly have viewed her letters as small litter. Neither will today's readers.

Many people have helped make this book a reality. The Moseleys and the Coes were fast friends in pioneer times, and much of the expense for the book's preparation has been underwritten as a memorial to the Limona Coe family by two direct descendants, Dorothy Coe Penn and Jean Coe Maynard. Dabney Adams Hart and Charlotte McClure, associate professors emerita of Georgia State University, read the letters at an early stage and strongly recommended their publication. Hillsborough residents Samuel A. Davis and his daughter Lona Davis Spencer, Nancy Maxwell Gentry, Joyce Washington, and Paul and Betty Dinnis read the manuscript and offered their insights on local history. Paul Kott's invaluable technical support rescued the initial computer transcription. Gloria and Judy Deese, Lewis Ellsworth, Peter and Renee Roos, and Scott Stephenson provided significant assistance in photograph preparation. To all of them, and to others who have encouraged this venture, our many thanks.

Introduction

The land that drew Julia Daniels and Charles Scott Moseley to Florida was east of Tampa, a growing town on Tampa Bay. The push of settlers from 1848 to 1860 had changed southwest Florida from sheer wilderness to a more penetrable land. Even so, when the Moseleys arrived in 1882 most of the roads were still sandy trails, and a railroad was several years away.

Tampa, or Fort Brooke as the area was called, after the fort established in 1824 at the outset of the Seminole Wars, had been accessible by boat and a network of military roads that fanned out to other posts. In the backcountry near Tampa, a few pioneers had settled in the hammocks, around lakes, near rivers, and on the occasional slight hill. Large, 160-acre tracts had been homesteaded by these scattered settlers, each of whom was required to clear five acres and put up a cabin. Throughout the 1870s and 1880s, new settlers bought land, cleared it, harvested timber, and planted vegetables and citrus. Some prospered by running cattle on vast tracts of unfenced land.

Stories of enticing weather began to be circulated to other sections of the country by word of mouth—first by early settlers, then by sailors and soldiers returning from the Civil War, and later through real estate agents' brochures and the published accounts of travelers. In Tampa the Orange Grove Hotel, originally constructed by wealthy cattleman William B. Hooker as a large residence, became known for its hospitality and for the

1. Numerous paths, long cart roads, and wagon trails wound through the thick hammocks and wetlands as well as through the higher pine woods. This sandy wagon trail led to the Durant area east of The Nest. The figure in the distance is Maude Pierce, a close friend of Julia Daniels Moseley. Ca. 1905–1909.

orange trees Hooker had planted around it. Sidney Lanier, poet and author of a Florida guidebook, stayed there with his wife in 1876; enraptured by the climate and by the oranges he could almost pick from his window, he wrote glowing letters telling of the beneficial Gulf Coast air.

Tampa's immediate easterly growth was limited by the federal government's ownership of Fort Brooke. East of the fort, however, a number of sparse, small settlements grew up, including Limona, where the Moseleys located. Limona, which took its name from the Spanish word for lemon, was established in 1876 by Joseph Gillette Knapp, a Wisconsin judge who had served the territory of New Mexico by appointment of Abraham Lincoln. His primary Florida interests were growing citrus, bringing in others interested in orange culture, and promoting the economic benefits of the climate. He was joined by E. E. Pratt, a surveyor and foreman of the Elgin Watch Company, who had been sent to find suitable Florida land for a winter retreat and for growing citrus. These men put Limona on the map.

In 1883 the U.S. government released the Fort Brooke property. This land did not go to Tampa and claims for it were in the courts for years afterwards; nevertheless, Tampa entered into a boom period. Henry B. Plant had brought his railroad to Tampa in 1883, and it was expected that Plant's railroad would do for Florida's west coast what Henry B. Flagler's was doing for the east coast. Plant's epicurean dream of the Tampa Bay Hotel was on the horizon.

Tampa had much to offer visitors and settlers alike. The town was becoming well established, with churches, schools, a courthouse, banks, trading establishments, an opera house, and a band. Above all, Tampa held the promise of a good port and exchange with Cuba, the Caribbean islands, and South America. No matter if residents still waded in deep sand in Tampa's streets; the area would shortly be known for its thriving fishing trade, an ice house with home delivery, and Ybor City, with its cigar makers and Latin culture.

Inland settlers were soon to have more rapid communication and trade as a result of the new railroad. For a brief period, however, the Moseleys would hear the nightly boom of the reactivated Fort Brooke cannon echoing across the pine flatwoods into their log cabin home, The Nest.

Come to My Sunland looks into the life of Julia Moseley as she embarked on her grand undertaking in 1882. She wrote about those days in letters to

2. Julia Daniels Moseley, ca. 1874.

her husband Scott and to her dearest friend, Eliza Slade. The Florida of her time was indeed a land of legend and to live there was an adventure.

Julia was not a beautiful woman, but she had presence. Although she stood barely five feet tall, people noticed her, often forming a first impression of her as a tall, stately woman. She remembered fondly a remark made by her uncle Bourland, the husband of her beautiful aunt Jule and a favorite uncle passionately fond of beauty and beauties. Seeing her as a girl of fourteen dressed in a shimmering pink tarlatan dress, her garlanded arms upraised in a June tableau (she knew her arms and neck were her strongest points), he had said, "I don't see how anyone could have looked at anything else after seeing our little Jule." He had often told Julia that she was the only girl who wasn't handsome that he had ever loved.

The second impression people received was of her clear, hazel eyes, shining with incredible interest and sympathy. Whether she was looking at a general or a boy in the street, a grand-opera singer or a woman working in the kitchen, whoever fell under Julia's gaze felt befriended.

The third impression was of her hair. Thick and smooth, it flowed over her head like a manifestation of her copious energy. It was of an astonishing hue and luster—from the red locks of babyhood, to the dark braids of youth and middle age, to the white glow of mature life.

An artistic woman with a verve for living, Julia reveled in the judicious use of color. Red was one of her favorites. She used its vibrancy for the excitement it brought to her pulses and the courage it gave her. On a white dress she would wear a red bow. Christmas and birthday presents for relatives and friends were dimes polished to whiteness, exquisitely wrapped in circles of bright red tissue paper topped with twisted fringes. The edges of her shelves she tipped in vermilion. She wove red into basketry and embroidery and used touches of red paint to decorate one of her finest achievements, a Persian-like wall covering of native Florida palmetto fiber.

The embodiment of great personal charm and fancy, she put her roots firmly down into the Florida soil. She was a Renaissance woman and a cosmopolitan in the wilderness.

Julia's parents, Elizabeth Preston and Carlos M. Daniels, had eight children. In this large, loving family, Julia early learned the value of an organized household. Her mother was quick in her ways and Julia inherited this trait. Elizabeth Preston Daniels had a great love of reading and a fabulous memory. Before she and her young husband set out for the West, her mother tucked into her trunk a copy of the Bible and a volume of Shakespeare's plays. Isolated on an Illinois farm during their first winter, the couple read through the Bible seven times and lost count of the times they read each play. Later, ministers delighted in questioning Mrs. Daniels on obscure Bible passages; she never failed to identify their sources.

Julia's mother remained a great reader while her children were growing up. If she had no time to read during a busy day, she always read for an hour before going to bed. Whenever her children asked her about history, travel, mythology, geography, or art, she could tell them something about each subject. Julia's character was shaped by this gracious woman, whom she daily observed making important family decisions in her husband's absence, as well as by her urbane aunts in Peoria. She had a background of the cultivated East overlain by the rambunctious West.

Julia's aunt Jule in Peoria exerted a special kind of influence on Julia, exposing her to the pre-Raphaelite painters. In her aunt's home Julia heard their ideas being discussed and saw samples of their decorative art. Visitors from England familiar with the movement also shared their ideas regarding the pre-Raphaelites.

Later, in Florida, Julia would apply these same principles to home decorating. She borrowed her designs, as well as some of her materials, from nature. The spiritual feeling of beauty and the love of Florida's natural environment, combined with its primitive heritage, stirred her senses. She felt that in Florida she was in her true element. From Rossetti, William Morris, and particularly Edward Burne-Jones, she drew much of her inspiration.

From her father, one of the few doctors in the newly opened territories of Missouri and Illinois and a man who always responded to a call, Julia learned to be fearless in times of illness and emergency. Her sympathies were easily aroused, but her father taught her how to be of the most immediate help. She learned the bones of the human body from his doctor's skeleton. She watched him mix medicines, and was fascinated by his skill in dressing cuts and wounds. In this family where strong feelings and opinions prevailed, she heard her father discuss the ideas of the day.

Julia met her future husband Scott in her hometown of Elgin, Illinois. She had returned to the family circle there from the cultivated home of her aunt Jule, ready to begin her mature life. Both her family and Scott's were Elginites, part of the push of pioneers into Illinois from the eastern states. Their paths crossed early through the flow of family and acquaintances. An inventor, Scott had worked for almost every watch factory in the country and was then superintendent of the Elgin Watch Company. When they met he was pouring his inventive genius into the development of assembly-line procedures for the production of finely tuned watches.

The son of a New England family from Westfield, Massachusetts, Scott was a genial man with a deep-seated love of nature and good literature. He had lost his first wife, but he loved Julia with a passion equally shared and enveloping them both. He wooed her with flowers and choice wild Indian pipes. She sent him pressed flowers, deep pink morning glories, and scented grasses.

Scott was the man who stood tall in Julia's life, his influence forever felt and treasured. When his look first fell on her, she knew it was the beginning of her true life. They matched, although he was forty-eight years old and she but twenty-six. He wrote to her every day when they were apart. Her letters to him were like a kaleidoscopic journal of shared thoughts, interspersed with snatches of favorite quotations, rather than a prosaic report of her days. Her prose sang like poetry. On May 18, 1876, Scott and Julia were

3. Charles Scott Moseley, ca.
1865.

married in Julia's father's house by a Universalist minister, the father of her good friend Eliza Slade.

By 1882 Julia and Scott felt it was time to embark on their own pioneer adventure. Their decision to move to Florida had not been made lightly: Scott's health was of grave concern. An asthmatic, he had recently suffered severe, recurring attacks. His two older children Frindy and Claude had inherited this propensity, and he had sent Claude to California when the boy was five, hoping the climate there might help. Now Julia and Scott wanted a suitable home for all.

In addition, there were Scott's business concerns. He had left the Elgin National Company, relinquishing his patent royalties to the company so its employees could benefit from his inventions. He now sought work as a consultant with other watch-making companies, helping them design more efficient assembly-line procedures. Creative ideas were throbbing through his mind, and he needed time to develop them.

Florida beckoned. After first temporizing with the idea of going to California, Julia and Scott responded to Florida's call, guided by the advice of some acquaintances and their knowledge of the state's geography and geology. They embarked for Limona.

Eons ago, when landmasses were being laid down, Florida had become the distinguishing long finger protruding from the southeastern end of North America. Tardily rising from and sinking back into the warm waters of the Gulf of Mexico and the colder Atlantic, Florida consisted mostly of sand and limestone. Each rising and falling had left distinguishable terraces, the last of which were clearly visible in the area east of Tampa Bay, where Julia and Scott settled.

Standing in the flatwoods formed from an old submerged estuary, they could look over thousands of acres and see the rim of the uplands, a relic seashore. Like water, the low land appeared to flow inward, seemingly loath to say good-bye to the Gulf. Water still stood over much of the area during the rainy season, and in the uplands sinkhole lakes gleamed. Julia and Scott found this land enchanting—much as Ponce de Leon had when he named

4. This round sinkhole lake was a favorite spot in Limona. Judge Knapp lived nearby in a log cabin he acquired in 1876. 1911.

5. Humorous watercolor sketch of the original Nest painted by Julia Daniels Moseley after the log cabin burned. Stumps of burned pines in the foreground, hovering rain clouds, and a buzzard flying overhead denote Julia's mood following this tragedy.

it "La Florida," a land of flowers. And they recognized the sinkhole lakes' salutary effect on mind and climate.

On these uplands, ten miles from Tampa on the old Indian trail to Fort Brooke was a piece of property held by Silas A. Jones, a relative of Judge Joseph Gillette Knapp, who had established Limona. Jones had become active as a real estate investor in Tampa and Limona. On this land stood a substantial but unfinished log cabin, erected by a prosperous planter before the Civil War and later abandoned. It had been used as a church until a new structure called New Hope Church was built farther east. That area would later be called Brandon in honor of the pioneer John Brandon, who arrived

6. North end of the Palm, showing the completed wall covering Julia made from the fiber of the saw palmetto, *Serenoa repens*, as a gift for her husband Scott (1886). Her attention to detail is apparent in the covered and decorated beam, almost hidden by the frieze surrounding the room.

in 1857. The cabin also had served briefly as a school where another relative of Knapp's had been a teacher. Although left unfinished it was beautiful, solid, and well built, awaiting another transformation into the Moseley homestead.

Julia and Scott fell in love with the spot. Even though they knew it would require hours of patient work to get the house to their liking, they bought it for the promise it held and for what they felt they could accomplish. They worked together, Scott designing and constructing some of the furniture with built-in lounges and cupboards. He finished the loft and the kitchen. Knowing what rugs, books, and "trinkets" could do for their home, they eagerly unpacked their boxes. Julia had a dream now, an incessant Florida dream of creating a wonderful palmetto-fiber wall covering for Scott. It danced in her imagination.

The seed of Julia's dream had been planted in her mind when she and Scott first explored the land close to them, enjoying the hammocks and the beautiful palm trees, and admiring the lowly saw palmetto. They appreciated the color of the wondrous fiber that surrounds and protects each new saw-palmetto frond and experimented with various uses for their fiber. Then one night as they lay in bed, Julia exclaimed, "Scott, I can make you a wall of this fiber." His succinct reply was, "Jule, it will take you a hundred years."

But these two could not have foreseen that their cabin would be lost in an early December morning fire, and that the fulfillment of Julia's dream would hang instead on the walls of the second Moseley homestead, which in 1886 would rise Phoenix-like from the ashes of the first. Instead of a hundred years, she had accomplished the wall in one year while Scott was absent in the North on business. Nor could they have foreseen that portions of the wall covering would be exhibited in the Agricultural Building, Florida Space, at the 1893 Chicago World's Fair. And not even by the utmost stretch of the imagination could they have known that the palmetto-fiber wall covering would last well over a century, remaining a unique achievement.

At the beginning of their Florida adventure, Julia and Scott threw themselves into establishing their first Florida home, where they could joyfully gather their family together again. Carl, dubbed "Carl of Lancaster" for the city of his birth, was joined from the North by Frindy and Claude, Scott's children from his first marriage. By the next summer another son, Hal or "Hallock of Florida," would join their family circle. These were wonderfully happy days—early days in Florida with their joy in each other, in their united family, and in the new home they were working so hard to complete.

In both her home and dress Julia expressed her freedom of thought and her sense of utility and beauty. The clothing she made, from underwear to comfortable red houseboots, reflected her own style. While other ladies dressed in ankle-length outfits with matching bonnets or great plumed hats and parasols, Julia shortened her skirts for outdoor rambles and work projects. She swept cobwebs in a special attire fit for the job. When they had a lawn, she mowed it in the rain in a bathing suit. Although her senses delighted in rich fabrics, she saved these for special dresses. She treasured old lace, writing that being half hidden in it was her only chance of looking handsome. Scott said that no matter what she wore, it took on a quaint air the moment it touched her.

Nor did Julia neglect her men in her sewing. While other men wore fine suits, high collars, and starched shirts for all business and church events, Scott dressed in the soft linen shirts and loose cotton jackets Julia made for general wear. She dressed her boys in the customary clothes—first skirts, then suits, then knickerbockers or long pants. But she also designed and made numerous informal and comfortable play clothes for them. Ahead of her time, she sewed extra pockets on a separate belt to be worn at the waist, ready to hold the gatherings of a boy's fancy.

She had learned to prepare many foods during the course of her marriage, carrying only one recipe in her head—that of a rich, chocolate dessert that required a dozen eggs. She now could turn her hand to anything that came her way—meat, fowl, fish, vegetables, fruit, homemade bread, and the mainstay peas and beans. She knew how to dress fowl, scale fish, and skin game. She welcomed these new challenges in the new land. But her utilitarian skills went hand in hand with her talent for fancier cookery: the chewy chocolates made late at night over a hot bed of coals in the log cabin's great clay-and-stick chimney, the rain and wind whispering outside; or the cups of hot chocolate served with whipped cream and mint leaves after she and Scott had spent a comfortable evening reading to each other.

Her love of beauty was a driving force in Julia's life. Without beauty surrounding her, she grew positively ill. Dr. Weightnovel, the Russian doctor who cared for her, recognized this, saying of one of her arrangements of wildflowers and foliage, "They are your necessities." Disliking mundane tasks, she let her imagination transform the drudgery of household work into stories. From early childhood she had absorbed the great fairy tales, reading them herself or listening as her cousin Clarence related them to her at her aunt Jule's when she could not sleep. Even as an adult, if she had peas to pick she named each group as it rolled off the pod, consigning it to the pot. Or she would imagine that a big goblin had ordered her to do a terrible task; if she did not complete it the goblin would call out, "Off with her head." She also used pet names for everything around her, and these became the fashion in the family.

Besides relying on her imagination to ease her workload, Julia was an efficient time manager. Early in her marriage she had developed the habit of recording her sewing accomplishments so that by the end of the year she could look at the work and feel satisfied. She learned to cut out five or six things at a time and sew them all at once. She also kept track of both incoming and outgoing correspondence.

When she couldn't spend time with the children Julia used a ticket system to schedule free periods during which she could give each child her undivided attention. She had learned early to cut out articles she wished to read; she slipped these scrolled papers into her pockets and read them when she was waiting for stagecoaches, wagons, or trains. Thus she ensured that her top priorities did not get lost. She was renowned in the family for organizing, for seeing through the confusion of too many projects, and for keeping things simple to handle them tidily.

When she was working on a project, Julia was able to help those around her who were slower without impeding her own progress. During the creation of the palmetto-fiber wall she laid out her work each evening, threading up a dozen needles and placing nearby the next pieces she wanted to work on. Frindy was delegated to read to her every afternoon while she worked without stopping.

However, she put aside everything else to be with her husband, for the hours spent with Scott were her golden hours.

Behind the curtain of Julia's skill and imagination lay a truth she could not avoid. The shadow of that feeling was with her even as her love leaped up to transform it. She revealed it in a letter to Eliza:

Do not breathe it to a living soul, it must remain a secret always but I abhor a needle. I loathe nine-tenths of things that go to make up the daily round of a woman's life. And if it were not for Scott and the children I'd rather die than plod through the days. Never from baby-hood did one little dream of the future hold anything bordering on monotony or drudgery. But you see I love Scott. I love him even be-yond my own fancies, my fondest ideals. A thousand things that but for that would make my life unbearable, I really find joy in. So in it all I breathe the breath of my love. I color it with the poetry of romance, and common things grow radiant. I can hardly keep from screeching sometimes when people say of certain vanities of work, "Now if I loved it as you do." How little they know the tricks I play with my fancy. How loud I have to call upon Hope to light the way for me through the dreary round of daily duty. Thank God the world can find a fair result in that my Love says, "You make my life brighter than my dreams."

If we could look through a window into the dear old Nest on any given day, we would find there waiting for us a table set with white cloth and a few choice dishes, flowers and vines mingling among them; and we would hear the conversation of Julia Daniels Moseley as she entertained us with stories of her time. These letters are our window.

chapter 1

Florida, Here We Come

March 1882, Limona, Florida—
The First of Our Florida Life

To E.S.[1]

Come to my sunland—come with me—
To the land I love
Where the sun and sea are wed forever—
Where palm and pine are filled with singers—
Where tree and vine are voiced with prophets.[2]

It was as happy a trip from first to last as ever a quiet old couple had in this
little world, from the wonderful breakfast at the St. James on the morning
of our departure to the final landing at Limona by starlight. It seems a long
way to go back to that breakfast but it would be cruel to leave it out. One of
the waiters who has always been "hand in glove" with Carl begged the
honor of arranging for that farewell meal the night before. What an array
met our eyes when one went in the dining room. We could not so much as
taste of half the dishes and such loving good-byes as were showered upon
Carl! We were wild to go south but for all that it was a little hard to say
goodbye to Cincinnati. To be sure we had been living in a hotel, and com-

fortable and pleasant as it was in many ways it is only half living to us, but we had met such pleasant people there whom one should always remember fondly. The Osbornes we liked so much and they have given us such happy hours. I had a long call from Mrs. Osborne the day before we left. And among our things is a very nice edition of Shakespeare—nice in its completeness and notes. It had been through Yale with one of their boys and is going through Florida with us.

Many years ago when my native state was "way out West," my father and mother and their delicate baby daughter Frances went from the East to Illinois. Nearly all of their earthly possessions were many months in reaching them. But tucked carefully away in my mother's little trunk grandmother had packed a Bible and Shakespeare. For over a year they had absolutely nothing but those books, which were neighbors, friends, newspapers, libraries, pictures, even knitting and sewing to them. They had nothing beside but each other, prairie and sky. They read them alone and aloud to each other. How many times they read Shakespeare my mother said they never pretended to count. But the Bible they read through seven times.[3]

All of our silver was stored among the things in Lancaster and impossible to get. Just before we left Cincinnati Mrs. Osborne sent me a little package containing six silver forks, teaspoons, tablespoons, mustard, salt and sugar spoons. They are so pretty and add so much to the most precious "china closet" in all Florida.

We started in the morning—which is the time to start always. We went but a short distance by rail and then took a boat and floated down the Ohio for a time. We passed President Harrison's grave, a little glimmer of white on a hillside among the evergreens. At Aurora we took the cars again. We had thought the water overflow at Cincinnati something to be wondered at. But it seemed nothing beside the mighty overflow for some hundreds of miles—countless homes abandoned, many with only the roofs visible above the water.

Way out in this wilderness of trees and water a little steamer came puffing out to take us on board and such a time as we had getting started. We had to make two or three starts to get clear of trees. Even then all along the way we had to stop to have branches cut off to let us pass.

At Cairo we were transferred to a larger boat and away we went down the Mississippi. And how beautiful it was with its cliffs and curves and wide expanse of water. About noon we were again transferred to an iron track and were flying on our way very speedily. It was Sunday and all the "Darkies" were out. Every station seemed swarming with them. For hours we went whirling through "old Kentucky." The little cabins all along the way were running over with "Darkies" and, as the chill of twilight came on, how cheery looked the fires in the old mud chimneys.[4]

The woods looked tempting enough with their little streams and ravines and great trees and mossy banks. We found plenty of places where violets hide and the first anemones.

Before nightfall we were in Mississippi. How delightful was the gradual growing of a warmer climate. When morning dawned we were in a new world—ox teams, mules and horses with well made saddles but nothing on wheels drawn by horses, fruit trees in bloom, green grass on all sides, woods full of wild plum and redbud, and here and there little early flowers. At Chatamia we saw the first barbecue ground and the first rose in bloom and a little farther on the first cowslip.

I was under the impression we were to go through Vicksburg and was so disappointed when I found I was mistaken. I have always wanted to see some spot made sacred by the war and that was associated with my brother Charlie. So many of his letters were sent from there. How well I remember the little flourish of his "l's." There are letters and there are letters, but who that has not experienced it can know the joy or the agony of a message from the war? I never sauntered when sent for my mother's letters but how I used to fly home with those, and how her little hands used to tremble in the undoing. And never was one finished with dry eyes. He was in the "thick of the fight" at Donaldson but before he slept he wrote a long letter—such a glorious letter—to his mother. It covered sixteen pages from a "secesh" account book.[5]

We passed through Jackson and could see the Capitol from the car window. On we sped, the entire length of Mississippi and then we were in Louisiana, at last in the great swamp that borders on the lake near New Orleans—cypress and pine trees covered with the gray Spanish moss, ground palmetto, tangles of vines, wild japonica, wild rice, cactus, birds and butterflies.

The foliage grew darker as the South came nearer and how beautiful and bewildering this swamp was! If there are ghouls, they spring from these dark shadows under the cypress trees and that misty shade of the gray moss. Under the blue sky and brightest sunshine it looks ghostlike and weird down there in those dark, dank recesses. What it must be on dark, rainy days, in dismal weather or on moonlight nights, I know not, but I am sure there are times when long limbed ghosts do hold high carnival in that swamp.

Then there is a sweep of gardens full of green things "fit for a queen." The train stops at a flower garden and troops of children with their misses and ladies with gay parasols come in the car laden with flowers and branches of orange blossoms. Ah! we are on the threshold of the "Crescent City." One more stop and we all clamber down and take a long breath.

We engaged a room downtown and took our meals where our fancy led us. We had a bath, a rest, and lunch. Then we strolled out in the twilight and saw beautiful homes and more than one lovely old garden. I wish I could send you a few yards of climbing roses. Think of a roof of white roses in February!

I never would be so unkind as to try and tell you all we did and saw. You would get too tired. We took little naps and rests during the noonday heat and were fresh for the rest of the time. Nothing we enjoyed more than walking up and down the streets at night. What an air of foreign life there is there! And such a gabbing in foreign tongues with faces from all over the globe. "Darkies" of all classes, from the high bred lady's maid who carries her head like a queen to the merriest little half-colored "Dark" who seems made entirely of joy and dirt. The only familiar face we saw was Henry Clay's. We met him on the square. He was bronzed from crown to back heels but we knew him at once. We spent a part of one day in riding among the homes. They are not like the fine homes of any other city I was ever in. But they were just what I wanted to find here in New Orleans.

It was charming out at the old Spanish fort. We sat hours and talked under the oak trees. We looked up the old Spanish church and rested awhile in the cool and quiet. We wandered among the strange cemeteries and through the parks. We spent hours at the levee and saw them unload oyster boats. I never saw Spanish sailors before. There were some of them that looked as if they might have fought against the English in the days of Queen "Bess." We are not the sort of travelers who stick to the beaten track and the most respectable places. Every bird store and china shop had a charm for us and our adventures and casual acquaintances driving down back streets and interesting alleys were a source of delight to us.

When I was a little girl I had a book in which was a story of "little Rosy" from the Spanish and a picture of little Rosy lying dead—with wreaths of flowers about her—and lighted candles. My first knowledge of death was in a very rigid, terrible way. To lie as did Rosy with wreaths of flowers and candles burning seemed a different matter from a darkened room and a long white sheet. As we passed down a narrow street the doors of a little house stood open, and I spied candles burning in the bright sunlight. I couldn't help it. I stepped within the room, softly and quickly, and there lay Rosy, wreathed about her the burning candles, and all alone. I stole softly out. Scott thought me very indelicate and I do not know myself but that I was. But to me there was something very lovely about it, the room so spotless, the wreaths of roses touching the very floor, the graceful dead, the lights in their long candle sticks, the open door, the morning sunlight . . .

The moon was in her full glory during our stay and enhanced every hour of our nights. We lived principally on oysters and oranges but there was one charming French restaurant where I used to get my coffee. We couldn't afford to get our meals there. It took too many "sous" but the coffee was so nice and the cups were so in keeping with my fancy that I was obliged to go. And then just to see the dame who was the grand madam of this spot was worth a good deal. She sat at one end of the room, spotless, dignified. Instinctively you bowed to her with deference, and yet it wouldn't have been hard to have thrown her a kiss. She looked kind. Underneath that inborn dignity seemed to linger a laugh.

Of course we went to the old French Market. What a morning to remember was that. We drank coffee from a shining urn before the dew was off the grass in the park just over the way. Before I was born my father spent a winter in New Orleans for a violent dyspepsia that came near being his death.[6] He says it is only dissipation that killed the men—the women never die. I never believed him until I went to market that morning. But upon my honor we saw some of the same old women that came over with the Spanish and Portuguese. There were any number that looked as if they might be seven to nine hundred years old. Ah, but that is a quaint spot, that market! Not spotless and fresh and sweet like the markets of Carl's Dutch Lancaster. They are as different as a daisy and a coconut. Bushels of squirming, pawing crabs, huge baskets of shrimps, fish as large as Carl, turtles big enough to run away with you, fruits from all over the world, hundreds of things I could not tell in half a day.

Carl was bewitching. It seemed as if all eyes followed him and everyone had a smile or word. Often someone would toss him up, saying, "Who are you, little man?" And always in a voice like a lark he would reply, "Carl of Lancaster," a reply that always won him a smile or a caress.[7] How often I wished Frindy could have seen him.[8] There are many things in New Orleans that would have pleased her dear eyes. But I doubt if one would have given her more pleasure than her little brother. The night before we left Cincinnati little Carrie Butterfield had come into our room and slipped a wee gold ring on his finger while he slept. It was hers when she was a baby but she had outgrown it and wanted Carl to have it. Tears were streaming down her cheeks and she looked so pretty and so unhappy.

I loved New Orleans. It was with real regret I stepped on the ocean steamer Mary Morgan and felt myself being borne away from all our happy days there.[9]

We enjoyed the ride down the river. For many years I had wanted to take that very trip. We passed many rice and sugar plantations. They lived like kings there once in their Southern homes with their broad piazzas and little cities of "Negro quarters" and wide fields beyond. I do not wonder they fought for slavery. The giving up meant desolation to them.[10]

The gulls followed us all the way and between three and four o'clock we entered the Gulf with a bound and by and by we were out of sight of land. The moonlight was wondrous. All the next day it was blue above and blue below. Carl seemed possessed with the spirit of a merry old "Tar." Climbing hither and thither over ropes and ladders, dancing through the cabin up to the pilot house and back, to and fro like a flash on deck, slipping in the pantry and issuing forth with fresh supplies, hanging on the steward's neck who always seemed ready for his caresses, riding on the porter's shoulders, on the best of terms with all the men from the captain down. The dearest, happiest little traveler imaginable.

Another night of perfect moonlight—a golden pathway across the Gulf. Soon after daylight land was in sight and by and by we saw the palms of the coast of Florida. The water was so beautiful. The sky above so blue and lovely, the air so soft, every breeze caressing. The palms in the blue distance had such a look of peaceful beauty that I looked up to Scott, saying, "I'm going to stay, Scott. I'm never going back." We landed at Cedar Key.[11] Some of the party were to take the train for Savannah and some going on to Cuba, we alone to wait for the Tampa boat.

We have long heard of the utter barrenness of Cedar Key but we had a good time there. I know not whether it is because we are overly wise or are not quite bright but we have a "good time" everywhere.

I walked slowly toward the hotel talking to some of our Cuba passengers who had come ashore for a stroll and Scott lingered by a basket of fruit and Carl wandered ahead. And when we reached the piazza, there Carl sat, chatting contentedly in the lap of a lady who proved to be a very pleasant acquaintance. She was from Buffalo and had come to Cedar Key on business and brought a niece with her for companionship. They knew all about Cedar Key and that was the cause of our having such a pleasant stay there. Carl has introduced me to more pleasant people than any other one person I've ever known.

We had some apple pie for dessert that excelled anything in the way of pie that I ever saw. I do not see how they did it. They must have been fine cooks for twenty generations back to have arrived at such perfection in one pie.

We spent the afternoon on the beach. I read aloud to Scott. The next day after dinner Scott and Carl took care of themselves and I went with the Buffalo lady, her niece, and a lady of the Savannah party. It was a long walk. We crossed a bridge and went on another island. We could smell the orange blossoms long before we reached the house. It was this place and its owners we had come to see. A sad little story. All that is left of a once prosperous and happy family of a Georgia planter, Capt. Harn.[12]

There were four children when the mother died and the father was married again. The daughters were educated in a convent and knew nothing of the world or care or poverty. The war came. Their property was swept away. The boys both died in the army. The father's health failed and he came to Florida in search of it, settled on that little island but in a few years died. A storm swept away the house he built but the poor whom they had been so kind to in sickness and trouble built for them the two small rooms they called home. There they lived alone, poor, helpless, two old "gentlewomen" braiding palmetto hats or any other simple thing they can do to keep the breath of life in their feeble old bodies. It was touching to see them.

One of them heard our voices and came out to meet us. They were clad like beggars but had they possessed all that heart could wish their greeting

7. The garrison at Fort Brooke, surrounded by the large oak trees that for many years marked this spot. The minarets of the Tampa Bay Hotel, later to become the University of Tampa, can be seen in the distance. Ca. 1900.

could not have been more kindly or more graceful. They were so refined and gentle, so perfectly at ease. I know not when I've been so charmed with a woman as I was with the oldest one, and what wonderful eyes she had, large, dark, pleading eyes. But such patience as looked out of them.

They know almost nothing of the world. They never seemed to have lost the innocence of childhood. All their early life was passed in a convent or on their father's plantation, surrounded by his watchful care. They seemed to worship his memory. One took us down a long path with a hedge on either side of wild jasmine and other flowers and vines to her father's grave. He lay under a canopy of vines with a large white wooden cross above. The daughter said, "He was Capt. Thomas Harn. He served his country in 1812. He helped take the battle at St. Marks. He fought under old Gen. Jackson and yet I can only give him this simple head board." "Do not let that grieve you," one of the ladies said. "This well worn path that shows how often loving feet have trod it and all these vines of flowers are more to him than the finest monument in the world." "Oh," she said, "do you suppose he does know and feels like that?" The tears stood in those beautiful eyes of hers. And another answered, "I think it is true. A monument belongs to the world but this quiet, lovely grave belongs to love alone." As she turned to lead the way back she turned to us, saying, "I am so glad I brought you here."

Those eyes of hers had a charm for me. I kept looking for them and she constantly turned her face to me all through our stay and when we left her she shook hands with us all but she bent over me and kissed me twice. I felt very proud of those kisses some way and I could not but feel that it was what we had said to each other with unspoken words that we should remember longest and understand best.

At five o'clock we were on our way to Tampa and a pleasant roundabout way up the Manatee River and the next day about four in the afternoon we were safely landed on the white sands of the city of Tampa.[13] The trees in the gardens were hanging full of oranges, the birds singing, the soldiers playing in their barrack amid such oak trees as one reads of in English stories.[14] I never saw trees to match them before.

chapter 2

Northern Newcomers,
Drawn to Health or Wealth

The next morning Scott and Carl started bright and early in an ox cart for Limona.[1] I waited and plodded knee deep in sand about the town of Tampa until noon. And just as the dinner bell rang, Dr. Pratt came to take me along the same road Scott and Carl had leisurely traveled earlier in the day. Ten slow miles. We did not reach Limona until after dark. Scott came out to meet me and how strange it seemed. The whole world seemed spangled with fireflies.[2]

We rested the next day but the next went with the Pratts and the Coes (both families are cousins) in mule teams thirteen miles from here to a Captain Smith's and spent the night. There we gathered our first oranges from the trees and took a walk through a Florida hammock in whose heart was a lovely spring with ferns to fringe its quiet, placid face and air plants and palms and many wild southern things growing in careless beauty. We cut down a tall palm to see its beautiful crest and to hunt out its heart.[3]

Captain Smith seemed bewitched with Carl. He hardly let go of his hand all the time we were there. He said he never saw a child that could compare with him. He would gladly give all his land for Carl. Sunday and Monday we rested but Tuesday our "traps" came and we are now in our own cabin, which I must leave for another letter.

8. E. E. Pratt, extreme right, on a sidewalk of the Tampa Bay Hotel gardens. Ca. 1886.

Our mail was a jolly sight, letters from everyone and bundles of papers. Mail day only twice a week. Doesn't it seem as if we had indeed reached a wilderness? There goes the "sunset gun" at Tampa. Goodnight.

        ❦   ❦   ❦

May 15, 1891

Dear boys,

The palmetto slab on which I painted "November in Florida" for Papa is from that same palm we cut down during our very first walk in a Florida hammock at Captain Smith's. Mama.[4]

        ❦   ❦   ❦

To E.S.

"To what country shall we go? Dear child," said he, "how would I know? Little, dearest, do I care how we go or when or where if from you I do not stray."[5]

It is in a log cabin and way down here in "southern Florida" under the pines and gray moss.[6] Little lakes are scattered all about us. There is no house in sight. Perhaps you are foolish enough to think it isn't much of a home but I assure you we never had a happier one and when joy abides who dare to pick a flaw? I should like those cliffs at Lake Erie and the great sweep of beautiful water. I should like to be able to climb upon the cabin roof and see again the "visions of a hundred hills" and catch a glimpse of distant mountains as I used to in Carl's Lancaster. I'd like the lovely ravines near "viende l'eau" and the deep, wild dells and rocky streams in New York and a broad river. But everything is never in any one spot and Florida is Florida and I cannot tell you how we like it.

The air is like paradise—so soft—so sweet—so satisfying. Out in the sun it is hot but in the shade with a breeze it is always pleasant. And above you hangs a sky of such heavenly blue. The nights are beyond words. Often at midnight the sky is a clear, deep blue and the moon is in full splendor. The stars look yellow on the blue dome. White clouds float lazily over our heads and often the mocking birds waken and pour forth some glad songs. You lie still and listen. The loveliness of the night seems to have hushed the world. The woods are full of birds. No bird in a cage ever sang as they do.

We live very simply. You would hardly believe people could live so simply and still live in "sweet content." We live in the open hall—eat—read—play cribbage—and swing our hammocks there. Carl builds his engines and steam boats in one end. Indeed it is worth all the rest of the house.

Our table is always lovely with its white linen and quaint old china, so delicate and lovely, and never without flowers. This morning it was water lilies and their pure white petals and melting hearts of gold made the table entrancing. There is one pale blue flower that fades in the noonday sun that we often have at breakfast. Its leaf is a mere film in texture but nothing could be prettier.[7]

❧ ❧ ❧

To E.S.

We have had some little "pleasure trips." One was to Lake Thonotosassa, a beautiful lake about ten miles from here.[8] We lost our way and Scott and I went in a "Cracker's" cabin to try and find where we were.[9] They were getting supper over a fireplace. It looked very tempting. I wanted to stay. We were lost, however, in spite of all warnings and how I enjoyed it. Until after 2:00 A.M. we plunged through the depths of the hammock. It was moonlight and the palms and pines and wonderful oaks and the labyrinth of undergrowth made it seem like the tropics indeed. Carl slept soundly. That little philosopher wisely adapts himself to "all ways and conditions of men."

Two nights we camped out not far from Tampa Bay.[10] On the beach we found a grove of palms in the white sand, nothing but palms and how strange it looked. The sand was so white and smooth that at a short distance it looked like marble and the trunks of the trees like fantastic columns, the crests forming a strange and beautiful canopy. To wander there looking out

9. Strolling on the gleaming white shores of Lake Thonotosassa, a popular sailing, fishing, and swimming spot. Earlier enjoyed by the Seminoles, who established a camp nearby, the lake became a favorite of visitors from Tampa, particularly after World War I. 1896.

upon the blue waters of the Bay seemed as if we might have strayed into the deserted hall of some old sea god.

We saw a rattlesnake that someone had shot. It measured only nine and one-half inches round its handsome body. He took all the poetry out of Florida for a time for me, although his skin I thought one of the handsomest things I ever saw.

We have roaches here that if they could be trained are large enough for watch dogs. And the ants, though small, are in great abundance and I've never seen one that did not seem totally depraved.

We have one "Darkie" family that is interesting in their way.[11] "Uncle Isaac" is the father of the family. He was fifty years a slave and it wasn't the "soft-side" of slavery down here. His wife goes by the name of "Andrew's Mother," Andrew being a young man who owns a "house and land" and is a man of promise. The "Darkies" had a debating society and the question before the house was "If your mother and your sister and the girl you were going to marry were all drowning at the same time and you couldn't save but one, which one would you save?" Andrew said he would save his mother. "A fellow couldn't have but one mother. There are plenty of girls he could marry."

Some of the family come often with vegetables and Andrew's Mother will not step on the rug in the open hall.[12] She seemed to think it an ornament for the floor. When she first saw my dishes she sat everything down she had and just laughed and tossed her head and kept saying, "Well, honey" and "Well, honey" and walked back and forth before the shelves, not offering to touch them but looking so delighted and laughing as if every one were an emblem of merriment.

Most of the "Crackers" are a thin, cadaverous looking people.

    ❧   ❧   ❧

April 15, 1882[13]

Scott and Carl just gone for the mail and by and by when they return they will begin to call me long before they are in sight and the woods will be filled with the echo. They looked so happy as they started side by side. Scott in a blue flannel shirt and white pants and a broadbrimmed hat and Carl looking up and in his sweet voice asking, "Do you see how tall I am, Papa dear?"

Scott reads to me when I am busy. I never pretend to work unless I can be entertained. The other night it was quite cool and rained and blew all night. We made a jolly fire in the old "mud chimney" and made caramels on the coals and played cribbage and read until nearly three o'clock. We no longer belong to the world and time is of no consequence to us. Our only law is our own fancy.

We go sometimes for days together without a sign of human life, seldom more than an ox cart in the distance. Of course, I except the Pratts and the Coes whom we meet often. (Mr. and Mrs. Coe and Percy, Miss Alma Pratt, Mrs. Coe's sister, Dr. Pratt, and the two young ladies, Miss Lizzie and Hattie, and Eddie, a young son.)

Carl sits for hours watching the clouds. "I cannot help it, Mama," he says, "they are so pretty." He was three the 5th of February and what a little glory he is in our fond eyes for only three years.

We hear from Mr. Osborne often. My mania for naming things used to amuse him. He happened to be there when we sent for our barrels, which I had named instead of numbered. And the dispatches read, "Send Dinah, and Martha and Jane by freight at once." And Mr. Osborne wants to know if I have all of the mosquitoes named yet.

The birds grow more and more beautiful. I shall never be able to take their music as a matter of course. It is a fresh wonder for me every day. The world will never grow green again in any clime that I shall not listen instructively for them and in my heart they will sing forever.

The joys we have known are always ours. I never so much as read of a rose that I do not again lay my cheek against the dewy, fragrant roses in my Aunt Julia's garden of gardens. Daily her beautiful eyes follow me. How many things bring back my mother's voice and touch. In countless ways I meet again my little precious Olive, and there is one so near and dear and tenderly beloved who lies and thinks of me and who is intertwined with so many of my thoughts and dreams. She seems to share my very life and the very places we have loved seem to remain ours.[14]

I grew to love the cliff at Lake Erie as if it had been a part of the dooryard at home. I owned the hills about Lancaster in the only way a beautiful landscape ever can be owned—I loved them. And they gave themselves to me. If I should ever again be fortunate enough to wander down the winding heart of the Fisherman's Ravine "at viende l'eau," belaced and bedecked with its ferns and trilliums and pink lady slippers and violets and hepaticas, would not the flowers and vines almost seem to know me and long to be gathered again by the hand that loved them? And the very lake smile upon me as of old? Ah! it is a blessed thing to have had, whatever the losing may be, and so we are thankful every day for our happy lifetime, however soon the days are over and whatever fortune has in store for us.

Long letter from Mr. Rounds saying how much he should love to see us and begging me not to let anything happen to the "pretty cups," and one from Mrs. Propp-Smythe in Santa Barbara. She says I'm "like her old school friends in Andover in whose society she used to revel" and adds, "Oh! why couldn't it have been California instead of Florida."

It is so early in the morning I've had to light the lamp to see to write. Scott and Carl are still sleeping but I was restless and am up to have a chat with you and a read. The birds are just beginning the day and are waking each other with songs. I have stopped to make a fire in the old mud chimney. It is blazing cheerily and makes the whole room glow. Do not ever expect to get a letter of any length with that fireplace left out.

You were the first one I thought of when I heard of Longfellow's death. I know how dear he was to you among the poets.

❧   ❧   ❧

April 23, 1882

To E.S.

We had a new recreation yesterday. You never could guess. We all went to a "rail splitting." About four miles from here lives a genuine New Hampshire old maid—that is, one variety of old maid.[15] I hardly imagine they are all alike anywhere. She will be 67 on her next birthday. She spent a good many years of her life in the Lowell cotton mills, but spent her money as fast as she earned it. (She doesn't look like a natural spendthrift either.) But she has managed to scrape enough together to get here and save a small crumb for a rainy day and has "taken up" a homestead of 160 acres.

She wears bloomers. She is homely, very tall, very thin, very awkward. She is kind, brave, true, honest, sincere, and in many respects very intelligent, and always unaffected. And yet in spite of all that you cannot help but laugh when you first see her, her ridiculous costume, her peculiar stride, the attitudes she strikes. She seems to have stepped from a pantomime. No matter how great your respect for her or your desire to show it, you might as well try to keep from sneezing after a big pinch of snuff as to keep from smiling when you first catch sight of Miss Averill.

While a neighbor was clearing land in a high wind, Miss Averill's fence was nearly all destroyed and the rail splitting is to help rebuild it. Her home consists of three little huts and a porch but an oak leaf after a summer rain couldn't have seemed fresher or cleaner. Mr. Chamberlain, a Philadelphian of education and cultivation, takes his meals there.[16] He has a place near. When he rose and bowed, I said to myself, you have bowed in more than one handsome parlor before you found your way to this wilderness. There is an exiled Russian physician who also takes his meals there who has a place near.[17] He is very odd, very smart, and has wandered nearly all over the world. He is a scholar, something of a writer and a lover of nature. He made a Gypsy soup out in the yard over an open fire. It had twenty-three different things in it and was fine. He sang us Gypsy and Russian songs.

We had a glorious day sitting in the shade out of doors, or around the long table, laughing and talking, a wild free sort of time, happy as larks. The only drawback was that there weren't many rails split. Nearly all the Northerners who come here are half dead with weak lungs or old backs or worn-out chests or softening of the brain.[18] Able bodied people stay away, and the result was that the fence didn't grow and flourish as it ought. But it was a happy day from first to last.

On our way home we went out of our way to see a freak of nature. Not long since a certain highway seemed in as perfect a state as usual when a man walking beside his oxen noticed a great hole in front of him. It was very nearly round, about seventy feet across, about thirty-five feet deep. At the bottom of this hole, looming up out of a pool of water, was the top of a pine tree. No one can for the present explain it.[19] If for a time no voice reaches you from this abode, just search in the bowels of the earth or send a dispatch to China. Perhaps we shall have fallen through.

❦　❦　❦

May Day, 1882

To E.S.

You could wreathe your Maypole with wild flowers here and crown your queen with loveliest garlands and carry palms to shade her young head, but you could never dance in the sand.

I am sitting on the rug in the open hall with the mail scattered about me—only eleven letters. Years ago someone said to Olive, "Jule was made for joy. I hope nature will make no mistake and send her sorrow. It would spoil a life that was fitted for as perfect happiness as a human heart could know." When Olive repeated the words to me I remembered how well they accorded with the time and place, and they often come to me. I am capable of great happiness. There is so much of exultation in my nature. I long so to be happy. I've such a horror of dull people and dull places. I seem impelled by the most irresistible forces toward bright and lovely things and it is so natural to flee from what is not. It used to trouble my dear Aunt Jule that I cared so very much how people looked and that it was invariably the first question I asked. To her, when she asked why I loved her, the first reply was always, "Because you are so beautiful." It is not the noblest of attributes, I know, to be carried away by the sense of external beauty, but it was born in me and from a child nothing could more quickly set my pulses beating than something that filled my eyes with delight.

It is strange how I love this land. It seems as if I had wandered all my life and, though the sea and the hills were gone, at last here I had found my home.

The very air caresses me as if it loved me. The birds sing to me as if they were confiding their joys to me. The sky looks down upon me as if I had guessed the secret of its loveliness. The flowers tell me clearly that they have been waiting in happy content for my smile of delight. Even the ghostly Spanish moss loves to have me gather it, and the solemn old pines trust me with all their family affairs. I can never go North to live. I belong to the summer and the summer belongs to me.

※　　※　　※

May 7, 1882

Yesterday Scott and Carl and I went alone to a beautiful hammock—the wildest and most tropical spot I ever saw.[20] The doctor was going to Tampa and took us in his wagon to the edge of the hammock. There were tall palms with some trunks bare and smooth, others full of the broken stems and they, in their decay, are such a medley of soft tints—delicate pinks, deep reds and soft browns, often covered with moss and tall ferns and air plants growing among them. Oaks with branches covered with ferns and often a clump of one very pretty variety of orchids. Old cedars, bushes of lantana in bloom, scarlet honeysuckle, and thousands of yards of trumpet vine trail in wild abundance down the moss grown paths, hiding huge logs that laid in its way, throwing a mantle of green over dead branches. I never saw such warm colors in a trumpet's heart before and each flower seemed to wear such a joyous air as if it held some of nature's happiest secrets. I always liked that flower. It seemed to be Gypsy all through and refused to be tamed and in that hammock it had grown according to its old wild, sweet will.

We saw red birds and humming birds, butterflies by the hundreds and a flock of paroquets. They lighted on a branch over our heads, chatted a moment among each other and flew away. Their plumage, a brilliant green,

10. Six Mile Creek hammock, showing early Limona settlers on a hunting expedition. Left to right: Mr. Carte, Mr. Lewis, Mr. Gooding, and Dr. Stone. This splendid thick cabbage-palm-and-oak hammock, located four miles west of The Nest, was one of the first explored by the Moseleys after their arrival. 1887.

11. The saw palmetto was the plant Julia Daniels Moseley used to make the wall covering in the Palm. She and Scott experimented with a number of possible uses for the palmetto before she had the idea of using it as a wall covering.

was very beautiful. There were nine of them.[21] A tall crane lighted on the crest of a dead pine, sat for a moment in dignified silence, then flapped his yard or more of wings and flew beyond our sight toward the bay.

In the heart of this hammock we found an old "still" where the "moonshiners" most likely made many a gallon of whiskey once upon a time. It was a choice spot for such a venture for a tidal stream led to it and in those days it was a place where human feet seldom strayed.

🍂　🍂　🍂

May 13, 1882

The Russian spent the day with us. He came through the woods singing snatches of songs. He looked more like a happy Gypsy than an unhappy exile.

He has some hobbies that he rides until you are tired out but when he too tires of them and talks of Russia and other things we enjoy him very much.

He told us of his grandfather who so loved his Gypsy "love wife" that he would have no other and he paid thousands of rubles to have her made his own true wife. There is a very lovely painting of her in the old home in Russia, and even the grandchildren have been taught to adore the memory of their Gypsy grandmother "stechsch."[22] I shouldn't like him often but once in a great while I enjoy him very much.

chapter 3

Reaching Out
to Cracker Neighbors

June 14, 1882

To E.S.

Why, my dear girl, it is over a month since I laid aside that half-written letter. So many things have happened, the chief event having been the moving into our own cabin. Think of it! Five acres of land and our own log cabin.[1]

I must tell you all about this mansion. There are two rooms about twenty feet square with an open hall fourteen feet wide, porches ten feet wide running across the north and south, and a kitchen ten feet wide and twenty feet long. There is no floor yet on the beams above the rooms so we can look up into the peak. No square beams are anywhere. All the house is made of hewn logs, magnificent ones, too. So that in spite of its roughness they have a regal air. The floors as yet are not laid anywhere save the kitchen and the east room. Not even windows are cut or the chinks closed up in the west one. It is like a huge corn crib.

The open hall with porches makes us a living room of forty feet. There are pines and oaks in the yard, a few baby orange and lemon trees and one little magnolia. That is all—not a well nor an old disreputable log fence. Yes, one other thing, equal to a small kingdom—an immense mud chimney. It is

12. Mrs. John Weeks on the wooden sidewalk in front of her cabin, southwest of The Nest. 1896.

13. Mrs. John Weeks' log cabin, which featured a clay-stick chimney, a well, a separate kitchen, and outbuildings, all enclosed by a wooden fence. She supplied the Moseleys with butter, milk, and eggs. 1896.

in the west room though and until we have a floor is only a prospective pleasure. But we are full of plans and expect in time to make a perfect bower of this little spot. We have such a view of the sunsets that would fill your heart with delight. Scott said last night he never saw a sky in California he thought so fine. We three sat in a happy bundle on the back steps and watched it for hours.[2]

❦ ❦ ❦

June 28, 1882

How I let my letters lie! Every hour seems so full. Each one has more plans than there are minutes to fulfill them. Nearly every morning Miss Lizzie rides over on one of her father's little mules. She is very pretty and has a very sweet nature but she cannot live many summers even in this soft clime. Sometimes she dismounts and rests a while on the hammock and sometimes she sits at the table and has a crumb of breakfast. Not because she is hungry she says, but because she always likes anything from off my pretty dishes. She often brings me flowers, among them such lovely roses. If anyone brings or sends her some pretty or delicate thing, she loves to share it with me. Not long ago she had a very painful night and the next morning her father drove her over and as he lifted her out said, "She wanted sunshine and I brought her to you!" I had just read to Scott one of Edward Everett Hale's charming stories and I read it to her.[3]

A young lady is visiting at the doctor's and I invited the three girls over to spend a day with me.[4] Scott and Carl had gone to Tampa with Percy. This friend was one of those dull girls with a dull face and chronic dull headache. I think it a great pity that stupid people aren't always good looking. Hattie made a pretty picture in the hall in a blue muslin and pink roses, sitting, knitting and talking, while Lizzie lay in the hammock.

Just as lunch was ready in came the Russian with a watermelon. He was charmed with the table. Each plate was wreathed with a little flowering vine with a deep red flower and leaves like satin. He said he would defy anyone to give me anything that with a twist I couldn't make of it a thing of beauty. He said I reminded him of a cousin whom they all considered the artist of his family. Once when someone said she, too, could turn anything into something lovely, the others said it was not true. There were things it was impossible to make of them anything but something ugly. When they went hunting they shot a hedge hog and, giving it to the cousin, saying, "There, make something beautiful of that!" The next day they all dined together and when dinner was announced and they were seated, a servant brought in the hedge hog. It was roasted whole and was lying on a fantastic bed made of its own quills and decked with flowers. A shout went up and they gave her the palm, which has never since been disputed.

I've been to a "Cracker" quilting, the only Northern person present. One old woman with a face like a squaw's seemed to take a violent dislike to me. She sat on the edge of a bed and smoked, scarcely taking her pipe out of her mouth all day except to dispute almost every remark I made. I held my own, though, and kept my temper and won her over so far that she invited me to spend a day with her. A dog (her dog and so like her) took a pound or more of my flesh in his mouth. How I happened to have the presence of mind to stand still I do not know, paralyzed with fear I presume. But I did and spoke to one of the women to call off the dog. Hogs, dogs and children were all under the house at once. It was not what I imagined it would be—a fresh and funny experience. It was sad and pitiful and awful. I couldn't even talk about it to Scott very much at first—women with their youth starved out of them, children who looked as if they never had had any childhood. So many of the people here look like the dogs—lean, old, starved, sly. Such human beings do not create a smile. They take all the mirth out of life and leave only pity and horror.

I have been to a "fish fry" and a sort of Sunday School festival. It was in a little church called "New Hope" out in the wood. By the way, our house has gone by the name of the "Old Hope" for, after the family went away who owned it, they used it as the church until New Hope was built. Our steps are made of the old benches. There are no window panes in the church building, just a long, rough affair. But there are doors at both ends and when they are all open and the shutters raised and the beautiful air sweeps in and you look upon a forest on all sides, it seems a pleasant place in spite of its uncouthness. Nearly three hundred people were present. It was the first entertainment of singing and recitations that a large portion of them had ever even heard or taken part in before. They came in all directions, in ox carts, in mule teams, on horseback and on foot.

Had one no sense of the fitness of things and not a vestige of reverence they might have remained only out of curiosity and made merry out of what they saw and heard, for it was a "motley crew." But their attempts at adornment were pitiful and their ignorance sad, and when one stops to realize that these wild shreds of humanity have had little better advantages than the birds and compare it with the enlightened North, your deepest sympathies are stirred.

Something seemed to compel me to raise my voice in entreaty to them and I stood up before them all and talked to the children of life and effort as I never dreamed of doing before.

Mr. Parker, the minister, afterward among other things concerning it in the Tampa paper, said, "Among other incidents that tended to make the day pleasant and profitable to us was the request of a lady present to make a few remarks to the children before the services were closed, her mind having been brought back to her childhood by what she had seen and heard. She, though a comparative stranger from a different state and young in years, made an impression on old and young not soon to be obliterated."[5]

The first book we've read in our new home was George McDonald's Warlock O'Glen Warlock.[6] It is full of good things. Among others is one on that well-known subject—the blessings that spring from troubles. "It may be your cloud has not yet passed and you scorn to hear it called one, priding yourself it is eternal but just because you are eternal, your trouble cannot be. You may cling to it and brood over it but you cannot keep it from either blossoming into a bliss or crumbling to dust. Be such while it lasts that when it passes it shall leave you loving more, not less."

❧   ❧   ❧

July 7, 1882

E.S.

Goose Nest.[7] I'm sitting on the back steps. Scott and Carl have just gone out of sight round the lake with their guns. Carl has a little wooden one his Papa made him. He carries it with ten times the importance of his father. They are a happy pair of comrades. Such love and faith and pride they have in each other.

The sun is setting—a beautiful vision is in the sky just at this instant. On a pale blue background is such a wonderful statue all in white and gray clouds, a figure not unlike a god of beauty, bearing in his hand a flaming torch and holding it proudly aloft over the head of a woman with uplifted face and streaming hair. I wonder if it is not Apollo with a flame of love lighting the way for Venus.

We all went miles away one day in search of a boiling spring.[8] The Russian and Mr. Chamberlain joined the party. We never found the spring but we had a splendid day and what greatly added to my pleasure was we were lost half the night. The Russian and some of the others walked beside the wagons carrying great flaming torches of fat pine. Carl went to sleep a little after dark, never waking until we were safe in The Nest and then all he said was, "I love home, Mama." It was a dark night and the world lighted only by our torches made every foot of the way a world bewitched. How weird the pines looked and now and then a cabin and bananas growing near and sometimes a cabbage palm.

14. Buckhorn Springs in dry weather, with the bowl of its light, bluish-green spring clearly visible. This secluded, privately owned site, surrounded by beautiful native growth, was located southeast of The Nest. It was a favorite spot for Nesters and other Limona residents alike. Ca. 1910.

15. Typical longleaf pine woods, with saw palmetto and other low understory plants shading off into more dense oak forests and hammocks. These woods lay slightly north of The Nest on the way to the Limona post office. Ca. 1905–1909.

August 17, 1882

Just at twilight. This is the month and the day and the hour that eleven years ago I sat in St. Paul's crowded church to see Didee Parlsifer married. How joyously she began her wedded life and how thick and fast sorrows swept in to mar it. Time is a cruel fellow. Yet, even he has his favorites. Some he leads with so gentle a hand they do not heed his touch or his footfall. And others he seems to clutch at every step as he hurls them along to keep pace with his mighty stride.

August 20, 1882

To E.S.

We have a bride, Mrs. Legate, pretty, young, well educated. We all like her and are so glad to welcome her. She has spent this day with us. Mrs. Coe spends a day or half a day with me often. I do not know as I have spoken of it but she is always sending me some little thing for the table—fruit or vegetables, a receipt for a new dish, a plant or seed, and anything they have in the shape of magazines and newspapers. Her library she gave us free use of long ago and she has that heavenly way of doing things that makes you feel that your acceptance and enjoyment were a sweet recompense to the giver.[9]

I wonder if I've ever told you of Mr. Chamberlain. We often see him and I think I simply told you he is a Philadelphian and obliged to live in a warm climate. When in one of his best moods, he is one of the most entertaining men I ever knew. He is tall, slender, with dark hair and eyes, and browned by our southern sun. There is not the faintest hint of effeminacy about him but he is the perfection of neatness and possesses not a gift but a genius for order. He is a thorough aristocrat in his ideas but is delightful to his friends.

We are always so glad to see him, for his coming means a bright day always. He has a white knapsack which he sometimes brings strapped upon his back. One morning when it was unfastened a hundred little yellow limes were within for us.

The next time it held a melon for dessert and the August Century because he wanted Scott to read the article on Bennett's beautiful steam yacht and me the charmingly illustrated article on "some English artists and their studios."[10] I tell you of those who interest us so that you can have some idea of the people we meet.

☙ ☙ ☙

August 26, 1882

You know perhaps that our John is way off in Oregon. He is the youngest one in my father's family. It hardly seems a year ago since I was telling him Jack and the beanstalk and for so long he was my little delicate brother. He says, "I have an office in a tent among big pine trees with the Columbia River right in front of me, and back of the tent I run up a bank a little way and see Mt. Hood rising 12,000 feet and all covered with snow at the top. I am content and happy. It seems horrible to think how dispassionately one gets to look on death. Sometimes I wish I had chosen an occupation among different people where I could have the benefit of more refinement. But as far as mountain scenery and lovely climate go, it is par excellence. If you could see grand old Mt. Hood at sunset! It looms up above the clouds all purple and the deepest crimson, while far down the side are the gray clouds and the foothills. Then the pines singing in the breeze and the great river nearly ten miles wide."

He is studying bookkeeping and keeping up his German. He has Chinese and Indians under him, to both of whom he gives their instructions in their own languages.

Letters come often from my brother Preston, who is with Charlie on his new place in Kansas. Perhaps you do not know that that gay brother of mine has just finished a very nice house on an old farm he bought there, a lovely place with an apple and peach orchard and a grove with many varieties of trees, among them an elm whose branches from tip to tip measure eighty feet. There are four springs on the place and a charming little stream, whose banks are bordered with trees, runs across the farm. They had two hundred rose bushes in bloom in May. Charlie writes me he never was so happy in his life before. He has some fine stock and little Harry, who is some seven or eight months older than Carl, has a pair of goats.

I've a very sore foot from the poison of a vampire on my instep. They are a wretched little insect. Scott went to Tampa today and we were up very early. I'm often very fond of that delicious, late nap but the morning is a beautiful time and lovely as it has seemed wherever I've been I've never found it so lovely as it is down here. The sky is full of bewildering tints. Then the sun bursts forth in such radiance. The voices of the morning are countless. The birds' music so varied and so sweet and there is such an indescribable charm upon everything.

If anything could surpass the mornings for beauty it is the moonlight nights. I read part of an article in Harper's one night by her bright rays.[11] The pines are so weird, standing sixty or eighty feet in height, the moss half veiling their gaunt limbs and the shadows lie along the sand like myriads of sleeping black ghosts.

August 31, 1882

Scott and Carl are asleep. I have on my gown and am sitting up here alone and have been reading until I can no longer see the words but I must not go to sleep until I have told you of our strange twilight tonight. Several acres adjoining our land have just been cleared. The great pines have dropped on the sand with hardly a groan, the logs stacked in piles. And this afternoon these huge bonfires were lighted. It has been raining since noon and every weed and treetop had that plumy appearance that foliage has when heavy and dewy with showers. The shadows were black where the wood was deep down in the bayhead. Great piles of logs were burning in the east. All the western sky was melting, mellow golden mellow. It was as if the sun had hidden behind a great cloud of moonbeams. I never stood in such a glory. The lake caught it and every ripple laughed up at the sky from a sea of melting gold. Even the green of pine and oak seemed to have been dipped in yellow dyes and the fires blazed gaily and the rain kept falling and there was a low, deep rolling sound of distant thunder. It didn't seem like our everyday world. I wonder if I wasn't wafted into Hades on a Gala Day.

☙ ☙ ☙

September 20, 1882

I wish you could hear our Carl use long words and the ease with which they slip from his young lips. I gave him a lunch the other day. The jelly on his bread was a kind he especially liked and he ran with it to Scott saying, "See, Papa, lemon jelly!" And his Papa said, "Lemon jelly! Aren't you glad, Carl?" And he replied, "Glad! I'm perfectly delighted." Not long since he bit a green grapefruit (a fruit bitter and sour beyond expression when green). He was telling me about it and said, "I suppose it was really nice, but, Mama, I was surprised when I bit that grapefruit." You would love him. You couldn't help it. His Papa found him washing everything he could find on the back porch, from the oil can to the umbrella and he said, "Carl, you know better than to do so. I'm ashamed of you." And he said it very sternly for him for Scott is so gentle with him when he is at his very worst. Carl looked up at him in his most surprised, unabashed manner, saying, "Papa, don't talk so.

It sounds hard and it troubles me." And it was very difficult to make this babe realize that he was not helping his Mama instead of the reverse.

But with all his mischief it is wonderful the steps his dear little willing feet save us. So cheerily and sweetly he flies to do our bidding and there is such cunning in those little brown fingers. He is a darling boy and we love him almost too much, if such a thing were not impossible.

❦ ❦ ❦

September 26, 1882

I had a delightful letter from Gretchen sent not long since. She has a very sparkling way of saying things oftentimes. She begins this letter as follows: "We had barley and cream for breakfast this morning, darling girl, and I said this tastes like Jule—soft and delicious with an excellent flavor with just enough resistance to let you know you are eating something with plenty of the cream of rich jokes and the sweetness of good nature overall. That's you, you little barleycorn." You remember what a happy morning you and I had

16. Frindy, Charles Scott Moseley's daughter by his first marriage, became for Julia Daniels Moseley the "dearest girl in the world." Although her real name was Florence, she preferred to be called Frindy or Frindolin. 1879.

17. At seventy-five, Frindy had long been the custodian of The Nest and her memory of people and events was prodigious. She could locate in The Nest's collections the exact item needed. If not for Frindy's courage, Julia Daniels Moseley's letters would have vanished in 1885 in the flames of the burning log cabin. 1941.

in the parlor on the hill when I brought all the spoils of that day in town with Gretchen and I told you of our lunch and our shopping and our hour in the gallery and our larks. And in referring to it she said, "I tell you, Jule darling, that one day was worth a whole year to us. It will always shine out brightly and, like Bella Wilfer, being such limited little beasts we managed to crowd into a few hours what one might have dawdled over for a few weeks. It was like a rush of a comet."[12]

We are expecting the children Saturday.[13] Scott and Carl are going to Tampa to meet them and I am to stay and make the welcome. I am going to have a bonfire and The Nest will be a bower of green. Isn't there a sweet ring in the words "coming home?"

Think of me with a daughter sixteen and a son twelve? Only the other night I dreamed I was a little girl again talking to my mother! Oh! heaven be kind! To think I never can talk to her again or see her face, save in my dreams, until I, too, shall have slept the white sleep and left a child to cherish my memory in their hearts as I cherish hers.

We all love you. I was thinking only a few hours ago how for over half my lifetime I have known and loved and trusted you. Your Barbara.[14]

🌿   🌿   🌿

To E.S.

Scott and Carl started bright and early to meet the children. It has seemed some of the time as if I should never see them again in this world. It is nearly a month since we first looked for them.

Carl had a long letter today from Jennie Glisson of Fredonia, N.Y. They are the family that loved him so much and had him so much when we were at the "Point" that happy summer.

She told him if they never saw him again he would always be their little Carl and no matter how tall and brown he grew they should love him just the same.

It is now 7 o'clock at night. Here I sit in my white gown with water lilies on my lace, waiting for those long lost bairns. The house looks like a nest, indeed, but not the nest of a plain goose but of some tropical bird. The open hall is hung so thick with palms and vines you could hardly put your little white hand on its walls without touching something green and fragrant. Even the ropes of the hammock are wound with flowering vines. This week we had a double doorway cut through into the west room, which has a smooth floor now.

When I gave Carl his supper last night he was very hungry and he kept asking for more and at last I said, "Well, Carl, I'd like to know how much you can eat at one sitting?" And he replied, "Oh! Mama, I'm sure I don't know but I suppose I eat an indefinite amount of mischief." He dearly loves Hattie Pratt and she is always so lovely to him. The other day he was going for the mail with Scott and Carl always expects to see Hattie when he goes for the mail. And he said, "I must put on my boots and then it's Limona and then Hattie."

One o'clock and still no signs of them. I am so anxious.

Three o'clock and still alone. The dawn is breaking and still not any sign of them.

❦ ❦ ❦

Noon. I think of ten thousand things but I can console myself with no good reason for this awful delay. I've not lain down a moment but walked the rooms, first one and then the other. If only someone would come to comfort me. Scott had hoped to be here in time for a 7 o'clock supper last night.

❧ ❧ ❧

Friday morning. They are here, safe and well. Came at three o'clock. The boat stuck on a sandbar in sight of Tampa and did not land until after nine o'clock the next morning.

I'm all worn out. So many anxious nights the past three weeks. For each one all during the week we expected them and I couldn't sleep for thinking of them during the journey. Then the preparation and the trip to town and the disappointment and at last that awful day and night when I could only walk the house and listen for the sound of their approach. I fainted away Monday and have hardly been able to sit up since. I hope soon to get rested. I tremble all the time. I was terribly frightened that night I spent alone. One time a drunken teamster drove into our fence and swore and stormed like a madman and an owl actually sat on a window sill and hooted at me.[15]

I only had a light now and then. I was afraid it would attract someone. The owls used to haunt this place before we came but none of these things could I recall then. I thought it a wild woman or an insane Indian at least.[16] The countless terrors mingled with my anxieties for my loved ones that night. I can never, never forget.

❧ ❧ ❧

To E.S.

The children are spending the day at the Pratts. Carl is on the floor close beside me drawing a steamboat. Scott has been very busy lately but he said I looked "tired to death" and he was going to devote the afternoon to me.[17] I lay in the hammock and he read to me and I soon fell asleep and did not waken until after three. Then I flew for I so wanted everything to look sweet when Frindy came home. It is always so "homesick" to go away to have a nice time and the bright side of one's neighbors or friends and come home to find everything upside down. Scott helped me and we soon had everything in order.

I think Florence is going to be a real comfort to me. She does love me I think more than anything else in the world and she is a good, sweet, unaffected darling.

❦   ❦   ❦

October 15, 1882

The children seem perfectly delighted with their home. I never saw more contented children. I wish you could have seen the three trunks unpacked. So many loving remembrances from so many friends. It was equal to a dozen Christmas boxes.

❦   ❦   ❦

November 4, 1882

Not but a trifle better. Cannot sit up. Will try and write next week. Doctor says I may have to lie still for a long time.

❦   ❦   ❦

November 22, 1882

I cannot tell you how sick I've been and every moment I've suffered.

Miss Averill is here. Came yesterday. Left her cottage and her cats and her garden. The noise is so terrible. Father Moseley and Will have come.[18] A family of eight. And only three rooms. Not enough furniture and bedding to make three as comfortable as they need. I hope you cannot even imagine the confusion and discomfort. Oh, it is killing me. Scott is putting up a little room, 12 by 14, several rods from the house so I can have the comfort of quiet at least. I am dying by inches in here. I am in great and constant pain and, oh, so tired.

❦   ❦   ❦

18. Naomi Noble Moseley in her Elgin, Illinois, home, surrounded by pictures of her husband Seth, son Charles Scott, grandchildren Carl and Hal, and Florida memorabilia. 1884.

19. Charles Scott Moseley's father Seth Moseley, a surveyor who left Massachusetts before 1860 to work in the newly opened country of Illinois and Missouri. Seth Moseley and his son Will also bought land in Limona, where they planted orange groves. Ca. 1870.

December 4, 1882

I have a new doctor, the Russian. Mr. Chamberlain thinks a great deal of him as a physician and Scott and Mrs. Coe have at last persuaded me to have him see me.

Do not look but for the merest word for some time. I am forbidden to do the least thing. Everything tires me. Scott devotes all of his time to me. He hardly leaves me for an hour in the day.

❧   ❧   ❧

December 11, 1882

Better and worse but I am gaining a little. Mrs. Coe has a delightful invalid chair and she has sent it over for me to use. I've sat up a little in that. We have our little room. It has windows on all sides. We call it the Whist for everyone has to keep still in it.[19] The birds dart through a dozen times a day and I have fresh flowers all the time.

I never tire of the lovely sky. Scott reads to me whenever I have strength to listen. The pain never quite leaves me even for a moment. There are too many roses in my life for there never to be any thorns. But I am not one of the natures that blossoms best in adversity. I'm most radiant in bright weather.

❧   ❧   ❧

December 15, 1882

It is nearly two months since I've had on my clothes. Everyone has been so kind to me. I did not know that so many people even knew of me and then I have so many letters and loving messages and yet I never was so depressed. I try for Scott's sake to keep up a stout heart but I seem unable to. It isn't like me to be like that. I've not much patience but I'm not a coward.

I heard a little commotion up at the house and someone say, "Carl, how could you?" And I knew he was in mischief. Soon he came in and I told him I was writing to you and asked him what I should tell you from him. He laid his hand on my shoulder and bending over me said, "Tell her I poured water in the molasses jug."

The other day Scott and Carl were going over to the store and Carl asked about a certain piece of machinery in Mr. Coe's sawmill—a little thing in use somewhere in the inside. Scott couldn't understand just what he meant and Carl said, "Wait, Papa, and I will show you." And he stopped and drew a plan of the machinery with this little piece in position. So Scott told him just what it was for. Scott thinks his powers of observation wonderful.

I had so longed for a beautiful Southern Christmas and I'm not going to even be able to sit up.

       ꙮ   ꙮ   ꙮ

Christmas Day, 1882

Seven calls today and twenty-five letters and packages in the mail.[20] Goodbye, 1882.

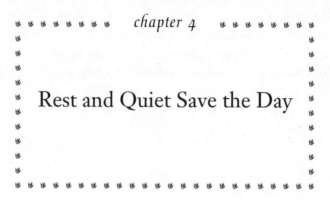

chapter 4

Rest and Quiet Save the Day

January 9, 1883

To E.S.

In the Whist. "Venice"—it is a great pleasure to write the word but I am not sure there is not a certain impudence in pretending to add anything to it. Isn't that charming? How it pleased me when I read it at the beginning of James' article on Venice in the November Century. Isn't it nice that I can read a little once more? Not a great deal but some. For weeks I wasn't able to read ten lines.

It has rained a good deal lately. The other day Scott was at dinner and I was alone. The west windows were open. Suddenly the wind changed from the north to the west and before I was aware of it my bed was drenched, though it was on the opposite side of the room. I tried to close the windows but I couldn't. I screamed but the storm was so loud my very voice was drowned. Soon Scott came out but the floor was flooded. I enjoyed it all. It didn't hurt me at all. It did me good. Scott has gone to Limona on an errand. He carried a pine torch to light him on his way. He is reading Black's *Shandon Bells* to me.[1] No matter how tired he is he always reads me to sleep at night. I get very tired by the time the plantation is hushed for the night. It is very hard for me to lie still and go to sleep until his dear voice quiets me.

Carl says, "Mama, look me right in the eyes. Do you really love me, darling?" Then we both laugh and he throws his little arms around my neck.

We have so many oranges. Our house is on the old "Indian Trail," the highway from Tampa to Fort Meade and long caravans go by here every week loaded with oranges. Some wagons are drawn by as many as twelve oxen. They are shipped at Tampa. Who knows but you have eaten some of the very oranges that have been drawn by our old cabin door.

I get very much discouraged sometimes. It is such a wretched way to live. I'm needed in a thousand ways and do have some wonderfully happy hours with Scott in spite of my restlessness and pain. He never is impatient—a sunbeam always. We have lovely times planning things, too, and I try to forget the present.

Miss Averill is one of those people that think everything belongs to the world. She says my voice and conversations are so fascinating. She thinks I ought to lecture if only I could "find something to talk about." I told her the

20. John Weeks and his son Levi with their logging team. One of Hillsborough County's primary industries from the 1870s through the 1890s was the clearing and logging of land. Levi Weeks later served in the Spanish-American War and for years traveled the United States as a skilled mule driver, highly proficient in the use of his long whip. 1896.

story of the girl who went to Fields, saying, "Oh, Mr. Fields, I have such mammoth ideas. If only I could find words to express them." I said if only I could find that girl and get her to furnish the ideas our fortune would be made.

Miss Averill is a comical old scrap of humanity. She drives me wild with her "set ways" but we all like her. She believes in all working together and having everything divided equally and she carries it out in everyday life to an absurd degree some times. One day she made a rice pudding, dumping in the lumps of cold rice in large lumps. Frindy said Mama always mashed them up fine. But Miss Averill insisted that that was a debasing principle to work on. It was not fair for one to break the lumps for eight. Let them mash their lumps as they ate their pudding. But the pudding went begging for the saucers were left nearly as full as when served. After dinner she came out to see me and the pudding was brought up and she delivered the same argument to me as to Florence in the forenoon. I told her it was said to be a poor rule that wouldn't work both ways and after this we would have the wood for her kitchen stove brought in in four foot lengths as it was hardly fair for one to do all the chopping and sawing on the wood. But like the sensible woman she is in spite of her perseverance she saw the point, burst out laughing, and said, "Mrs. Moseley, you have caught me once." And a few days after she made another rice pudding that soon vanished on account of its creamy smoothness.

She and Carl are wonderful friends. She has one very rare quality with children. She always is willing to confess when they are in the right, though it proves her in the wrong. We correct Carl's speech and he is to remind us of any mispronounced word and when she came she wanted him to correct hers. She is always ready and willing to learn. Carl has a wonderful appreciation of clear intonation or any sweet sounding word. Last night he pronounced a word wrong and I reminded him of it, giving him the right one. And he said, "So, that is the proper way, is it? So that is the correct way? I must let Miss Averill know. I'm sure she will be glad. She wouldn't want to say what wasn't correct, would she, Mama?"

If you could hear his voice and watch his earnest face. Off he goes to his old friend and she holds him on her knees and listens as respectfully as if he were thirty instead of three. And then she takes out an aged atlas she never travels without and from it Carl has taken his first lesson in geography. He loves the book and nearly every day they sit down together over it.

❦ ❦ ❦

January 19, 1883

Home from a little ride. Have been up to see the Coes' new house. Large rooms. Wide open hall. Broad piazzas running around three sides. Large, airy chambers. A nice house for Florida and they are just the people to enjoy and deserve it.

I have been thinking of my mother today. What splendid health she had and what a fine woman she was with her unusual memory and power to recall what she saw and read and heard. I do not think there was ever a day that illness did not prevent that she did not spend more or less time over a book or magazine. She was often obliged to sew and mend in the evening, with father's slender purse and their flock of children. But no matter how late it was she said she couldn't rest without that hour of reading. It was worth more than sleep. I really think during her last visit to us she met more people in Lancaster who really liked and admired her than I did in all the three years of our stay there.

21. The Lyman Joel Coe home was built between 1882 and 1883 near Whittington Lake, northeast of The Nest. The Coes, great friends of the Moseleys, had known Scott Moseley in Elgin. This, their second home in Limona, was situated in the middle of a fine seedling orange grove. Ca. 1915.

Rest and Quiet Save the Day   57

This morning a lark sang to me for a long time. How Olive loved a bird. I think I never knew anyone that loved them with the intensity that she did. No matter where I was she always sent me word when she heard the first robin. No one could have been freer from all personal vanity than she was. But she was a born Philadelphian with her quiet, unselfish nature and sweet voice and, while she liked Darwin better than a novel, she seldom spoke of such things. Her fondness for what was highest and best was too real to be spoken of lightly. She was modesty itself. Nothing in nature she loved as she loved a brook and the birds. How many books we have read on the banks of a brook. How many hours we have sat talking to each other as it babbled at our feet. When she died Scott said, "She was the most beautiful woman I ever knew and yet how few really knew or appreciated her."

🐾 🐾 🐾

January 23, 1883

Am up and dressed a part of every day now. Read aloud all the evening to Scott. Perhaps he wasn't proud and happy. He sat with his eyes hardly lifted from my face from the first to the last sentence.

🐾 🐾 🐾

January 26, 1883

Went to the house yesterday for the first time.[2] Carl sat looking at me and at last exclaimed, "It seems as if we have a visitor!" And he often came and kissed my hand or my dress or my hair.

Think of me often—Love me much, Your Barbara

"Carl of Lancaster presents his love and compliments to his darling Papa and requests the honor and joy of his company to his birthday supper to-night at 6 o'clock.

Goose Nest, Limona, Florida

February Fifth, Eighteen hundred and eighty-three (four years old)."[3]

I was able to make his birthday cake and trim the table with flowers. I put a wreath clear around the border of the cloth and we had a very happy time.

🐾 🐾 🐾

22. "Carl of Lancaster," Julia Daniels and Charles Scott Moseley's first son, is shown here at age five. He was named for his Pennsylvania birthplace. 1884.

March 18, 1883

To E.S.

I may not be able to write you very long or frequently before fall. My health is a constant source of pain to me. But by and by I shall be radiant in my pride and newborn joy or looking down upon you from Paradise.[4]

❧   ❧   ❧

March 24, 1883

Today I painted a frieze for the west room which is to be our sleeping room and we shall call it the Little Heart as it has the open fire and will really be our brightest room for a time. The frieze is made of heavy white canvas-like cloth, fringed five inches and on it I've painted a stream of scarlet poppies, yellow sunflowers and a blue blossom.

We can have nothing for a time that costs money but we cannot live without something sweet and lovely about the house.

❧   ❧   ❧

E.S.

The other morning Scott found our first morning glory. Carl was with him and he told him that it was my favorite flower. I did not have one last year, the first summer of my life that I ever went without. I was so delighted to see this that the next morning as soon as Carl was dressed it was his first thought. And he ran forth to see if one had blossomed and then back to his Papa, begging that he might be allowed to pick it for me himself. It amuses me when people speak of the children's taking care of Carl. Carl takes care of himself and waits upon us all and is our fun, our delight, our life and light, our bit of wisdom, our little rock. His little arms reach round us all. His little heart holds us all. You should see him flash if a word is breathed against a soul in The Goose Nest.

"Gretchen" is Clara Mayo. She married Col. Mayo of Mayo on the 28th of February.

🐾   🐾   🐾

Carl has a very sore finger and this morning he hurt it terribly. He said to me, "Mama, I just screamed and rattled and yelled when I hurt my finger. It was such a terrible hurt." I held him for over two hours and then I read to him. When he was ready to go he tucked the sheet all round me very snug and nice and I said, "What is that for, Carl?" and he looked up saying, "Oh! just to please my little love."

One of Carl's stories

"There were four girls of Lancaster and one fell off from a house and one fell off from a barn and one fell off from a horse and one fell off from a mule. And when they got up they couldn't tell which fell from the house and which fell off from the barn and which fell off from the horse and which fell off from the mule. And they had a terrible time and never could tell."

🐾   🐾   🐾

April 24, 1883

A genuine rainy day it has turned out to be and Scott and Carl are off miles from here in search of shingles and orange trees. They must be wet through but I can imagine the philosophical manner in which they will both take it wherever they are.

Later. My "boys" safe at home. Mr. Chamberlain was to go with them so they drove there.[5] They took off everything from poor, drenched Carl and arrayed him in a dry flannel shirt of Mr. Chamberlain's and put him to bed. He had a good sleep and was as contented as a kitten. They stayed all day for the rain did not cease until nearly dark. Mr. C. is coming to spend a Sunday with us. Scott is at this moment setting out trees by the light of a lantern.

❦   ❦   ❦

May 7, 1883

All my days are full of pain. I cannot write of them. Scott says if he were younger he would like to take Carl after his education was finished under his own care and impart to him all of his experience and knowledge.[6] He feels that he might fulfill the dreams and ambitions of his life for with his ingenious little brain and splendid courage and force of character he could accomplish wonders if set in the right direction. I know we have failed in many ways but Scott's work in this world is a fine inheritance to his children. And the world has been vastly richer for that ingenious brain of his and the future is not yet over.

❦   ❦   ❦

May 8, 1883

We sat up and played cribbage and read and forgot the hours were flying. It was one of my nervous nights with little pain. And when I feel better I do not know I am alive. I'm so happy. At last, Scott said, "I believe it is later than we realize" and it was four o'clock in the morning!

❦   ❦   ❦

May 11, 1883

Burt Coe had a little dancing party last night. Frindy was there and looked so sweet and fresh. They had bonfires and Florence said it was lovely.

❦ ❦ ❦

May 18, 1883

Seven happy eventful blessed years since your father with a tremulous voice and tears in his eyes pronounced the sacred words that made us "man and wife."

Carl stands beside me drawing a sailing fleet and explaining as he goes. I do wish you could see him draw. He is left handed and we never would allow anyone to try to help him to be otherwise. I glory in that little left hand. It possesses more cunning than many a pair of right ones. It is just as easy for him to draw anything bottomside up or sideways and it makes no difference where he begins. He is as apt to begin with a man's feet as his head. He will make the machinery of a mill or a ferry boat and then put the framework of the mill on top or the framework of the boat and everything fits as if they had been erected first. He draws like a flash. His fingers scarcely seem to touch the paper.

❦ ❦ ❦

May 19, 1883

We slept in our new room last night. The Little Heart is quite complete and I will tell you all about it. The closet is finished even to the shelves and hooks, the front of which is draped by a pair of yellow satiny finished hangings that we bought in Buffalo a year or more ago and never had used. Gray and pale blue flowers are sprinkled over them.

The frieze is up. Scott had a band four inches in depth put round the walls after they were sealed for the frieze so it would hang out from the wall. The effect is much prettier and the breeze catches it and tosses the fringe.

A dark olive curtain hangs across the double door into the open hall. And on the north we have what we call the "Dutch door." It opens half way and a little shelf runs across it. It is so quaint and pretty. We have the largest washstand I ever saw and about the daintiest and yet it is for use. A large

23. Impressed by boats at an early age, Carl was five when he made this sketch.

mirror hangs the long way. It is an old one I bought of the old "Captain" among the other things at the Lake.

Nothing we have is more delightful than a twelve-foot lounge that runs across part of the south side and under a large double window. It is made to open and we use it as a storeroom for many things. The mattresses fit so nicely and the large, soft pillows give it such a look of comfort.

We have just put up a long, broad mantel over the great fireplace and over it hangs Tadema's "Vintage Festival."[7] Beside the mantel, high up, Scott cut me what we call the picture window. It is a window about three feet square and is just to let in a picture of sky and treetops—an exquisite touch in the room.[8] Then comes the "swallow table"—a stand with a background of cream with flights of swallows in shades of brown, a scrap of French cloth

I bought in New Orleans. On the table are piled books and sometimes a basket of flowers or a bowl of something, while in the corner is a shelf to hold a jar of palms. That corner, with its "picture window," its palms, and "swallow table" is so pretty.

The bright flowers on the white frieze light up the grim walls. The curtains are soft and pretty and everything on rings so we can put them out of our way when we want all the breeze or all the light.

Just as we were through arranging the Little Heart a wagon drove up full of our friends—the Coes and Pratts. They all seemed perfectly charmed with everything. We all enter into each other's joys and sorrows in the most earnest way. I think in a new wild life people get nearer to each other's hearts in a great deal shorter time than in more civilized places. We depend on each other. We are obliged to and we dare not think of each other's shortcomings.

ﾟ ﾟ ﾟ

May 21, 1883

Mr. Chamberlain spent the evening here, which we spent in the Little Heart. He, too, was delighted with it. Lizzie told me she could hardly keep back the tears when she came in the other day. It seemed so like a lovely picture or like a room in a dream.

I do not look sick in the least. Scott says it is enough to make one feel well just to look at me. But I am never free from pain and some days I am very ill and everything tires me out. But soon I shall, indeed, be better and everything of any worth must cost someone a price sometime. There is one terrible thing of which I cannot speak. It haunts me sleeping or waking and that is to see Scott go north as soon as he feels safe in leaving me.

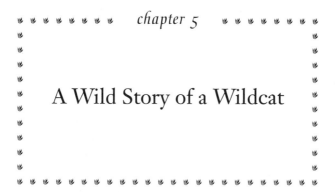

chapter 5

A Wild Story of a Wildcat

June, 1883

Carl said to someone, "And, don't you know my mother, my beautiful mother? Oh, but she is beautiful." Little Toodles McAsker came in with his jacket all torn off from him and his eye nearly gone. He had tried to thrash a boy that said his mother was better looking than Toodle's. Mrs. McAsker was a splendid woman. A woman that has been a mother to five adopted boys besides her own generally is—but she was not at all handsome and when she told Toodles that the other boy spoke the truth, poor Toodles threw his loyal arms about her neck, explaining, "I guess I know how you look. You are the most beautiful mother in the world."

Carl may possibly go with Scott. How can I ever live through it?

        ❧   ❧   ❧

August 4, 1883

To Scott.

Dearest. Go from me. Yet I feel that I shall stand
   Henceforward in thy shadow. Nevermore
   Alone upon the threshold of my door
   Of individual life, I shall command

The uses of my soul, nor lift my hand
Serenely in the sunshine as before,
Without the sense of that which I forbore,
Thy touch upon the palm. The widest land
Doom takes to part us, leaves thy heart in mine
With pulses that beat double. What I do
And what I dream include thee, as the wine
Must taste of its own grapes. And when I sue
God for myself, He hears that name of thine,
And sees within my eyes, the tears of two.[1]

As I stood watching you in the early morning riding out of my sight and beyond the sound of my voice and the sweet child at your side it seemed as if my heart must break. Never has it known such agony. But in spite of the pain and heaviness and sadness of that hour, the thought came to me that we were each other's though Death itself had borne one of us away and this beautiful sonnet of Mrs. Browning came to my mind with a truth and sweetness it had never known before and I wrote it for you to read again.

Your broad brimmed hats I hung side by side on the wall of the Little Heart. And your brogans in which you had tramped together over so many miles of Florida sand sit side by side near the "Dutch door." I've filled them with flowers.

Tell Carl everyday how his mother loves him.

Sunday I tried to write but I couldn't. Tears hid the page. My hand trembled.

We are having a beautiful shower. The water is sweeping in from the southeast in great sheets. Hallock is sleeping sweetly.[2] The thunder seems to fairly lift the house but he does not stir one little eyelash.

You can see all the dark, changing clouds and the hurrying storm through the pines. The glad blue of the sky by and by when the sun bursts out again, the plumy softness of the green and the laughing, dancing drops of water on every tree and leaf. Ah, how sweet it is to know we have seen it all again and again, side by side. And when I tell you in a letter "it storms today" you are here in an instant and can see it all without the telling.

Oh, Scott, come back to me, come back to me.

Little Carl, little Carl, you are my heart's delight.

❧   ❧   ❧

Your beautiful letter came today. You seemed near as I read. Oh, my love, how dear you are to me. Every thought and word and look is for you. Constantly you are with me and a part of me.

Hallock is just a month old today. And each day he grows both large and wise.

Every hour I long to weep but I keep back the tears and try to live as bravely as I can. I will not have the children feel that this dear home of ours is a house of woe.

Carl, sweet Carl.

I am so glad of all the little things you tell me of you and Carl and what he says and how he looks. If you knew how I sit here in the empty home with my baby close to my heart, thinking, thinking, thinking all day long you would understand how precious is the least word concerning my wanderers.

         ❦ ❦ ❦

August 7, 1883

This is my birthday. We had such a garden of morning glories on the breakfast table. Oh, Scott and Carl, my flower of flowers, come back to me.

         ❦ ❦ ❦

August 9, 1883

The time seems endless. The hours refuse to move. I was telling the children at lunch some stories from the Old Testament and really I wasn't sure whether the Queen of Sheba visited Solomon before you went North or since for it seems so unspeakably long since I beheld your face.

My new time table runs like this—
60,000 seconds make a minute
60,000 minutes make an hour
60,000 hours make one day
60,000 days make one week
60,000 weeks make one month
60,000 months make one year
Come back. Come back.

Soon I shall hear of the voyage. "Go softly, go safely, oh! boat of my lover, oh! boat of my lover that bears him from me." Tell Carl the ocean could not hold his mother's love for him.

᭙ ᭙ ᭙

Hallock is a lovely boy but sleeps but little. The embodiment of life.

The birds are singing. The mornings are as fair, the sunsets as bewitching as when you were here. But without you to share them their charm seems gone, like a delicious repast offered to one whose appetite has vanished.

The garments you have worn, the books you last touched, the playthings of Carl's, all speak to me in such pitiful voices of my loss that I think sometimes I must hide them to keep my heart from breaking. And then I know that every log and crevice of the old cabin would remind me of you and if I burned it down, the earth whereon it stood and the sky over it would still speak only of you. I can never go far enough back in my memory to find anything that will not in some way remind me of you and Carl.

᭙ ᭙ ᭙

The mail bag just here and in your letter from Savannah the very words I wanted. The name of the boat, the hour you were to start, and the time you were to arrive in New York, and that you loved me. I so well know that. I could not doubt it if I would. And yet always the words are like dew to me. What a meager scrap of a letter awaits you in New York. But soon as I know where you will be this long one will be flying on its way and what long and blessed letters you are sending. But for them I could not live.

Blessings for Carl.

᭙ ᭙ ᭙

Hallock commands me morning, noon and night. I shall not be able to do anything to make the home more lovely for your return. But if I keep this little pearl of a son well and give him to you all joyous and beautiful in his bewitching babyhood you will think him gift enough I know.

Carl, dear Carl.

❧   ❧   ❧

August 16, 1883

Every twelve hours that I rock back and forth with Hallock it is 26,640 times. I counted.

I've lived through this day better than any other since you left me. And yet I told Florence that if I could have my choice to see you this day for half an hour and then die, or wait until Christmas and live, I would say, "Let me die if I can but see and touch them once more." But I must be brave. I know I'm a miserable coward. I seem to have lost all power, save the torture of your absence.

❧   ❧   ❧

August 17, 1883

I am happy, so happy for you are safely over the voyage. I was worrying that Carl was ill. But never for an instant am I troubled with anxiety over him. I know that a love wiser and tenderer even than my own watches over him. What have you not been to him these four years of his young life? And hard as it is to be separated from him, it is a constant joy to me to know that a part of my very self is always near you in my beautiful boy.

Tell Carl how I love him and how proud I am of him and that never in all the years that are to come must he do aught to wound my love or lessen my pride in him.

Tell Carl he wouldn't know his little bed. I've had new pale blue curtains and canopy and the Sistine Madonna hung at the foot. And when the curtains are looped up and little Hal with his skin like a pearl, his hair like a mist of gold so fine it is, lies on the little white pillow it is a pretty picture. But Mama never watches him that she does not think of that other boy so inexpressively dear who slept on that same pillow a little while ago and in her dreams he lies there still. Cover him with kisses for me.

Keep well. Keep a brave heart. Be happy. And remember that you are the life of my life. Your Trix.[3]

August 20, 1883

Your tenth letter came today, mailed at Philadelphia. They have all invited me to spend days with them and I think it would do me good but Hal and I belong at home. I like it best. And the coming back and not finding you here I cannot do. They must come to me instead.

Evening. I'm sitting on the lounge in the Little Heart. All the house asleep. A beautiful shower today. The clouds were magnificent. All through my life in cloud and shine I need thee.

❦ ❦ ❦

August 25, 1883

I sent off your second long letter this morning. I shall have such uneventful days to recount, dear Scott, that these letters will be of little interest, save that they tell of our health and bear ever the message of a faithful heart.

❦ ❦ ❦

August 26, 1883

There is a broad rainbow over in the southeast and the trees in the bayhead have caught the glory and are blooming in pink and purple. The clouds are magnificent. The entire heavens look down in black and gold and mellow burning colors with dashes of crimson. Thunder is roaring as if it would tear the earth to atoms. Lightning is flashing. The rain is falling thick and fast and yet amid it all the sun is shining with an unusual brilliance. Come home. Our little world down here is a world of splendor tonight.

Carl, my bright, sweet boy. Why are you not sitting beside Mama?

❦ ❦ ❦

August 28, 1883

We have our meals "on time" nearly always and however sad I feel I try never to be so at table. We always talk of pleasant things and the table is always lovely with its order, its pretty dishes and its beautiful flowers. No matter how little we have, it is served sweetly. My children must never remember a shabby or unhappy table whether we dine on stuffed peacocks or dry crusts.

September 2, 1883

I've on a white dress and water lilies. The room is as fresh as a wild rose and flowers are everywhere. Little Hallock is asleep and the curtains are drawn. But should I lift them and you could see the picture within, you, too, would feel that nothing more beautiful could meet your eyes anywhere, seek where you would.

One little hand is tucked under a pink cheek. The other lies on his breast. The morning breeze tosses his soft yellow hair. The child so still, the white spotless bed, the pale blue of the curtains, the lovely Madonna and the cherubs looking down upon the living picture. I've been again and again to look that I might never forget it. Some day if he lives my Hallock will be a man and "hold his head to other stars" but while life lasts I shall have the sweet joy of his babyhood in my heart. And now in my loneliness I so cling to him and his beauty is such a joy to me. It may seem strange coming from a mother's lips but he is so much more of a joy to me for his perfect little body, his exquisite skin, the masses of his wondrous hair, his round and shapely head, his beautiful eyes. His very beauty shortens and brightens the hours for me.

Tell Carl I have so longed to hold him in my arms and know neither sea nor land divide us. And if I long to behold Carl, how then must I long to behold the face of my love who is dearer even than my little child in whom I have such pride and joy?

We are blessed, Scott. We have health and in our love for fine things, nothing can debar us from possessing many. We have such love and faith in each other. I know we have had and are having great money troubles. But as long as we are so rich in some things, let us never repine or get down-hearted. What would kingdoms and crowns and seas of gold be without the other? I've always known it but this separation is burning it into my very soul.

* * *

September 4, 1883

The children have spent the day with friends of theirs. Hallock and I went across the field to meet them in the twilight. Does it not seem strange to think of him and I [*sic*] going over fields and watching flocks of curlews and the nighthawks and singing all the way? How he does laugh! I'm going to teach him so young to love all beautiful things that he can never remember when he did not.

I read aloud to the children a good deal. I do not suppose Hallock really comprehends very much of it but he looks wiser than any of us. He follows me with his eyes everywhere and when I turn and bend over him he laughs aloud and his voice is like the air of his native state—clear and sweet and without a flaw.

᙮ ᙮ ᙮

May 22, 1891

Note—Dear boys.

The following letter dated Oct. 2, 1883 was written to Papa for fun. He was where he had much of interest to write me, while my life was as quiet and uneventful as a life could well be. It seemed to me as if he must grow tired of my sky and my Hal and my flowers and nothing else. So one day when I sat down to write I thought how monotonous my letters were and exclaimed, if someone could burn out or I could shoot a Wild Cat, I could send an interesting letter. And I thought I'd write of those things. Mr. Chamberlain had had word that his mother and sister wanted to come and see him. But he had no way to make it pleasant for them, as they were people accustomed to much elegance. Judge Knapp was our postmaster. The letter instead of amusing Papa as I intended and his taking it as a joke made him almost indignant with me for he believed it and it came near bringing him home in a hurry. At the time this letter was written, the law against killing a pig in Florida was very severe—much more so it was sometimes said than the killing of a man. I never wrote any more romances to Papa, ever after adhering closely to facts and the weather. Mama.[4]

᙮ ᙮ ᙮

October 2, 1883

To Scott

Limona, Florida. Dearest. Greatly as this letter will surprise and perhaps alarm you, do not allow it to distress or disturb you. Remember that great as the danger and excitement have been, they are now over and we are living as serenely and quietly as before. So full of strange and startling events have the last few days been, it seems as if I must have been living through some horrible nightmare.

On Thursday afternoon Florence and Hallock and I were here alone. We saw a smoke in the direction of Mr. Coe's and it seemed as if it must come from the very spot on which the house stood. And Frindy would have gone over at once to make sure but she did not want to tramp over sandspurs and brush heaps a second time for nothing, as only that morning I had seen a smoke and sent her flying and the fire was a fence half a mile from there. But the smoke grew so dense we felt that we would like to feel sure it was not the Coe's and Florence flew for her boots. Before the last one was on I was sure I heard not only voices but the roaring and crackling of burning timber and by the time Frindy had reached the spot the school children, the hands from Burdick's Mill, and everyone within call was there.

But nothing could be done. It was discovered too late and scarcely an article was saved unharmed and now the house in which we have had such an interest, whose doors were always open wide to us, whose welcome and friendliness was stamped upon the broad piazzas and open hall, the home our friends had planned and built hoping to make of it a home for their old age is now a heap of blackened logs and ashes. And yet it is wonderful the calmness with which they bear this calamity. Mrs. Coe says the things she cannot get over are family letters and a few sacred things no time or money can replace.

There can probably nothing be proven as to where the guilt lies. But there is little doubt where the fire originated. I could write a long time on this subject alone. But must hasten on to an adventure that will strike terror to your heart, though bear in mind, my darling, that we are safe and "all's well that ends well."

When Will was over and shot the hawk and I saw how easily he handled the little pistol and what a simple thing it was I determined to use it myself and begged him to teach me. I practiced a good deal and, though it may sound vain, I've made some pretty fair shots.

I know you have always considered me too reckless to handle firearms, but when you realize that this little pistol has been the means of saving one or more of our lives you will never regret the experiment and will preserve the pistol as something almost sacred.

When Claude came home from school Friday afternoon we were out of milk and he was obliged to hasten back to town for it so Frindy and I were alone. She had gone out to shut up the Whist and do several things for the night as it would be nearly, if not quite, dark before Claude returned. I had given Hallock his supper and was singing him to sleep when Frindy went out. As soon as his eyes were fairly closed I laid him down and walked out on the back porch to watch the sky.

The sun was gone but in the west were a few clouds of strange and somber beauty. And while I stood watching them and the landscape before me, I saw the tall dog fennel moving to and fro over by the fence as though something were creeping through it. At first I thought nothing of it, so absorbed was I in the change all nature was undergoing in the gathering dusk, but suddenly I noticed that whatever it was, it was not only near the house but heading directly toward it.

You know my greatest horror is a snake and immediately those huge rattlers from Dopp's Hammock[5] came to my mind and I flew into the house and snatched the pistol which lay loaded on the mantel. By the time I reached the porch the creature had begun to emerge from the taller weeds and I could make out the outline of some object stealing toward the house. I thought at first it was a pig and even laughed aloud at the thought of all the dire mishaps that might befall me should I be so unfortunate as to have shot a pig in southern Florida.

But I determined he should not sleep under our cabin at least and called to Frindy to come and help me get him out. And then, oh! Scott, how can I ever portray the horror of that moment? There crept forth a Wild Cat and crouched ready for a spring, only a few feet from me. But before he could make that fatal spring, I had fired. He was hit and in the head but only wounded. And had I not flung my left arm quick as a flash across my throat no one can tell what the end might have been. At this moment Frindy reached us and most blessed chance she had the ax in her hand. Among the things to be done at night is to bring in the ax and put it near the Dutch door and when I called her she had just completed the last thing to be done and was coming in and bringing in the ax to put in its accustomed place. And what did the brave girl do but raise it now in my defense and strike the animal such a blow that he loosened his hold and fell backwards. I fired not once, but three or four times and two bullets fortunately entered his head and our enemy lay quite lifeless.

My left arm was badly torn as it received almost the entire force of his final spring and a terrific scratch. But the Russian dressed it before morning (for Claude went for help soon as he came back and half the town was here in a few hours) and I may be obliged to wear it in a sling some time yet.

Mr. Weeks is dressing and preserving the skin for me and when you return I will lay it at your feet with pride unspeakable.[6]

I could write a good deal before I told you all that has been said and done over this strange adventure. Everyone that has heard of it, both far and near, have been to see the place where the Wild Cat was shot and over to see the skin at Mr. Weeks'. Sunday several were out from Tampa. Judge Crane and his wife spent the day at Dr. Pratt's and came over here to call upon us in the afternoon.[7] The Judge said he not only forgave me for keeping his book so long but was proud to have had it in the possession of so brave a woman.

It is evidently a young animal and probably not fully grown, but large enough to have raised such a furor as you would hardly have thought possible in this wilderness of pine and sand.

I must tell you of one more item of interest before I close this somewhat unusual letter. Mr. Chamberlain's illness decided his mother and sister in their desire to come to Florida. They started within two or three days after receiving a line from Mrs. Coe saying he was ill. They made up their minds to come, prepared to keep house and give him the benefit of a home for one winter at least. They even brought a cook and maid with them. But on arriving, Mr. Chamberlain, being able by that time to ride so far, met them at the steamer and soon convinced them that it was utterly impossible for them to remain in Tampa. But they insisted on being near him and clung to their first determination to keep house and after much arguing and some maneuvering on the part of Mr. Chamberlain they succeeded in renting New Hope Church for the winter and early spring and are fully established there now. The room is curtained off in Oriental style and Mrs. Coe writes me that the effect is charming. Soon as possible they will have a cook room and servants' quarters put up outside. I am quite anxious to see them and their home. They are very interesting I hear, though aristocratic and somewhat ascetic in their tastes. But Mr. Chamberlain has not seemed so contented and in such good spirits since we knew him.

Judge Knapp arrived home from the North Sunday with a bride of thirty-three, very good looking and nice appearing with the exception of a slight limp. And report says something of an heiress.

The mail is waiting. I've only time to add that facts have come to such a stagnant pass here at The Nest and our community that there weren't enough left to make a letter of and I was obliged to resort to romance. Ever yours and yours only, Trix.

❦ ❦ ❦

October 10, 1883

There is such a stillness over everything today. I'm alone save sleeping Hallock. No sound save the singing of the birds and the buzzing of the insects. One enraged old bumble bee is flying about and banging his head under the roof. Two wasps are having a fight in the doorway. And some yellow butterflies are madly waltzing over the bed of scarlet cypress. Two grim old buzzards are sailing round and round in the blue sky. The needles of the pines glisten like polished steel. The gray moss moves lazily to and fro. How gracefully the tall slender autumn grasses bend to each other. Everything seems steeped in sunshine and peace and stillness. Hallock and I seem alone in the world and even Hallock sleeps.

Carl, my little Carl, why do you stay so long?

❦ ❦ ❦

October 29, 1883

Dearest.

A letter just here from E.S. and I want to copy a little for you for they were words that made me so happy. She is telling of your call with Carl. "I was telling him how Louie Waldron said only yesterday that I had so many things to remind me of Jule and he asked in what way. And I said in the little things all about. I've never known anyone else who could be so generous with so little as Jule. She puts so much thoughtfulness into all she does and always makes so much brightness out of trifles, more than any other one I had ever known." And she said you answered in your quiet, undemonstrative, impressive way that I must know so well and that must be so dear to me, "No one else does it" just as we would say, "God loves us."

It brought the tears to my eyes to hear that sweet praise from my dieudonne whom I love best of all women on earth and echoed by the one who is the love of my life.[8] And then she says of Carl, "Carl is Jule's own boy

24. Limona's tall older pines were vulnerable during summer thunderstorms. Those tapped for turpentine, such as the one shown here, were particularly at risk during sudden shifts in wind direction. 1908.

and what can I say more?" He is so frank, so bright, so original, affectionate and self-possessed. I want him with me everyday. He was looking at some views through the glass and he turned to me saying, 'These stereopticon views look as if they were in the world.' Whatever he may be to others, she says, to us he is the most beautiful child in the world."

Not a time since you went away have I so longed to show you the night as it was a few days ago. The sun had gone to sleep. All the sky was a blush of pale pink. The trees looked black. The moss like plumy shadows. There was over all the world a mist and the atmosphere and hour was such that it was a pale pink. It seemed as if the world was trying to hide itself behind a roseate veil, so intangible and unreal it seemed as if it might be some rare perfume trying to reveal itself in the very breath of a color. It was indescribable but to see the trees, the flowers, the sky itself as if looking through these heavenly tinted tissues was lovely beyond words. Never before in my life have I seen nature in such exquisite delicacy.

I do not wonder Gypsies and Indians never can be quite tamed and they refuse to give up their free life. I love Florida more and more. I never want to live for long again where this soft air cannot find me, where this radiant sky is not over me. And I love the pines as I've loved the rocks and cliffs. Now and then we can fly away and see the mountains and the sea and have a great breath of the world. But in this climate let us live and die.

Listen! Listen! Do you not hear that voice? That little laughing, sunny voice, the very music of sunshine. It is your Hallock, your own beautiful boy, who will gladden your heart while you live. Praise heaven. He seems like a draft from the fountain of youth, such a living embodiment of joy is he.

Make haste and come to me. I can wait no longer.

❦ ❦ ❦

November 7, 1883

To Carl of Lancaster

Come quick, most precious Carl. Little Hallock is waiting for thee. The blocks are ready and all the old playthings. The scarlet cushions are ready. The long lounge, the hammock, the big rug down by the fire. The sun shines on the south porch. The sky is blue. The air is sweet. The birds are singing. A few wild flowers still linger for thy dear hand to gather and Mama, oh Mama, is dying for thee. Hurry my little Carl, hurry.

＊ ＊ ＊

To E.S.

My beloved dieudonne, I must begin your letter before Carl and Scott get here for I want it to seem like life and if I wait until they've come it will be all joy and that isn't life at all.

Scott's eightieth letter came Friday and such letters as he sends.[9] They keep me alive. We think and talk of nothing now but that homecoming. We expect not only will the sun shine in all his glory that day but the moon and stars ought to be out and if possible a comet. I wish I could make you see Hallock as he is. Not only our friends and acquaintances talk of his beauty but the "Crackers" and "Darkies" and the people who go by and ask for water on the way stand and look at him and sometimes come back and look again.[10]

I have many things to tell you but I have so little time that I can only hurry them through. It seems a little strange but I have not known physical fear here at all until I went to the Coes'. Mrs. Coe drove up one morning and took Hallock and me to their place at Seffner where they are for a time and where the new railroad is going through.[11] I had a nice time. Mr. Chamberlain is there, too, and their oldest son, Burt. While there Burt was shot one night. It was a bright moonlight night. He sleeps in a cabin a short walk from the house where we had all been having a happy evening together. He had not been gone but a few moments when he came running back with his arm all blood and his shirt sleeve burnt off. He flew upstairs for the gun. Mr. Coe took a pistol and followed him and Mr. Chamberlain with a bowie knife. It was a serious waiting for Mrs. Coe and me but soon they returned and I dressed Burt's wound, which happily was only a flesh wound. He was shot by a "Darkie" for his money but the man was never found. He belonged to the railroad gang who are the very worst kind of "Darkies" that the South has, so the Coes say and even warned the people against them. They are not always of this order, sometimes sober and respectable. I was terribly frightened and could not get over it but was full of terror every time I waked in the night after my return and am to this day.

Mr. and Mrs. Coe came up and spent a day and night with us, sleeping in the Little Heart. Mr. Coe says it is the quaintest room he ever saw.

Scott's letters are full of Carl's pictures. The little darling tries to send me pictures of anything he sees. When in New York he said, "Papa, take me down to the Chinese laundry again." And when Papa asked why he wanted to go there, he said, "To study the Chinese. Mama wants me to send her pictures of everything and how can I draw the Chinese unless I study them."

Everywhere the child makes a host of friends. Scott writes, "Carl is so sweet when I can get a word with him alone but he is a perfect society man now." I wonder what Carl will think of Hallock. Before he went away he would insist upon always talking to him in a whisper and when I asked why he did so he replied, "I cannot talk aloud to him, Mama, he is too tender."

No words can tell you what this separation has been to me. I sometimes wished I had never known the joy of love that I might not know its pain. There have been nights in which I've walked the sands til daylight—my dear ones seemed so far away I could not sleep and the torture was so great I couldn't lie still and endure it. There was no voice to comfort me. No one to whom I could say that life seemed too hard. I do not know but it is a false kind of courage but I could never endure to hold any other than a gay face to the world. Few really care for our troubles and nearly all have more than enough of their own and to many it seemed a simple matter to live apart from one's husband and little son. But to me it meant the joy of my own self and the agony of anxious fears known only to the heart that loves beyond measure and beyond measure.

※　※　※

November 22, 1883

To E.S.

"It is mere accident that makes life sweet at times. It has nothing to do with years or place or beauty."[12] This past week has been such a sad one for me. I presume Scott has sent my letters telling of my illness. To think how near I came to missing both my boys. I've had congestion of the lungs before and they are more delicate on that account perhaps. I wanted to do so much. I had so many plans. Everything must go now and I must be content just to be alive.

※　※　※

25. In this 1883 sketch Julia Daniels Moseley depicts herself sweeping down cobwebs from the open porch as she joyfully prepares for Scott's return from a business trip in the North.

December 5, 1883

To E.S.

This is the day that the boat sailed across Tampa Bay with my precious freight. Every door is wreathed in palms. Beautiful roses and oleanders are in the rooms. We are all dressed and waiting. I am trembling with joy and fear. Bonfires are ready to light and I can do nothing but hold my breath and listen.

        ❦   ❦   ❦

They are here safe and well. They were the first passengers on our new railroad, the South Florida. Scott and Carl and my brother Preston. Scott says they told him I looked well but to him I looked sad and as if I had been in sorrow and I had. But I shall soon be better now.

Scott says Hallock is the most beautiful little child he ever saw. He is shy and allows no one he does not see very often to hold him. But he went with a laugh to Scott and when I went up to him a little after, he nestled down closer as if he wanted to stay.

Last night the Russian was here. He said, "Your children lack nothing. I hope they will live long to make you proud and happy." Few things in life are sweeter to a mother's ears than praise of her children.

It is fun to hear Carl describe people and places. One charm of his is his apt words.

꙼   ꙼   ꙼

We had our dinner out-of-doors with morning glories on the table. I rocked little Hallock to sleep out under the stars. The doors and windows open all day. Such was Hallock's first Christmas.

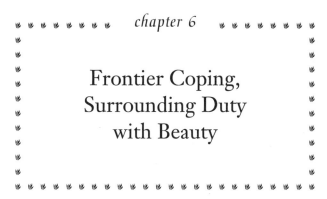

chapter 6

Frontier Coping,
Surrounding Duty
with Beauty

February 15, 1884, The Little Rest, Peru, Florida.[1]

To E.S.

We are on the banks of a southern river, six miles from The Nest. Scott thought a change would do me good. There is a little cottage here we have named the Little Rest, as it was to rest that we have come. In the cottage we live and get our meals but we sleep at Tamarind Hall, a few steps from here.

The house is a dingy, old affair. All the woodwork inside is stained burnt umber. Just imagine the gloom of it if you can. Our chamber is huge and high and grim, extending over the entire house. I told Scott it looked as if it had been built and decorated expressly for the funeral of some black-hearted old goblin. I said that it seemed as if a man who could have conceived such a room with its diabolical paint, its little cracks of windows with their grimy blinds and solid shutters, its very floors and walls begrimed, its high, far-away ceilings where bats could fly forever and ever and not be caught, it seemed as if such a man could murder people just for a pastime. But, indeed, he is nothing of the sort, but hospitable and kind and his little wife is good and sweet with a pure heart.

The house stands on a hilltop—at least it is a hilltop for Florida—amid an orange grove. It looks out upon a broad river. Pines stretch away in the distance. Cedars, yuccas, palms stand along its banks. The wild jasmine clambers down along to the water's edge. The tide comes in from Tampa Bay, five miles away. Boats sail up and down and now and then a steamer puffs by.

One night Scott and I lay in wait for the moon and the world was beautiful. We stepped out on the balcony. The moon's kiss had enchanted everything. The dark green of the orange leaves glistened to be in harmony with the bosom of the river. The pines stood silent and black. The tall, stately palms with their white velvet trunks seemed to be made entirely of moonbeams. An owl sat in a distant tree and sounded as if its vile heart was made of woe. The soft air seemed to fondle us and its touch was like the poetry of a breeze. Indeed, dear, this climate is the very love song of a climate.

Scott and Carl have gone fishing. The babe of the House of Moseley is sweetly sleeping among the scarlet cushions on the floor. I think your foolish heart would melt if you could see him. He has just had a bath and his clean white dress is so fresh and spotless. The fine lace frills curling around his neck and wrists, one lovely arm lies over his head and the other is lying a sweet little line of plumpness down his side. His yellow hair falls over his forehead and closed lids. The wind catches it and tosses it to and fro like little golden sunbeams.

The work is all done in The Rest. A white pitcher of blue violets and ferns stands on the table. The sunshine comes in at the open window and lies a stream of light across the room. A lark is singing to me of the morning. The breath of wild flowers and treetops is in his voice and I think lovingly and longingly of you. Are you shivering in the cold while I'm basking in the sunshine? I'm not well yet, not as well as I wish I was, but I've forgotten everything but that birdsong and this morning seems made of joy.

❦   ❦   ❦

February 24, 1884

Home again and there is no place so excellent and so beyond all compare and good as home. It was a charming ride home. I sat in my own little Dutch rocker and nearly every foot of the way was over violets. The sand was blue with them.

I wish I could write you of one ghoulish night we had there. It stormed and after the boys were asleep Scott and I descended to a little, low room somewhere down among the eaves where there was a fire and a blackened old chimney. The lord of Tamarind Hall had been in the diamond mines of South America and had seen some strange things in his day. He was not a miner but there in some capacity connected with the diamond trade. He converses very well when interested, is quite a reader, indeed partly supports himself with the proceeds from his pen. One story was frightful. The people were in rowboats, a shark followed all the way and a body was buried on the banks of a river. And another was of a woman buried at night. He has a low, rather impressive, harsh sort of way of telling such things and that with the smoldering fire, the black walls, the moaning of the storm outside, one small sickly lamp, and the lateness of the hour made one feel as if they were in some evil place where death was liable at every moment to creep in and clutch or smother one. And to go from that uncanny room to our own great, black chamber was if anything more frightful still. I felt of the children to see if they breathed. We shall never forget that night. I'm a little chilly now as I recall it.

One night while there I supposed Carl was asleep. He slept the entire length of our room from us. He said, "Mama, sometimes when I was away I used to shut my eyes and try to think of your voice. All the time I was gone I never heard anything so sweet." I think he has such lovely thoughts and then at times he expresses them so sweetly. There are depths within depths in Carl's nature I think and surely it is not all in just my foolish heart.

❦ ❦ ❦

March 3, 1884

Scott brought me a great leaf from a cabbage palm, the stem nearly nine feet and the leaves measured seven. When he asked where he should put it, I said, "Nail it to the ceiling" and so he did. And then we made a mad fire in the great chimney and then had supper under this exquisite canopy. And after supper when Hallock had had his evening bath and his pretty white gown, we laid a scarlet comfort on the floor under the palm and put the darling on it. You should have seen the picture it all made—the quaint room, the garden of flowers, the palm, the beautiful little child on the bright floor, and over all the dancing firelight.

The large, white blossoms I sent you are of that pure whiteness of new snow. I use them a great deal, especially on the breakfast table. And when that breakfast table stands upon the south porch, these sweet spring mornings with the sunlight falling in great riffs along the rough beams and the birds are singing love songs as only wild, southern birds can sing, and on the table is the delicate old china, then the flowers seem as much at home as in their own hammocks. They are beautiful, too, in a great mass under the sad, tender face of St. Cecilia.[2]

ʷ   ʷ   ʷ

March 22, 1884

Our sweet Hallock of Florida has five teeth through. He says Mama all the time now and Papa quite often. He is indeed a joy forever for from morn til night or asleep or awake he is "a thing of beauty." Scott has made him a lovely highchair of cabbage palm stems and his face with its beauty and vivacity adds greatly to the charm of our table for he behaves very sweetly and is quite an honor to us.

This is the twenty-sixth day of the month and I have cut and made twenty-eight garments this month. I hardly see myself how I have accomplished it for I have been so far from well. Some were Hal's waist and skirts which were very simple and I could easily make three or four in a day. But I'm in a hurry to get the necessary sewing done before May, which is the most disagreeable month in the year to us. Had I gold and to spare, never a needle would go between my fingers.

I must tell you of one thing I did just to show you that even the things that we dislike are not all disagreeable. Jenny sent Frindy a delicate blue dress. After it was fitted I laid it aside and made it when she was away and I painted some ribbons to wear with it and made her a bundle of Indian muslin ruffles and other things she needed and folded them all in a basket and sent a note by Carl to the room she sat in telling her that her fairy godmother had left a basket on the queen's bed for her. Her delight was so sweet. She is such a guileless child it was not at all hard to surprise her. And but for some sweet surprise or happy holiday, the countless stitches are torture to me.

But for the romance and the beauty with which I surround the common-place duties I should lie down and die from despair. When I was a child and had to shell peas and string beans and pick over strawberries and rip off buttons I always played games with them. It was never a pea I took from the pod but a pearl from the shell. The beans were a terrible task set by an ogre and to be done at such an hour or my head must be whacked off. How my fingers flew and when Grandmamma used to ask why I always played games I used to tell her that I couldn't do sober work things like other people. I had to make them into other things or I could never do them. And it is the same now among the real duties of life. Often people say they do not see how I can spend so much time over my flowers about the rooms but it is the beauty of these things that make the sweeping and dusting possible and takes from me the hardest part of the fatigue. If my table was not exquisite the drudgery of the meals would be a terror and so it runs through everything and in the beauty of my life lies forgetfulness of so much that is dull and ugly.

❦ ❦ ❦

May 10, 1884

We have had some company. An Elgin party surprised us one day. They seemed charmed with our home. Three ladies from the North spent a day. Mary Lizzie Pratt spent two days with us. She is back from the North where she spent some months. She is very frail.

❦ ❦ ❦

May 11, 1884

Our dear old "Pet" is today among the Ten Thousand Isles, eating bananas, pineapples or coconuts or mangoes or custard apples or some other tropical fruit. They have had fine weather for their trip and perfect moonlight.

One night while Scott was in Tampa we killed a fox. Think of it, my dear girl. While you are lying so safe in the heart of a town, I'm in the wilderness and rising in the dead of night to help slay wild beasts (no romance this time—stern facts). His pretty skin lies before the swallow stand in the Little Heart now. Beauty is a power. I felt as if I wanted to set him free because he was so handsome.

Hallock has a sweet little trick of raising both arms when he wants anything and holding them toward you with the little palms outspread in such a supplicating way. Carl says, "He is a very praying child. I suppose he talks to God a great deal."

I've sent Gretchen a lock of Hallock's hair. She always calls herself the little boy's godmother and she wrote, "Tell my little godson how I have a bit of sunshine from his wise little pate for peeps on rainy days. Why, it is just like light and surely it spoke louder than any words which he will learn to utter ever can. For what is so sweet and pathetic as a lock of a tiny baby's hair."

The very day that sweet expression came, "Andrew's Mother," the old "Darkie," came around with blackberries. She had never seen Hallock and I brought him out for her to praise. Up went her arms with a perfect shout as she exclaimed, "Oh, where did he get his pretty candy colored hair?" Could anything more perfectly portray the difference that lives in my little witch of a Gretchen and this poor old slave born in a southern wilderness?

When I came out to breakfast I was very tired from a sleepless night with Hallock and had slept late. Everyone kept so still. There stood the table so fresh and pretty in the open hall and fish just caught in the lake. And Frindy had cooked it so brown and crisp for me and my chair was full of water lilies Claude had gathered. I felt new all in a minute—no longer old and tired. Scott always reads to me to rest me and no one in the world was ever so charming a reader as he. Some day when Birdie is especially sweet, get her to read to you "The Legend of Padre José" by Thomas A. Janvier in the Century for July '83.[3] It is exquisite and by a dear and intimate friend of our friend, Mr. Chamberlain. He has told us delightful things of him and of his very gifted and lovely wife.

A mere shadow of a man called here the other day but tall enough to have been raised in a bamboo thicket. He was so long and so slender it seemed more appropriate to offer him a reed than a chair.[4]

❧ ❧ ❧

May 19, 1884

It has seemed as if sorrow was sweeping in on all sides since I wrote on the 11th. The dispatches containing the word of Auntie Mama's death never reached us and I heard of it first through Cousin Mary's letter and a package containing lace and a ring that Auntie wanted sent to me as a parting token. Then came Charlie's letter with his little Harry's death.[5] It seemed doubly hard for me to write him sitting here with my two boys to give me back my caresses. Charlie worshipped his little son. Another letter gave an account of the death of Ulrich Fairbanks. I knew his mother so well that summer at Lake Erie. We have had many a happy hour together. And he has taken me out for a sail with her in the twilight and was always so lovely to Carl. He was just through school and so full of promise and hope.

At five o'clock today we buried Lizzie Pratt. Her grave is beside her mother's under a group of pines in their own yard and the grave is ripe with cape jasmine. They wanted me to arrange the lace at her throat and I laid two half-opened water lilies among the folds. When she spent a day with us a little while ago there was a large pitcher of water lilies in the room and when she went home she said, "You do not know the pleasure just that one pitcher of lilies is to me." How little I thought then that before a week was gone she would be lying in her grave with my lilies on her breast.

chapter 7

Real Events Happen
in the Heart

June 4, 1884

To E.S.

I've not been able to write. Not ill but so sad and my love is soon to go North again and it is beyond my strength or courage to talk of it even to you whom I love so well.

Hallock walks splendidly and alone everywhere and is the glory and beauty and sunbeam of this house.

July 2, 1884

To Scott

In the Cheer. Dearest. You have just gone. I could not wave you goodbye from the porch. It doesn't seem quite so much as if you were not coming into the room again if I do not see you riding away. It almost seems as if the world had died but I will try and get over the sad hours and this agony of loneliness and live for you.

Yesterday Carl was playing alone in the east room and as I passed the door I heard him talking and, thinking he spoke to me, paused to listen but he had not seen me and was talking to himself. He was sitting on the floor with his hands clasped over one little knee and kept saying over and over, "Oh, I wish Papa would come back. Oh, I wish Papa would come back." I stole softly away. I felt that even I couldn't comfort him. He is asleep now. I went to his bed and lifted the curtain a few moments ago to watch him as he slept. What a dignified looking fellow he is. I almost wondered as I stood looking down upon him lying there, so tall and shapely with that grand little air of his, how I ever dared shake him. But he is naughty enough sometimes and I've not only a very human son in my Carl but he has a very human mother in me.

At lunch he burst out, "Oh, dear. I just wish I could step into a depot or some sort of a nice place and come across Papa." We were standing on the porch this morning and talking of you and he said, "I tell you, Mama, I feel like fainting away when I think of Papa. Oh, I cannot tell you how I feel when I think of his going away so far and not taking me with him. How could he do it?" Of course, he is full of fun and mischief but he seems to just mourn for you at times. "Oh," he says with such an eager look, "I wish I could hear that whistle and he would come and not go away again." You know how he loves you. I need not tell you.

Tonight as I lie and watch the old familiar pines through the south window I shall think of you on the beautiful Southern River. I will think loving thoughts until I fall asleep to dream that the waiting is over.

❧ ❧ ❧

Scott

It is little Hal's birthday. A year ago this morning we heard his voice for the first time. This is the day that you are to be in Cincinnati. I wonder if you are in the pleasant home on the bluff talking to the Osbornes. I can see and hear it all so plainly, from the dishes and exquisite linens to the diamonds in Mrs. Osborne's ears. She was made for diamonds and fine laces. Such things seem hers by every right. I can hear her saying in that pleasant voice, "Perhaps you will be more comfortable here, Mr. Moseley." All their chairs are comfortable and one found it hard to leave them. I think one can tell so much of the life of a home just by the chairs and the way they are arranged.

❧   ❧   ❧

July 9, 1884

Already you must be missing this matchless climate. These soft breezes are in love with Hallock's hair. How they toss and toss it, down to his blue eyes it falls like a shower of sunbeams. Then a little breeze will come flitting through the hall and stops and lifts the golden mass and covers with kisses that white, beautiful forehead. Then hurries on and another and another and another hurries in. But they all stop to offer a caress to Hal, sweet Hal. The happy sunbeams and every gentle wind that blows love him. And, alas and alas, so do the mosquitoes.

I asked Carl how often he thought of you and he looked up with the utmost surprise, saying, "Why, Mama, I'm thinking of him all the time. I can never stop thinking of him." This morning Hal came tripping across the south porch and put his sweet head through the window and I called out, "Hello, sweet, who's a blessing?" And the little darling piped up, "Papa, Papa."

Last night the sky was so beautiful that I sat out on the porch until it was quite dark and held Hal, singing him to sleep, and little Carl lay on the rug at my feet and sang, too. The night hawks darted over our heads. Now and then one bold fellow flew under the roof. Last night I slept but little and this morning Frindy would not waken me. Carl was very impatient to see me and Frindy said he kept coming softly to the bed and would kiss the curtains and then steal out. He said, "Mama, I love you millions more than my tongue can tell. But still I cannot help but love Papa a little more than anyone else. Oh, if he would only come back." And then his eyes fill with tears and he sobs, "I need Papa. I do need him." My eyes are dim as I hold him close to my heart and answer, "So do I, Carl."

❧   ❧   ❧

To Scott, five o'clock.

I'm sitting on the lounge in the Cheer. I've on the pale blue French gingham you like so well and your pet kerchief and some wild yellow flowers. Do come to supper with me. All the charm of my meals has fled. You seem near as I think of you. It seems as if I must look up and meet your eyes and how heavy grows my heart when I whisper to myself, "A thousand miles, a thousand miles."

❦　❦　❦

Last night in the twilight we walked down to the shore of the lake. It was a dear little walk through the red weeds with their white tufts of blossoms, an exquisite sky overhead, a pink blush on the water. Carl had a little wade but little Hal only trotted back and forth on the white sand.[1] Today Carl said, "Mama, I love even the rain in the North because it touches Papa." He stands and looks at your picture as if he would never be satisfied. He looks at it as a mother might look at the picture of her dead child. He leans on his little elbows and says (all the time his eyes are fastened silently upon your face), "Mama, I love his eyes. I love his hair. I love his cheeks. I love everything about him. Oh, how I wish I was with him. Oh, dear, how I wish I could hug him. Mama, you don't know how I'd kiss him. I never kissed him as I'd kiss him now if he would come in. And yet his picture is a great comfort. I don't think I mind so much his being gone as if I did not have his picture. You see I can look at it everyday and almost think it's Papa."

You remember every intonation of that clear sweet voice and just the expression of the eyes. Everything is "Papa, Papa, there is no one like Papa." He says, "Papa's the king, Papa's the flower." He is good most of the time, very bad now and then, but only for a moment or two.

I read a delightful page or two in the Critic on Charles Reade.[2] I've always thought nothing he ever wrote equaled his lovely Christy Johnstone and have often said that was enough to keep his memory green though he had never written another book. And I was so delighted when I read today his epitaph should be: Charles Reade, author of Christy Johnstone. It was one of the first books I read to you after we were married. I read it in the beautiful hall on the hill with some winds blowing through, wild flowers on the tables, and you lying on the lounge and watching me as I read sitting in your grandfather's tall chair. You were so near I could put out my hand and touch you, and now—

Be sure and send some special word often for Carl for he stands at my elbow as I read your letters, kisses the words and asks with such a sweet, yearning little voice, "Did Papa say something for me?"

❦   ❦   ❦

July 20, 1884

You cannot make of Hal a proper chap at all. He will now and then break all bonds and throw decorum to the winds. And yet with his grace and his beauty and his flashing little face he is such a sweet witch you forgive him everything in a twinkling. We all ran from the supper table to look at something and when I came back in a very few minutes there sat Hal with an arm on each of the arms of the chair, his head resting on the back, sound asleep, and a little foot planted on the table. It was such a sweet little saucy picture, the attitude so full of independence and comfort, the foot so pink and so shapely, the sleeping face so full of innocence, health and beauty. The table was charming with its bowl of flowers and quaint glasses and my dishes a history in delicate china.

Carl says I know Papa needs me.

❦   ❦   ❦

July 21, 1884

I've been so busy today. All the edges of the shelves in the kitchen I tipped with scarlet. The cups I hang now and have arranged the dishes so prettily. It is so much easier to work in a pretty room. I've made some lovely bread today, feathery and light just the way you like it. And I've baked a little fat chicken for supper and stewed some plums that looked just like rubies.

Your letter has lain untouched but the next one shall be longer. Just come and take tea with us. It is going to be uncommonly nice. The frescoes of our dining room are new every night now and never the same. We sit out here in the open hall and watch them change to gold or crimson and little Hal alone would adorn a feast or melt a heart when he sits like a human sunbeam in that dear palmetto chair.

Last night just after supper I said I ought to do some little task that I had forgotten and gave a great sigh as I fastened my apron. And Carl ran to me saying, "No, Mama, you look so tired. Take off your apron and come and climb in the big chair Papa made. Turn it so you can see me and watch me while I build the new cottage and talk to me about Papa. That will be so much nicer." And after a little he came and laid his little cheek against mine, saying, "You know, Mama, Papa doesn't want you to get so tired." No one comforts me as Carl does. His little heart mourns and cries out for you the way mine does. We love and we suffer together, he and I. Our first thought is that absent face, dear beyond every other face we have ever known.

❧ ❧ ❧

July 31, 1884

I'm sitting out here in Carl's bower. I came out here that I might write in perfect quiet. I awoke tired this morning and perhaps a trifle depressed. I felt old and sad and lonely. Life seemed too hard and some things so bitter they seemed to hide all the sweet. I felt as if my youth was slipping away and my life had amounted to nothing. I turned over and leaning on my elbow with my cheek on my palm watched Hal as he slept. As I lay there looking at him and thinking, those old lines came to my mind:

"The Roses of Life"
Oh, fair is a life when youth trembles and glows
With the odor of love and an innocent heart.
And the bud unrepressed opens into the rose
In transitions of beauty surpassing all art.
The Roses of life were a bloom in her face.
The freedom of health in her step and her words.
Her smile was a sunbeam no cloud could displace.
And the voice he loved best was clear as a bird's.
But time, ah, how it withered his rose in a day,
The rose that he gave when his heart was beguiled.
But the rose in her cheek that was stolen away,
She has found it again in the face of a child.[3]

In some way the memory of the words, the vision of my beautiful sleeping child, the youth, the promise that lay in my boys, the knowledge that no matter what is best and finest in their natures is due to you. Still it may have taken me, just incomplete impatient me, with all my faults, freaks and fancies to have made them the very boys they are. I felt comforted and made fresh vows of patience and courage.

Carl said he dreamed of Papa and I asked what and he replied, "It was just a dream of how much I love him." Oh, the stockings I could darn, the patches I could put on, the seams I could sew, the ruffles I could hem if I did just that if I didn't spend so much time writing to you. And writing what? Why, a postal would have held all there has been worth the telling from July to December and still leave room to ask you not to forget to bring me that bottle of olives.

You have written me over two hundred pages since you went away.

❧ ❧ ❧

July 31, 1884

I wish you could see Hal dance. Someone will say, "Come, now, give us a dance." And he will glance up with a laugh in his eyes, toss his head, lift one side of his dress and the little feet will break away in such a little joy dance, back and forth, from side to side, round and round, that always ends with a laugh and a great rush into some pair of arms. How people look at him when they come for water or to ask the way or to wait through a storm. They always watch him, always speak of his hair and seldom depart without a word of praise for Hal. Sometimes it is, "You have a beautiful little child, madam." And again with the "Cracker" drawl, "That's a mighty purty baby." It is all the same to me. I always comprehend and never criticize any praise that falls on Hal's dear head.

I've had glimpses of things years ago that I've never forgotten and I think Hallock must seem like that. In a city full of elegance and wealth and beautiful children dressed like princes it would be different. But to travel dusty, tired and burning through this monotonous forest and to come upon the old cabin and step under the huge grim roof and catch a glimpse of cool palms and flowers, books and trinkets, and to find this little smiling beaming face so full of witcheries, his hair of gold, and the dainty matchless coloring of cheek and lip and eye, his shy roguish glance, his graceful dancing motions, and then his fine delicate dresses. I'm sure it must all make a vision as refreshing as a vision can be. You remember the little lines from Goethe that have always been somewhere on the wall of my room since I was sixteen: "We must read a poem, listen to music and see a picture every day."[4] Frindy says, "Hallock is all of that."

Our home is in many ways very sweet even now but it is only the beginning of a home and I want to stay here. I want to go into the world now and then, of course. I want to make of this an oasis of rest and beauty and to have it for our home. The climate is fit for paradise and while there are many things to annoy and torment us, still there are many to woo and charm and wherever we may go there are things at times to drive us half mad with worry and anxiety. Those two terrors are large enough to fill a world and yet they can slip through the tiniest crack and, as to disagreeable people, one can never get away from them. Wherever we may go we will always find some that ought to be annihilated, and the more I think of it the more I feel that here I want our home.

Little Hal brings me my slippers and stockings in the morning and hands me my brush and comb and is I doubt not the most lovely page that ever graced a lady's chamber. The doctor said the German who brings us vegetables told him—"Mrs. Moseley has the most beautiful baby he ever saw." I just like that man.

I'm often sad and I am always missing you but I am not a lonely soul. I am too busy and life is too full for that. Once in a great while the monotony in my life comes over me in a mighty sweep. I never go out of the gate save to gather wild flowers or cut fresh palms. I never think of a break in my day save the joy of your letters which illuminate all the hours. I live for you as if you were beside me. I try to be an honor to you although there is no voice to praise my deeds, no soul that seems to comprehend my sorrows or my efforts, but to turn back or to falter would be madness. I feel that however monotonous our lives may be, we must still live our best, still look upward to our ideal, still strive to reach it, still struggle to be fine, still feel that we do live though the world has forgotten us and solitude alone remains to answer our questionings.

❧   ❧   ❧

August 2, 1884

Carl built a most lovely palace on the south porch out of his hundreds of blocks. He spent much time upon it with the inside as well as the outside. Its towers and turrets and battlements and drawbridges all are there. A chicken stalked up the steps in hot pursuit of some buzzing insect and raised sad havoc with the beautiful palace. Carl was standing near playing with a palmetto stem. He gave a cry of rage as he saw the walls demolished and flew at the chicken, giving it a blow with the palmetto. It was only a little stem but it came down with such force that the chicken lay like one dead. Carl felt very bad. I took the little stricken thing out and shut it up, thinking it might revive.

I wanted Carl to realize what it was to give vent to such a violent temper and told him when he was all undressed for the night that he must remember that while he was lying so safe in his clean soft bed the poor little chick was in pain from his blow. He looked up at me with such an appealing look, saying, "I suppose you can never say dear Carl again." But I told him he was always dear Carl to us, and that we loved him even when he did wrong but before anyone in the house was awake he had stolen out to see how the little chicken was. When I opened my eyes he stood with such a glad look on his face, saying, "It is all right. It can run as fast as any of them." He constantly mourns for you. I am three times as patient with him as I would be were it not that I knew his little heart was constantly grieving for the one it holds dearest. Whatever I may be to him I can never be quite so dear as that beloved Papa, from whom he has had always such patient love, such tender care.

You know the little trick he has of reading imaginary stories. Yesterday while he was reading one I wrote down each word just as he related it and will copy it for you. It is wonderful how smoothly he talks. He sits down and describes things he has seen as if he was accustomed to entertaining rooms full. This is his story without one word altered or suggested.

Carl's Story

Once there was a good little boy. (It wasn't me for he was always good.) And he had two sisters and they were good, too. They were just as big as me and just of a size and that made them twins. They lived with their father and mother in a large forest. And there was a depot close by and a narrow-gauge railway and one day their father and mother wanted to go to Africa and they asked the children if they thought they could be good and keep house for a week. And the children thought they could and the father and mother said they would bring the children nice presents and then they went down to the depot and asked the baggage master if that narrow gauge went to Africa and he said it did. So they got on the train and in two hours and a half they were in Africa and they stayed two days and one more which made three days and that made a week and then they went home. They found the children all right and they had been good and they gave them their presents. There was a real baby for the little girls to play with and a little carriage and pony for the boy to drive. That is all. They lived in the forest always.

❦   ❦   ❦

August 3, 1884

Dearest.

This little silver tress, gray and fine enough to have been cut from the aged head of some old gnome, is from the root of a very coarse, stiff grass. While we want every green thing left to help cover the blank countenance of the sand, I did not like this variety of grass. It is so stiff and ugly and while out for a little dig among the sandspurs I pulled it up. What an exquisite surprise it was to me. Perhaps that makes you smile. But the sand was damp from a late shower and the root came up softened by the moisture and lay against my hand like shreds of old lace and it brought such sweet fancies to my mind. How I longed to call you in the dear old way and lay it against your hand, too.[5]

It reminded me of people who are made after some of nature's uncouth patterns, large and stiff and homely to look upon but gentle and refined, possessing a sort of inward grace without the power to reveal it. You have a feeling when with them that it is there but yet they never really manifest it. And you sometimes wonder if in "other worlds" with greater possibilities there may not be a sort of resurrection and they be set free from the outward husk and the finer parts revealed like this little root of grass. It seemed almost pitiful to me that it should stand in the garden among the countless vines and blossoming things, looked upon with scorn, and yet knowing that just below the surface its root was growing in such exquisite delicacy as would put the choicest rose bush to the blush.

I've read some since you went away. Not a great deal. At first I could not. I could get my mind on nothing. I was in despair when I tried to keep still but of late it has been different. Oh, Scott, what can compare with those blossoms of the mind, speech and the gift of expression? Just think, darling, of the companionship that I've had for an hour now and then when the house slept or in the early morning before it was astir. I've not been in a Florida wilderness with no human habitation in sight, save a "Cracker's" cabin. While I lay on the old lounge, fanned by soft southern airs, I've floated on the bosom of broad rivers and sat upon mountain tops. I've listened to fine thoughts and wandered down more than one shady lane with cool turf beneath my feet. And once, just for half a minute I heard an orchestra and felt the hush of the music.

How happy one can be just in a book. Into what charmed circles they lead us. I do not wonder that strangers lay flowers lovingly upon authors' graves, that thousands of people contribute to the erection of a great writer's monument whose living face they have never seen. They have perhaps blessed their lives more than some who have lived near them ever since they came into the world. I do not believe there are thirty people that I know who have given me the unalloyed happiness that just Thackeray alone has. And do you know, my sweetheart, that we have never read one of his books together? Do hurry home and let us read one, right away. Which shall it be? The Newcomes, or Henry Esmond or dear old Pendennis, or Vanity Fair, or all of them?[6]

There is a storm coming up and we will have a shower before the moon comes up and perhaps it will be cool enough tonight to have a fire in the old chimney and we will put the palms in the corners and they will make such lovely shadows on the wall and you shall lie on the lounge while I curl up in my great chair among the scarlet cushions and read to you. And now and then there will be something very merry and we will glance at each other and laugh together. Then there will be something very tender and we will find each other's eyes again and Frindy will sing Hallock to sleep on the hammock and Carl will stand at the table and draw and Claude will sit lost in St. Nicholas.[7] But by and by they will all go and we shall be left alone and the moonlight will steal in at the picture window and will come in with a great sweep of light through the broad window and door to try and make love to the fire light or she will peek through the little Dutch door from the north and beckon to us to come out in the garden, down the walk, among the shadows.

Shall I get the fire ready to light and trim the lamp with special care and take the book down from the shelf? And would you like just for a treat, the night so cool and cozy, a cup of chocolate with whipped cream and an oleander in the saucer? A thousand miles, a thousand miles. No wonder the silence almost breaks my heart and that no answering voice comes back to me.

Later. We had our shower and everything was dripping and running wild with water. And then a rainbow and sunshine, and far as the eye could reach diamonds and emeralds seemed throwing back sunbeams into the face of the sun, and such clouds—dark masses of blue, great garden plumes, caves of silver and seagreen, a million hues and tints floated in billions of changing loveliness.

And then such a light as suddenly fell upon the earth as if all this splendor, the dying sun, the beauty of the day, had all melted into an unspeakable glory. The treetops in the east turned to gold. Every shrub and tuft of grass seemed bathed in pale yellow and while we stood looking on in hushed delight a flock of more than a hundred curlews flew over our head and across the lake to the forest beyond. You should have seen Hal's face when he saw them. He held up both hands and with uplifted face and such a long, wild cry of delight as rang out and up from that sweet mouth. It seemed as if every bird answered him, so many voices came back to him from among those white wings. Sweet Hal!

I'll have nothing worth showing you when you come home and yet there is never a day that there is not something that I want to share with you—the sky or a flower or a stray bit from somewhere or to listen to a line from a bird's song or feel the soft air or to see Hal's golden head against your breast. Something, always something. No joy can ever be really mine unless you share it. You are my love and my life and my joy.

🍂   🍂   🍂

August 7, 1884

All the children were invited out for the day and everything had to be left to get them ready. As they were about to start Carl came up to me, saying, "Mama, I've just a mind to stay at home and help you. You look so tired and Papa doesn't want you to be tired and if you should drop, what would become of me? I don't know what I would do if I should come home and find no Mama." Isn't he a sweet fellow? And you can see him as he speaks, his pretty attitudes, his graceful movements, I often think there is more expression in Carl's hand than in many a face.

Carl says he wants you more than ever when he doesn't feel well. I feel a little anxious over him. He is not strong. I can never give up my first born. He is to fulfill some of the dreams of both of our lives.

Ah, how brave and beautiful my boys looked last night as they slept. I lighted the lamp several times before morning just to look at them. I went first to one bed and then to the other. I kissed Carl a hundred times and laid my hand on his forehead. What a splendid brow it is, so white and broad. His little heart flutters unevenly. He takes all things in that intense way that I do, only he takes it all more seriously. Mine is overbalanced by my mirth that flies hand in hand with it or it would have burned me up years ago. Carl gets furious over things, too, as I do. I was talking to him the other day about getting out of patience and said I did sympathize with him more than he knew perhaps for I had a hot temper, too. And he gave a sigh from the very depths of his heart, exclaiming, "Yes, I know, Mama. And it's too bad I'm so much like you in some of those things." It is needless to say I felt somewhat humiliated but he loves me with all my faults. He told someone not long ago, "Mama isn't very good. She says so. But I think she's the nicest Mama in the world."

Hal and I were sitting in the little Dutch rocker. I noticed Carl watching us in that quiet, intent way he has at times. After a little I said, "What are you thinking of, Carl?" His face lighted up and he said, "Oh, Mama, I was wishing I could make a picture of you and Hallock just as you look now to send to Papa. I know he would like it."[8]

Carl says, "Mama, I do not suppose I ever was like Hallock, so beautiful and so sweet. But you always loved me, didn't you?"

❦ ❦ ❦

August 13, 1884

It has been nothing but illness for days. Anxious nights and anxious days. I cannot be comforted by any memory. I want you. The boys are safe now. The fear is passed. I am too tired to rest.

❦ ❦ ❦

August 14, 1884

I wish you could see the Cheer. I was going to share it with Carl but I've only room for my chair and a spot large enough to set an ink bottle. His papers fill every chink and corner. As soon as he is up he runs in here in his white gown and draws before breakfast, often before another one in the house is awake. He flies in between his games or after a walk or a meal and always it is to make pictures for Papa. Dozens of them, daily loom up here in the little Cheer.

I'd give a fortune for a picture that looks just as it looks. So tiny. Its three windows, one on the north and one on the south and one on the east and a door on the west opening into its own little open hall. The vines running over it, the garden close by, the wild sweet light within and its hundreds of quaint pictures scattered everywhere, pinned to the walls, piled up in each corner, knee deep in places, and beside the table our Carl of Lancaster standing, while over the table bends the face we love so fondly, and the dear little left hand traces the strange and varied fancies of that young brain. Through the open windows, the blue sky looks down and the soft breeze steals in. "Mama," he says, "I often see visions of Papa, as plainly as I can see him when he is here, and in them I'm looking up at his face and saying, 'Sweet Papa.'"

❦   ❦   ❦

August 16, 1884

To Scott

In the Cheer. Dearest. This afternoon when we went for wild plums I looked over every shoebag to find a pair of old shoes to wear out in the wet grass and I came across that pair of walking boots you had made for me in the spring of '81 that were made in that little shop on King Street in Lancaster, into which for more than one generation many a dame has gone for perfect fits and shoes that are well worth the sous that they cost.

And as I walked across lots and through a young orange grove I thought of all these shoes had seen and the tears came to my eyes and my pulses beat fast. I tramped through the streets of Carl's dear old Dutch Lancaster for the last time in these boots, peeked into the garden where I had sat so many happy times with you, down the shady lanes and droll alleys where the boughs met overhead and strolled through the markets and bought a flower for my love or a pretzel for Carl. Stole into St. Anthony's to see its fresco just once more. We took our farewell walk among the hills, across the bridge by the old mill. We went for the last time down the familiar streets and watched the busy life along the square. Then that little trip with only a glimpse of Philadelphia and that delightful day in New York and the park and the beautiful cathedral, the "good-night" down at the pier and Carl and I going out of sight in the boat with the band playing and all the beauty of a summer evening on the water. The two weeks in Boston, the day of days in Albany and Troy, the trip on the Hudson, and the summer at Lake Erie climbing the cliffs again and again and the woods with ravines and gorges, and that one weird waterfall in the depth of a moss-covered forest.

Oh, I wonder if often the little brown people who dwell in its chinks and crevices have guessed from the outside world who carry away so many happy memories of their grim, abiding place as did we. There was that wonderful day at Niagara and then that homesick October with you in New York and me in Illinois. Many a time did I climb the hills in those boots to have one unalloyed hour with my dieudonne. One early morning I crept away to my mother's grave and with my face as wet as the dew on the grass that covered it, wept for her who in this world I could run with glad feet to meet never again. Those two or three hours in Cousin Emma's lovely French chamber and back to you. One wade in the snow a day at the Point with our beloved cliffs icebound, then away to Cincinnati and the walks among the Ohio hills and then south with its wandering about New Orleans and to Hallock's Florida. And they have carried me many a happy mile through the sands among the hammocks and under the solemn pines. Who can say they were not well-made shoes and of good "stock"? Alas, that they are so well-worn.

❦   ❦   ❦

August 17, 1884

This morning early Carl and I went down to the hammock for fresh palms. Everything was glistening in the sunshine. The young pines were covered with dew. You know how prettily they hold up their crests. And Carl said, "See, Mama, the gas in all the chandeliers is lighted." Carl's eyes are quick to see and how sweetly his little tongue can recount his visions.

When we had gotten home with our spoils and the leaves were arranged, I did so long to show them to you, but above all else it was Hal I wanted you to see. The great chimney these warm summer days I keep filled with palms. Hal was sitting on the rug and over him bent the palms. There were some branches of white flowers and one wild, tall slender weed that looked like a breeze grown into a blossom of old gold. One reckless sunbeam had stolen through a crack in the old chimney and touched Hal's hair and shown through the leaves of a young palm just over his head and for love of Hal had hung a string of emeralds just above. Crane's Baby Opera lay open on his lap, a book he dearly loves.[9] I can never tell you how beautiful was the picture it all made. I shall never forget it.

❦   ❦   ❦

August 20, 1884

A scorpion stung me. A huge black spider ran all over me, refusing to go. A vampire bit me in three places. All those things happened in the night.

I was in the woods this morning all alone walking slowly along, absorbed in meditation, and looking up suddenly found myself face to face with a black cow with long straight horns, gazing at the bright bands that trim my blue frock. She had an inquiring, doubtful expression as if she was wondering if I meant anything personal in wearing red trimmings and a scarlet poppy in my hat. I never scrambled over a fence faster in my life than I darted over the one close by and turned with a supplicating glance over my shoulder, expecting to see the cow frothing at the mouth and with death in her eye, plunging after. But she was contentedly grazing and had evidently forgotten all about me.

We had a shower this afternoon and in closing shutters and bringing in the rugs and pillows from the porches Hal was forgotten. And when I ran to look for him, there he stood under the eaves, singing like a lark, water running in streams down his yellow head and filling his tiny shoes. And when his wet clothes were off and he well-rubbed down and I had turned around to pick up his dry things, off he darted into the storm, scrambling for joy—the prettiest little "god of mischief" you can well imagine.

I teach him to kiss your picture and letters and even the flowers you send. I think it would have been a sight to stir your heart could you have come up softly to the south window of the Cheer and looked between the leaves of the passion vine and seen him standing with his elbows on my knees, holding the bundle of your letters that came today, and kissing them again and again and looking up in my face with bright, loving glances and then hugging them close against his sweet little heart. It is so hard to keep up and not die without you.[10]

Carl's first pants were finished today. You should be here to witness Carl's joy and pride. That you cannot see him is all that is lacking to make this a perfect hour to him. There is a little pain at my heart as I follow him with my eyes. My little child is quite gone and this tall boy in jackets and knee britches can bring him back to me never again. But my little son, my sweet rare Carl of Lancaster, no change can ever make you anything but our beloved son as you have been these five, beautiful years.

I must tell you of a little conversation Carl had with a Mr. F., who has charge of the doctor's grove over here by us. He came to the house for water and while resting on the back porch began smoking, and asked Carl if he didn't wish he could smoke. Carl told him no and that it was a filthy habit, and when Mr. F. asked if you did not, Carl indignantly replied that you wouldn't do such a thing. And the man said, "He eats bread, doesn't he?" "Yes," Carl replied, "he must live." And then the idiotic Mr. F. said, "Well, that is just as bad as tobacco." Carl lashed out in the most indignant manner, "No, sir, tobacco is one of the worst things in the world, bread one of the best, and you know well enough we would die if we didn't eat it." Mr. F. continued in much the same, senseless train as he began and Carl at last sprang up, saying, "What nonsense. I think you talk silly. Indeed I think this conversation has gone on long enough. My dinner is ready. Will you come and eat dinner with me?"

I could have hugged Carl then. He seemed so like you. His argument was so reasonable, so entirely to the point and concise. But he ended the conversation in that easy, offhand way with such a polite invitation to dine and a smile that seemed to say— "though we differ we would scorn to quarrel." Forgive me if I seem too proud of Carl, if I praise him too much. Remember he was but five in February, that he was "my firstborn" and that I love his father.

Your beautiful letter, like a great breath from northern woods, sweet with lavender, came today. The scarlet leaves were like flowers when they reached me but the Indian pipes were black as jet. I, too, hope the time will come when we can wander together in those beautiful places and amid the woods you haunted when a boy. It seems a long way off now but without hope, how can life be borne.

Nothing grieves me more in this separation but that you are losing so much of Hal's childhood. This lovely, bewitching age will soon be gone, never to return. This tender, innocent beauty will pass away and you will have had so little share in it. I try to tell you but one might as well try to put in words the freshness of the morning, the song of the lark.

🍃   🍃   🍃

August 31, 1884

When I awoke Carl was beside me and lying as still as the bed on which he lay. I asked him what he was thinking and he said, "I'm thinking of Papa and how I love him and how dear he is to me."

My birthday present to myself was Mrs. Carlisle's letters.[11] The book came yesterday and tonight feeling restless and having tried to go to sleep without any success, I lighted the lamp and began to read. I knew I should like these letters but I did not dream I should be so enraptured. Here I sit with pillows at my back, the owls singing to me from one of the lonesome old pines, the moonlight sweeping in with great yellow radiance, little Hal in his beauty asleep beside me, until it is 1 o'clock and I hate to lay down the book even now but I must and I am going to try to forget Jane Welsh Carlisle and go to sleep.

Later—two a.m. But I couldn't. I've been drifting into them again. They charmed me so I could not sleep. I hardly am able to tell just why it is, I'm sure, but while you are reading you forget they are printed letters, written years ago by brave little hands that are to touch pen and paper never more in this world. And they seem if not really written for you, at least letters you were intended in a measure to share and before the second is finished you are bewitched. There must, indeed, have been wonderful magic about her if in these old letters there can be such warmth and sparkle. How she doted on ham and bacon. I can sniff them even now and I wish I had some, I'm so hungry and I would like an egg with it and brown sweetening. You know I'm no delicacy about an egg. I want mine turned over and browned on both sides. Never tell, for it isn't a nice taste at all. I was always ashamed of it.

Later. Morning is almost here and I might as well sit up and be here to welcome the new day and just skip just one little night. But before I turn a fresh page, let me copy just one little note for you:

"I have only him, only him in the whole wide world to love me and to take care of me, poor little wretch that I am. Not but that numbers of people love me after their fashion, far better than I deserve, but that his fashion is so different from all these and seems alone to suit the crotchety creature that I am."[12]

It is so like your love for me, the only love in all the world that satisfies me and that seems fitted just to me.

❦ ❦ ❦

September 3, 1884

As soon as Hal awoke, he gave a scream of joy as he looked about. It seemed like a glad cry of welcome to the bright morning. He flew for his Baby Opera that he never spends the day without, ran with quick feet down the steps, and sitting down in the sand, out in the clear sunlight, began to turn the pages in his own sweet fashion, trying to outsing the birds. There never was a more charming fellow. I can hear his happy feet running up and down the hall, and from room to room, as I write. If those feet were to stop running over my home and heart, half the music in the world would have gone for me.

I am so enjoying Mrs. Carlyle's letters and one pleasant thing about them is that the charming book of Caroline Fox, both letters and memoirs, was full of some of the same people.[13] And it is like meeting old friends to find them again. I am marking choice bits to read to you when you come.

What strange memories must have crowded themselves thick and fast upon you when you saw the house where you were born, the mountains you had climbed so many times, the streams where you learned to swim, and all the dear familiar places. What wild dreams I used to have as a child but I never dreamed of a joy so great and satisfying as has been your love to me. And some day we will go over the scenes of your childhood together and you shall look in my eyes and tell me out of your heart that I am more to you than all the beautiful castles in Spain that you built among New England hills those twenty years before I was born.

I felt very homesick and forlorn this morning and went alone for a walk. There are times when your absence overwhelms me. Nothing but to go out alone in the woods will give me peace. I came home comforted as I always do. Nature speaks to me when I am sad in a voice no human speech has power to utter. I turn to her when the ways of human life are too strong for me and she gives me the peace I need and fills me with strength and sometimes a touch of gladness for I must have come to a sad pass, indeed, when I can take a walk in any woods, from the wildest beach of Maine to the sunniest tip of Florida, and not find something that I love and that loves me.

                    ❧   ❧   ❧

September 6, 1884

Carl and I have turned Hal out of his nest and taken possession of my bed ourselves. I've come in here behind the white curtains early for a long read and Carl is to have his papers and draw here beside me. We play it is a yacht with white sails and we are floating down a river. Carl thinks nothing ever was so cozy and sweet. When I arose from saying my prayers tonight, Carl said, "Shall I just whisper to God, Mama?" I told him to say anything he wished. So, kneeling in his little white gown with his hands clasped he said, "Please save Papa." From you he is never apart. You are the burden of his thoughts as your safety is his prayer. Everything that is dearest, brightest and best in his young life is embodied in that absent Papa. He is more than a son to you, but a faithful lover who never forgets, whose very dreams are of absent love.

He has just this moment finished this picture of a solemn and wise being. You surely will smile when you behold it, for in spite of its solemnity it is mirth provoking. What would you not give to see him now as he lies crosswise of the bed and his little fingers flying over the paper and a sweet contented look on his dear face?

Hal loves all the growing things and brings me butterfly wings or any little wild thing that he thinks will please me. This morning he came in with his face beaming and, holding a great spider by one leg, he held it up to me with the greatest pride and a little screech of delight. I couldn't help but laugh. He seemed to think he had such a choice bit and do you suppose a spider would bite him? No, indeed.

26. "Hallock of Florida," born in the old log cabin Nest to Julia Daniels and Charles Scott Moseley.

He leads a charmed life. Just at this moment he is playing peek-a-boo with himself in the mirror. He hides behind the curtains and then runs forth with a shout and a sweet picture it is—the little graceful figure in a little pale blue dress, the yellow hair in a shower on his shoulders, the old gold of the curtains for a background with its streams of flowers. Then out he darts and hides behind the door and screams to the vision to come and find him, all the time playing little tricks on himself and doesn't know it.

Isn't this a cunning little bit of Carl's? I just saw it under his pencil on the table. What's the little fellow made of that he gets such effects with a few scratches of those baby fingers?

Carl was greatly distressed that I should mark the pages of a new book as I am doing Mrs. Carlisle's letters. But when I explained that I wanted to have the best ready for you he quite forgave me and not long after I found that he had marked Mother Goose and Kate Greenaway, all through and through. And I said, "Why, Carl, what have you scratched your books up for?" And he coolly replied, "I've only marked my favorite poems to have them all ready for Papa to read to me when he comes home."

September 8, 1884

That black-eyed "Cracker" of whom we buy butter and milk said that I was a plumb-honest woman, adding I tried her lots of times but she's always plumb honest. Just think of her laying pitfalls and snares for me to fall in. I wonder if she is plumb honest. She looks so full of Indian blood that I cannot but think it was not many generations ago she might have enjoyed my scalp.

The plumb honest reminds me of the German woman in Lancaster who sewed for me when mother was there and said, "I told them at home that your mother couldn't be beaten for nice." And, she couldn't.

Do you know that that rogue of a Hal pretends to get sandspurs in his hands to see us search for them and to see us console with him and to see us fly to get them out quickly? And then he will laugh and dance about so happy, but do you not love him from his saucy feet to the crown of his glorious yellow hair?

This morning everything was in such perfect order in the Little Heart—fresh flowers and palms and the room looked fit for a princess to breakfast in. We were all in the yard busy over some new plan and Hal was forgotten. And when I went in, there was my spotless bed loaded with sardine cans, stove wood from the kitchen, a wash basin, clubs, dolls—to say nothing of books and papers and odds and ends of clothing.

He has of late fallen in love with my little, old leather-covered dictionary and carries it about, tucked under his arm. He pats it lovingly, saying, "Dic, dic, dic." He is too sweet, too cunning, too beautiful and much too bad.

* * *

September 12, 1884

Your letters are full of sweet praise. I know one should do one's duty because it is one's duty and not to be praised or to have it known of others. Now I care more for the praise than the duty. A slow-going old duty is purgatory for me. Praise I love and I can hardly live without it.

I've been only half-alive for two weeks—on the bed or the hammock more times than off it. The hardest part of being ill for me is that everything gets so ugly. The flowers wither. The rooms lose all their charm and I so love to have things look lovely when my head aches and that crooked side refuses to allow me to walk or turn over. I always use my pretty dishes, though.[14] Sometimes I think I will not use my choice cups all the time. They are so delicate. If I knew some sweet little granddaughter with a weakness for old things and curious things and such a soft, soft spot for dainty dishes should one day be happy in their possession and hold them deftly in her pretty hands and say, with just a trifle of tenderness in her voice, "This was my little Grandmother Moseley's. She was something of an imp in her way but she did love a pretty dish." But, alas, some fiend will have smashed every one before that day can come about and I'm just going to sup from them three times a day and enjoy them while they last. Old Lorenzo knew of what strange fates our fortunes are made when he said, "There's no surety for the morrow."[15]

*   *   *

September 13, 1884

A little scratch of a letter from my father. After saying that he loves us, he adds, "And, now my babes, God bless you all." He never wrote me a genuine letter in my life. Once or twice a year he writes and tells me that he loves me and that is all. But I some way always feel that it is just the same. He does love me and he loves us all and he abominates writing letters.

27. Dr. Carlos Daniels, Julia Daniels Moseley's father. After studying in the East he completed his medical education in St. Louis, then considered to have that region's finest training. 1892.

September 14, 1884

Carl says, "Here is a little gentleman in armor for Papa and if he isn't little enough, send him this one."

Carl has a habit now of making speeches. He stands in my large, square chair and Hal sits on a little stool near and listens. Carl talks for a time and then says, "Do you catch my meanings?" And Hal nods his head and Carl continues. Some of these speeches are very funny. This morning I jotted down one word-for-word. I wish I had captured more of them.

A Speech of Carl's

"It would have been a sorry day for the people if the world had never been made. The world is made of sand and water and is called the earth. There are a great many liars on the earth. When men were made, they were only little babies. But now they are grown men. The spots on the moon they used to think were spots but now they know they are mountains. The stars are gold."

❦ ❦ ❦

September 21, 1884

Carl has taken a fancy to Anthony Trollope's picture in Harper's and has tried to draw one. Mrs. Trollope stands on one foot, with the other tucked modestly under her skirts. He has asked all about Trollope and I have told him his entire history as far as I know.[16] Then he chanced upon Alfred Tennyson and tried to make a sketch of him.[17] He has a wonderful memory for names and I am so glad since it will always be of service to him.

❦ ❦ ❦

September 22, 1884

This morning I beat an egg for Carl as you used to and he said, "Oh, this reminds me of dear Papa. Mama, was there ever such a darling as Papa?" And I smile upon him saying, "No, Carl, but he has a little child who knows how to love almost as much as he." When I was putting the Cheer in order he came in, saying, "Mama, when you have finished the Cheer, won't you come in the Little Heart and have a little loving time with me? I am so lonesome for Papa."

28. Carl's drawings depicted whatever was being read to him, and anything else that captured his imagination. As the reader explained the story or author, in this case Tennyson, Carl would draw faster and faster.

I've sent you mere shreds of letters but I've had no heart to write. I'm worried almost beyond words over Carl. He's better than for a few days but he is far from well. He is thin, with dark circles around his eyes. There is an old look in his face with his quaint, strange expressions, his sweet voice. His dear little hands, how sweet are those hands, so full of cunning. You know, I've always feared he would not live to be a man. But the doctor says I must not fear for him. I must be very patient, very tender, very watchful. And we must teach him nothing and that he will be stronger soon.

Oh, Scott, I cannot bear it all alone. The fears are tenfold with you not here to share them or to comfort me. One day when he saw me watching him very closely, he said, "Mama, are you looking for the love in my eyes? It's there just as strong as if I was well." For five days he lay so still, scarcely eating or talking. "It hurts me to have you with me," he would say, "because I know you are too tired. If Papa were here he would lift me so easily and so nice. Papa would read to me. Papa would be so sorry for me." And yet the doctor says that in a week perhaps he will seem as well as ever. "I do not want to die while I am young," he says. "I want to live to be an old, old man."

I've worried so over him and lost so much rest that I had a nervous chill last night. But he is better and I mustn't be foolish. So many things that would not seem very hard were you beside me become agony in your absence. And then I talk to no one of my sorrows or fears and I know the silence makes them heavier than they are and harder to be borne. But my friends are far from me and I am quite alone in the real things that nick or mar my life.

I read to Carl a good deal. He says, "I do not know which I like best— Harper's Young People or St. Nicholas or the Scientific American."

Carl says, "Tell Papa a boy couldn't feel more well than me. I feel unusually well." The doctor has given him stimulants and he begins to seem like our boy.

Here is a letter of Carl's. He is much interested in your walk and boat ride with Mr. Higginbottam.

"Darling Papa, how does Mr. Higginbottam look? Can you not send me a picture that looks like him so that I will know? Please bring me a soldier suit, a little sword, a pair of red-topped boots, a pair of little gloves, a pair of little brushes for my shoulders. Mama says I mean epaulets and I do mean epaulets, a drum and a nice pair of drumsticks. Are there any nice people in the factory and do they like you and is everyone good to you? Nothing else but love, and so great a love, and kisses, Carl."

No one has added a word or made a suggestion. It is just Carl's letter. I told him there was a possibility of your not bringing him all those things but he said, "Perhaps not, but he won't mind if I ask him. He would just as leave I ask him for anything."

❦   ❦   ❦

I asked Carl how often he thought of you and he said, "All day, every minute. And I wonder if they that are with him love him and are good to him." So often he talks of this and fears you are not loved enough and adds, "I know Papa needs me. He always needs me. I wonder what he would do if I should run in softly and put my arms around his neck." He talks of you more than he talks of everything else in the world put together. We must keep him. He is a joy. The brightness of his life must help to shed a radiance upon ours to the end. There can be but one Carl of Lancaster and he is ours. Ours for always.

Hal says so many words—all our names, yes, indeed, pretty, moon, chick, bird, milk, hurry, sandspur, ants and other little words. At this instance he is admiring himself in the glass as he stands under a Chinese parasol. And it seems to him a very funny picture as he is laughing as hard as he can laugh.

❦   ❦   ❦

I never saw the world that it seemed more lovely than it did last night. We had one of our rosy sunsets. The entire sky an unbroken cloudless pink, and as the twilight waned the pines grew black against the warm background.

Then the moonlight came later on. There is nothing one could put into words and yet it was so very beautiful that when I walked out alone among the trees and lifted up my face to watch the matchless heavens I could have wept remembering that you were not here to see it.

❧ ❧ ❧

Hal does more mischief in his few years than Carl did in seven. Carl said today, "No one can be angry with Hal if he is all mischief. He looks at you with such a pretty face and even if you did not care for that, his voice is so sweet." Carl is reading Tom Brown at Rugby to me.[18] Just here Hal spied me. I had come out on the south porch and kept quiet, hoping that rogue would keep out of my sight for one little hour, but he came down the hall and caught a glimpse of my dress. Such an exultant "Hi" he gave and the mad charge he made, throwing himself upon me as if he had been tossed by a whirlwind. Over went the ink bottle. Everything was scattered and I escaped alive by stopping and having a little play with him. I cannot say we all really fear him, but we all obey him, that's certain.

❧ ❧ ❧

October 4, 1884

Dearest.

Only a little time before supper, which is to be by lamplight and moonlight out on the south porch. Moonlight and wild flowers—they are sweet additions to a full meal. But it will be a very nice meal tonight. The bread is fit for the queen of Sweden. We half live in the open hall or the porches. We sew and read and work out here. Hal has his daily baths on the back porch and swings to sleep in the hammock on the south one.

It is so lovely out here at night. The old beams and logs look so dark amid the shadows. And when there is a light in the Little Heart it makes such a pretty picture with its flowers and palms and long lounge with its bright cushions. Through the windows and the open doors, one looks up to see a sky as blue as June. The great moon shines down, the tall pines look like black marble wrought into weird shapes. The shadows on the sand are like black velvet and the air is as soft as the down on the breast of the bird.

It is a lovely world then and I long for you. But then the others are awake and we are reading together or talking or watching Hal dance. It is when all are asleep that I want you most and I steal out here alone and sit silent among the soft, tender glory of the night and think of you with no human sound to break the silence.

❦ ❦ ❦

October 11, 1884

You know I've given Carl the Cheer. I often like to surprise him by making it especially pretty. And today I put a wreath of flowers and little palms clear around it. Then I sent for him. But when he walked in, he clasped his hands together, gave a little shout, and said, "Oh, it is so lovely and Papa cannot see it."

Hal is learning to talk so fast. He lisps after us in a voice sweeter than wine more words than we can count.

❦ ❦ ❦

October 14, 1884

I'll often send you trifles from Carl's little fingers—the dear little fingers that even in the night I often kiss for the absent Papa he so loves. A more faithful, loyal, loving little heart the world does not hold. He is naughty and trying at times and often very perplexing to me, but he is a good boy and a delightful companion, so reasonable and thoughtful, so intelligent, so fond of everything fine and beautiful, so quick to see and feel what is wrong, even in himself.

At breakfast the table was strewn with morning glories. If I were writing flower fables I should tell how Aurora on opening her eyes with the sun on a perfect June morning was so charmed with the freshness and beauty, the song of the birds, the sweet promise of the day, the thousand awakening voices of nature that she drew a breath of delight.[19] And the breath became a flower. And the flower was called the morning glory.

Carl says, "Someday I shall be sitting in the Cheer and I will hear a great rushing and a voice saying, 'Oh, dear, dear, stop.' And I will fly out of the door and into the hall and how I will hug Papa. Oh, how I will hug Papa."

Last night when I was holding Hal he came and put his arm around me and his head on my shoulder and, looking down at Hal, said, "Mama, look at his happy, shining eyes. There's nothing so sweet as Hal." Again, he said, "Mama, you are beautiful to me when you are happy. I love to be with you when you are happy. I wish you were never tired and always happy."

        ⱴ   ⱴ   ⱴ

October 25, 1884

Such a stack of mail came tonight and I stole away to the Cheer to have a quiet hour by myself and to read my letters in perfect peace. As I sat curled up on the lounge in sweet content I heard a little sound overhead and looking up saw a night hawk sitting on the beam above looking down on me in the most unconcerned manner. He wasn't afraid of me. He knew I loved every one of his beautiful brown feathers and the white bar across his wings.

But it does seem strange to think of you amid cold and frost, among hills and mountains, sitting beside fires, and walking among streets and people while I read your letters in the Little Cheer in a pine forest in southern Florida, clad in thin, summer garments while the soft autumn winds are playing with my hair through open windows and doors and night hawks sit above my head.

Last night an owl walked across my room twice and flew the last time through the chimney. Do you suppose she was searching for bats? I wasn't afraid of her. She seemed to be in harmony with the rest of the wilderness and I only sent a laugh after her as she soared to the chimney top. But when a little while ago one awakened me in the dead of night as she sat on the sill of the picture window, I fairly trembled with fear for a time. I thought nothing less doleful than a band of Seminole squaws, howling for their dead, could sound so forlorn and so tremulous.

Carl has hurt his knee so he is quite lame and can hardly move without pain. This morning he was talking of your coming home and he said, "Oh, if I could see a little white speck far off and I looked longer and saw it was Papa coming, how I would run to meet him. I'd never think of my knee or anything. I'd not mind my pain but just know Papa was coming. Oh, Mama, don't you think you would faint away you'd be so glad?

        ⱴ   ⱴ   ⱴ

I'll send you another of Carl's stories. He sits and reads them as he lies on the lounge. It is too bad I haven't kept more of them but unless I do it just as he is saying them I do not care to for I will not have a word changed. I want them just as they come from his lips.

Carl's Story

There was a dear man and he was so good. His name was Andrew Dickerson. One day he was out walking and he saw a cave. He went into the cave and there was a large dragon. The dragon clutched him and hugged him. Andrew Dickerson called, "Help, Help." He screeched and screeched, "Help! Help!" And soon some men with guns and knives rushed into the cave and killed the dragon and saved Andrew Dickerson's life.

Andrew Dickerson had a little girl called Sera. She had curling hair and a smiling face. Andrew Dickerson had a son called John Alber. One day Sera and John Alber went out walking in the woods and they saw a little fairy sitting on a toadstool holding a light in its hands, a darling little fairy that looked like a dainty frog. Sera said, "Dear little fairy, happy little fairy, cute little fairy, who would hurt a little fairy?" "What does he flop his wings for?" asked John Alber. "Oh, I don't know," said Sera, "to keep the flies off maybe."

They were very happy. "Now let us talk of ants," said Sera. "Did you ever see an ant, little fairy?" And the fairy said no. "There are several kinds of ants," said Andrew Dickerson's daughter. "There is one kind called the Ant Lion." Then the fairy said, "If you are telling a lie, I'm sorry. The most provoking thing I know is a lie."

Then they had a very instructive conversation on fools. The fairy said to Andrew Dickerson's daughter, "Now I've heard of fools that are such great fools they do not know how to talk and if there's anything funny about they do not know enough to laugh at it." Sera said she never heard of any fool so great as that. "It's a very strange thing to me," said the little fairy, "but it's true."

Then Andrew Dickerson's daughter told the fairy if he would come and live with them they would get him a beautiful little cage like a bird's. But the fairy said, "I do not mean to be selfish but I do not want to live in a cage." "Will you come and walk in the forest?" the children said. "Or, will you sit on your toadstool. You must come and walk or we will leave." And they left.

"I do not know why it is," Carl says in that sweet voice of his, "but Papa's face is the most beautiful face in the world to me."

❦ ❦ ❦

October 30, 1884

I cannot tell you the comfort it is to me to know that every Sunday you give to me that you go away from the world as close to nature as you can get and write me long letters and fill them with New England woods. Or read thinking of me. Soon it will be too cold. Even you will not dare venture from the fireside but I shall be in your thoughts, that I know. Oh, Scott, though seas and lands divide us, we are never really apart.

I wish you could have seen Hal the other day. He tucked Mother Goose under his arm and marched down the hall and across the porch with that air of blissful content that sits so naturally upon him. But by some mischance, just as he reached the top of the steps, he tripped on something and rolled to the bottom. Not a sound did he utter. Not an appealing glance did he raise. But when he landed there he lay and, coolly taking Mother Goose from under his arm, began to look at the pictures, sweetly conversing the while with his old favorites within her pages. I saw it all from first to last and when he fell my heart stood still but when I saw the droll coolness of the "wee bairn" my pride knew no bounds. I did not disturb him even by a word but I loved him exceedingly.

❦ ❦ ❦

Saturday, November 1, 1884

Our dear old Pet goes today. We had breakfast on the south porch—a perfect morning. It was hard to see him go. It was hard for him to part from us all, but especially from little Hal. They have been such friends. Happy, innocent little Hal. He does not understand the sting of farewells. He does not know that he will feel his gentle loving arms no more. Sometime he may come back to us and may we all be here to welcome him. But never this little baby Hal of today. He is slipping past into quite another being.

❦ ❦ ❦

Real Events Happen in the Heart   121

The other day Carl was asking how long it would be before you came home. And when I said perhaps in five weeks, "What!" he said, clasping his hands and his face fairly radiant with happiness. "Papa home in five weeks, in five weeks!" Then, lifting his eyes upward he exclaimed, "Thanks be to God."

He says, "Mama, Hal is beautiful enough to be a king's son."

❦ ❦ ❦

November 25, 1884

To Scott

This rough old Nest suits me and chimes in with many of my moods and fancies. Not that I am rough but I am a little wild in some ways. At least I love unsullied things with nature's touch quite fresh on many things. And in some things I've always refused to be quite tamed. And I like a nest where the outdoor life seems to settle down and seems at home, where the flowers in the house look like corners from happy gardens, where palms seem to be

29. The house built by Isaac Preston Daniels, or "Uncle Pet," while he was in Florida helping to rebuild The Nest. Carl Moseley is seated beside him. Pet's property later became part of the Moseley homestead. 1884.

30. Julia Daniels Moseley's sketch of the picture window. The sketch also provides a general impression of the log cabin, showing its notched logs and its clay-and-stick chimney. 1882.

as content as in their own hammocks. When I bring the wild things in here to glorify the hall and the rooms, they do not seem stolen away and in bondage. They look as if they belonged here. They seem to laugh in my face for very gladness and tell me they are so glad we have found each other at last. These mellow old logs have a beauty of their own. Each one holds the secret of a hundred summers.

Last night when I braided my hair I cut off two inches or so from the end of each braid and Carl could not endure that they be burned up. They were very precious to him because they were from his mother's head. He put them up carefully in tissue paper and this morning I found them by his side. They had fallen out of his hand when he went to sleep.

We were talking at supper about your coming home and I said I so feared you could not get away as soon as you had planned to. "Never fear, Mama," Carl said, "Papa would die if he could not come home soon and kiss you pretty soon. He loves you so, he couldn't stay away much longer. Don't you worry, Mama. Papa will come."

We had morning glories on the supper table. The afternoon shadows come so early on the east side of the house. Last month when you wrote you supposed there was a full moon floating about somewhere. But it was impossible to find it because the weather was so stormy.

Your little Hal was in such ecstasies that I could not make him come in and go to sleep like a well-bred babe. He lay in the sand and rolled over and over, clapping his hands and shouting. You never saw anything prettier. It was in the back garden and the castor bean trees throwing such beautiful shadows amid the orange and the lemon trees and among them lay Hal rolling, tumbling, shouting, gone mad with the beauty of the night—a night so brilliant I could have read your letters by its light.

I'm too busy, always too busy, but I have great happiness in many things and I strive to find something of interest in everything I touch. The Russian laughed at me the other day. He came just as I was finishing my kitchen floor. I was down on my knees giving it a bath. He always tells me I work too hard, that I get too tired and gives me many little lectures. He often laughs and says I find something charming in everything and often says beauty is my chief necessity and will ask when I'm busy over things if I find any in the task whatever it may be. And I often, just to keep the best of the battle on my side, will conjure up some little romance to prove that I do. And this day he said with a twinkle, "Well, you don't find any beauty in washing floors." And I said, "Oh, yes, indeed, doctor. In the first place cleanliness has a beauty of its own and then I would never have known how beautiful the boards I walk on every day of my life were had I not polished them so many times and found how lovely their grain was." How he laughed! "You are always a philosopher. You are always a wise woman," he said. And later when I sat down at table in a fresh dress and a bowl of such beautiful roses on the table, he looked up at me with tears in his eyes, "You never forget, you never forget. They are your necessity."

I know that in many things he is a heathen, that in some things we dislike him, that people think him a terror in some ways, but I doubt if there is one among all our American acquaintances down here that appreciates my struggles and endeavors or appreciates my determination never to let the ways of misfortune really touch me as does he. Then I love to talk to him on so many subjects. He tells me so much that is new to me. We often fight over things but we do not allow such things to really mar our friendship. The little boys adore him. They rush upon him as if he was their friend indeed and he does love them.

Hal is not what you would call a patient or bland fellow but he is the courageous one. He makes very little noise over his bumps and scratches. Today he flew to the window at which I was sitting and shouted, "Bite! Bite! Oh, bite! Bug! Bug!" He was almost covered with stinging ants. His neck and face and his entire body were covered with bites. His clothes were off in a moment but fast as I worked the ants worked faster. But not a tear dimmed the luster of his sweet eyes nor a groan issued from those brave lips. He can yell, though. Do not imagine he is always silent when things go crooked. Wait until you see him "mad."

ꙮ ꙮ ꙮ

December 6, 1884

Dearest.

I've sewed one hundred and four seams today, counting long and short ones. I'm wild to get my sewing done before you come. I wish we could wear leaves and feathers. I'm quick with a needle or what would become of me. And then I sew strong because I hate to mend. In your letter of today you say you are to send for Harper's and Century for me. I've ordered the Young People for Claude and the St. Nicholas for Frindy.[20] So we shall have that much of the best of the world for one year at least.

ꙮ ꙮ ꙮ

December 14, 1884

Evening. What would I not give to have you beside me tonight? Carl has croup and I feel so powerless and so utterly alone. All are sleeping save me. I am sitting alone with Carl and watching him constantly. Last night I was up all night. I dared not even try to sleep. He has been so patient all day and seems better tonight. He said, "It would be dreadful if anything happened before Papa saw me in pants. Papa would feel very bad if he never saw me again. Papa loves me, Mama." I lay my hand on his head and say, "Oh darling, do not fear. I'll save you for Papa." And he kisses my hand and answers, "I hope you will, Mama" and falls asleep.

He told me this morning I was the most beautiful and the loveliest woman in the world. And when I laughed and said he had forgotten how many beautiful women there were in the world and many beside whom his little, tired mother would look quite plain, he put his little hands up and took my face between his palms and said, "To me there is none so beautiful as my little, tired mother."

᭥   ᭥   ᭥

Carl is better. A lark is singing even if it is December. There are birds and there are birds, but a lark is the bird of my heart. If I die first and go to some Persian heaven where souls sometimes return, I'll beg that mine be sent in a lark's song to be poured out in some glad song to you.

᭥   ᭥   ᭥

Christmas Eve, 1884

The children, all three, gone to something at New Hope Church and Hal and I are alone. I wish you could see him hold your picture and say, "Sweet, Papa, sweet Papa" and then kiss it all over on both sides and press it to his heart. "Never mind. Never mind," he said when he fell a little while ago and nearly broke in two the prettiest head in all of Florida.

The Russian was here today. I love to have him see the children often. I feel worried over Carl and he knows so well just how he is and always gives me courage. He says all I need is rest and I told him he must not stop me for I accomplished nothing now. But he only said, "Who accomplishes so much? See how many you have to care for. And yet no one does so much that is beautiful."

I showed him my collection of wild flowers and roots of grasses. The sheets are nearly two feet square, a pale tint, and in the center on one side or wherever they look prettiest, a square of some other tint, some in deep reds, or pale blue or sea green or rich brown, and over all of this lie the flowers and wild life. The effect is beautiful. It has been a great task but I love it. The Russian had never seen it. He said he had seen collections in several countries but only one so perfectly prepared and that was a French collection in Paris that had every possible scientific means to perfect it. And

126 *"Come to My Sunland"*

even that was not so artistic. I never saw him show so much delight over anything. Mine, you know, is not scientific. It is simply to show the artistic floral beauty of Hal's Florida. It is only begun but there are eighteen of these lovely sheets and they are the work of many hours besides being the result of many a long tramp. I want to make dozens of these bewitching pages and when people say, as indeed they are always saying, "You have no flowers in Florida" I can say, "I beg your pardon" and unfold my lovely proofs.

ﻉ   ﻉ   ﻉ

Christmas Day, 1884

The children have been so happy. Carl asked me the other day if I couldn't make a stocking for him to hang up. He said his was so little Santa Claus couldn't get hardly anything in it. And I've made one four feet long with stripes of eleven different varieties. We hung it in the middle of the Cheer from the beams above. Every book and trinket that has been coming from the North for some time went into it and all sorts of funny things we conjured up down here. It had around the top in large letters the words, "The Christmas Stocking of Carl of Lancaster and Hallock of Florida." When they were led in this morning they gave a shout and walked around and around it.

It has been a lovely day. On the breakfast table we have morning glories. The doors and windows have been open all day. Frindy and Hal and I have worn our white dresses. We had a beautiful bowl of freshly picked roses. The children have just run wild. Tonight we are to have a bonfire. I wish you could see the open hall. The rugs are strewn with books and papers, toys and happy children. The great table is littered, too. Its yellow cover with its deep border and fringe and wreath of scarlet poppies makes such a pretty corner piled with books and trinkets and the bowl of roses.[21]

I dare not even write that I miss you. These happy holidays in which we have been so happy together are a pain to me without you but whatever the years may have in store for our children in the future, they must have as many happy holidays to remember as possible and I must not give up to loneliness or homesickness. But I am both today.

ﻉ   ﻉ   ﻉ

Eleven o'clock. I'm sitting alone in the Little Heart. The old year is almost gone. It has been perhaps a quiet year viewed from some standpoints but to me it has been a very eventful one. Miss Thackeray says, "The real events of life happen silently and in our hearts."[22] I was a young girl when I read that sentence and even then it seemed to burn with truth. "I have so laughed and cried with you I have half a mind to die with you. Old year if you must die—[23]

The moonlight is lovely. When Hal came through the hall and saw that moon shining in the sky he shouted, "Hello, moon, pretty, pretty moon" and ran down the steps as if to greet a friend. And the moon sent down a little beam of light that kissed Hal's hair and eyes and face while he stood there just outside the shadow of the bananas, like a child transfigured.

Tonight when he kissed me for you, he said, "Sweet Papa, sweet Papa" and Carl stood near and throwing his arms around me said, "Oh, Mama will he never come? Oh, how I long for a sight of the face dearer than life itself and that lies on a pillow a thousand miles away."

♨   ♨   ♨

To E.S.

My dear dieudonne. A few days before Thanksgiving a letter came from Scott in which he said it was a great sorrow to him that I had to spend so much of my time in ways that were so distasteful to me, that I was made for the brightest side of life and he wished he had wealth that he might give me an existence such as he knew I should enjoy. But he said I did possess wealth in my two eyes that nothing could take from me for I found beauty in all things through them.

I do want a great deal that only money can bring but I do not repine. My love is to me the best that life has to offer and because we have had misfortunes does not make him the less dear. I am proud to share whatever fate has in store for him. But I do love to have him feel that all good things belong to me. Whatever a woman may seem to others, she never wants her husband to think her commonplace.

After reading the letter I thought the idea of wealth in one's eyes a pretty idea for a child's story and on Thanksgiving the children, having been invited out to dine, a few quiet hours happily fell to me and I wrote Scott the little story I enclose.[24]

The Wealth of Hildegarde

Hildegarde lived with her grand-aunt in a garden of sweets. A wall ran around it like a caressing arm. Vines clambered over the wall and trembled in each passing breeze. Birds sat on the branches of the old trees and even on the broad window sills and sent little love songs into every corner and crevice of the cottage. Flowers grew and blossomed in the garden as if it were a joy to bloom for the grand-aunt and Hildegarde.

They had very little gold and only one or two jewels but still they were rich. The grand-aunt had a wise head and a kind heart and little Hildegarde had a fairy godmother.

They lived very happily until one August day a little imp called Envy crept slyly into Hildegarde's heart and embittered each summer hour. A little maiden named Wilhamena came to live in the castle on the hilltop. Wilhamena wore soft silken gowns. Tiny jewels twinkled almost maliciously up at Hildegarde from the buckles on her little shoes. The web the grim, black spider spun on the old south wall was scarcely finer than the delicate lace that lay about her dainty neck.

Years ago the mother of Wilhamena, who was then an orphan like Hildegarde, lived in the old castle with her grandfather and daily she spent hours with the grand-aunt, either in the huge castle on the hill or in the little stone cottage in the valley.

The grand-aunt taught her to sing and to read and a scrap of Latin. They read history and the poets and many things together. She taught her to sew seams, to make edging for her wee night caps, and to darn her pretty hose and a hundred bits of knowledge.

And although she was the governess of the little lady of the castle, she was in many things a rare mother to the lonely child. And when she was fifteen and the grandfather took her away from the dull, old castle into a bright, gay life there was nothing in all the world half so dear to that young heart as the brave, sweet soul who dwelt alone in a simple cottage.

The maiden grew into a lovely woman and in time married a gallant officer, who died in a foreign land when their little daughter, Wilhamena, was hardly old enough to lisp his name.

And so in after years that her child might see and perhaps learn to love the old castle, Wilhamena's mother came again to the home of her childhood.

Hardly a night had passed after her arrival before she rode down into the vale where the home in the garden stood to see the friend of her youth. There were tears of joy in both their eyes and they looked in each other's faces. And the mother of Wilhamena laid her hand on Hildegarde's head and said she must go back with her to the castle and cheer up her little daughter who was lonely already up there on the hilltop.

And so gaily they rode away, innocent little Hildegarde and the mother of Wilhamena.

That was the beginning of discontent. The beautiful rooms, the richness and elegance overpowered Hildegarde. The books, the trinkets, the lovely trifles everywhere were fit for the queen's children. Ah, if she, too, could revel in such ease and beauty. How poor and rough and commonplace the little cottage seemed. How ugly grew the little frocks and kerchiefs. What a stupid little life it was after all. The weeks flew by. A great part of her time was spent at the castle. The summer was over and the autumn fast slipping away but the pain forever gnawing at Hildegarde's heart would not heal.

One morning the grand-aunt sent Hildegarde into the forest to search for mushrooms. The good doctor and his wife were coming to tea and mushrooms were his favorite dish. Hildegarde had filled her basket and stood leaning against a tree, looking wistfully in the dancing waters of a little brook, when she heard her own name softly spoken. She turned quickly and there, sitting cozily on a bed of moss, was her own fairy godmother. Hildegarde gave a cry of joy and, sitting down beside her, told her all her trouble. And though there was a twinkle in the fairy's eyes she lost not a word, and when the confession was at an end she said, "There are many kinds of wealth, my child. Now and then dame nature in some happy mood bestows wealth, the possession of which is sweeter by far than the gold a prince or a baron drops into the laps of their grandchildren. Little Wilhamena has her troubles, too, and her discontents are as bitter as thine, my Hildegarde. Have a care or thou wilt beggar thyself. To enjoy what thou hast is more to be desired than a king's crown. It would be out of all reason for one person to possess all the gifts or all the blessings and even a king must hold to reason.

But thou must make haste. It is late. See, the shadows are almost straight. The good grand-aunt's dinner will be cooking and her heart anxious. I cannot give thee the wish of thy foolish little heart but I will teach thee a lesson, my Hildegarde. Thou shalt change eyes with Wilhamena."

Supper was over in the little cottage. Hildegarde had sung her evening hymn sitting at the feet of the old doctor. She must go to sleep a little earlier than usual the grand-aunt said so that she might be ready for a great holiday on the morrow. It was to be Wilhamena's birthday and she was to go to the castle almost as soon as the sun was up. She kissed them all good-night and ran lightly up the crooked little stairs to her own room among the eaves, undressed in the moonlight, and was soon fast asleep.

The new day was there in all its glory before it seemed to Hildegarde that she had had time to close her eyes and they had come from the castle to carry her to the birthday feast. But, what is the matter? How strange it all seems. She rubs her eyes and tries to waken herself. She eats her breakfast as if in a dream. Did the little flower that the grand-aunt never failed to lay beside her plate always look like that? What has robbed the quaint little room of all its cheer and freshness? Everywhere in the house and out of it, it is the same. The world seems changed. How wildly her heart always beat with delight when they swept around that curve and came in sight of the river, but she does not care to lift her eyes to see the ripples on its bosom or the dark line of trees beyond. And the rocks are only dull, brown rocks, not a million tints and shadows full of wild and rugged beauty. It was never so before. What ails the dear old rocks this morning?

Ah, Hildegarde, little Hildegarde, that was thy wealth—those eyes of thine, those rare, sweet priceless eyes that sought beauty everywhere and found it in each happy glance. In the velvet blackness of the shadows among the moonbeams as they stole into thy tiny chamber and lay across thy home-spun coverlet. In each tree and shrub, flower and leaflet, vine and tendril— oh, how the birds sang to thee, filling thy very soul with sweetness and not one soft shade of plumage, not one toss of the gay little head was ever lost on thee. What pictures in the firelight those eyes of thine have seen. And even in dreamland, when lost in sleep, they still do bless thee.

Hildegarde stepped from the carriage door and crept slowly up the castle steps. Wilhamena, with a face like the face of a young Aurora so full it was of the glory of the morning, stood ready to receive her. For an instant Hildegarde stood still, unable to speak, so overwhelmed was she with the vision of beauty before her. Then she sat down and buried her face in her hands saying, "Oh, I understand it all now. Wilhamena has my eyes, my dear old eyes." And with a sob awoke to find her head pillowed on her grand-aunt's breast and a lark telling her that the morning was here.

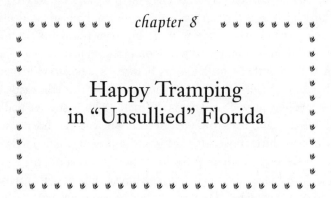

chapter 8

Happy Tramping
in "Unsullied" Florida

January 1, 1885

Dearest.

"My wife the long, long day sweeps by the cocoa tree
And my young children leave their play to ask in vain for me"[1]
These last days move so slowly. It often seems as if time had forgotten
that he was never to stop and was resting in motionless forgetfulness. But
still I do know that in reality he has not lost an instant and the hour is
steadily approaching that shall bring us together.

Today I said, "I love you, little Carl." And he looked up, saying, "Say thee,
Mama. It sounds so soft and smooth and sweet when you say I love thee,
little Carl." Has he not an ear for all things harmonious? "Mama," he says,
"when you were talking to Hallock, making love to him tonight, I couldn't
say a word. I could only stand and listen. Your voice was so sweet."

January 6, 1885

We can talk or think or dream of nothing but your homecoming. Carl
says, "How I love him. How I love him, that old Papa of mine. Indeed, I
know I'll cry for joy when he comes for just to think of it makes me almost."

January 23, 1885

To E.S.

In the Cheer. I'd love to have you see this little room. The Russian says it's like a naiad's bower. One corner is all from the sea, even the blue cup that came from Spain that Pet brought me. It hangs there.

We have one such pretty thing about the house that I never told you of— a little bridge. It runs across the open hall from loft to loft. There is no floor across the hall. You look up to the rooftop. And this little bridge has a railing and lattice of palmetto stems and is so quaint and pretty.

Sister Jenny sent me a piece of old brocade of pale blue and yellow. She has had it over twenty-five years and it was old then. It is lovely. I arrange it first in one place and then in another. It is a treasure in my eyes.

Tonight I was making chocolate and Carl stole in and laid his head against me, saying, "I don't feel satisfied and I'm so tired." And I said, "Why, Carl, what is the matter?" And he put his arms around me saying, "I feel so melancholy." But after a little while he was happy. He has to be left to his own amusement often and these busy days when I find little time when I can read or talk to him he misses it and is lonely. Not long ago he was not very well and I had the house kept quiet and darkened his room and let him sleep late. And when he came to breakfast I had arranged a little table with great care to tempt his appetite and his fancy. When he saw it, he exclaimed, "It's enough to make a smile come to any mouth and joy into any eyes to see such a lovely little dinner as this."

❦ ❦ ❦

February 24, 1885

To E.S.

Today Scott was reading to me and, spying Hallock in mischief, laid down his book and ran to stop him. Without deigning to do so much as glance at his Papa, he waved with a majestic sweep, saying, "Nay, nay, go on reading." The whole thing was so droll and so impertinent his Papa couldn't resist him and returned to his book and Hallock to his mischief.

❦ ❦ ❦

The mocking birds are in full song now and the larks sing every morning. There is to me no music like the song of a lark. They send sunbeams clear through me.

Little Hal comes up the steps every day, and sometimes a dozen times a day, from little walks. And his first words are, "Where is Mama? Oh, where is Mama?" And when he has found me he hurries to my side, radiant with pride, and offers me his two hands full of flowers.

Yesterday I had much work laid out to do but Scott begged me to go with him for a long tramp. We took a lunch and a book and such a happy day we had.

Can you imagine a neglected corner in the Garden of Eden where you could look up fifty feet and see air plants growing on the branches of great oaks and hundreds of ferns nodding to you up there in the sunlight and the gray moss like a mist? Or magnolias with their cool, dark leaves and tangles of vines running up the oaks to hug the ferns and the air plants? Or at your feet ferns almost tall enough to touch your cheek? And, then imagine the palms that I should miss anywhere if I had to go away from them.

I am a very busy woman. Few of my friends realize how much really hard work I am obliged to do but I would not live in a commonplace way whatever might come. I doubt if I'd carry my head any higher if I had a maid to dress my hair or my feet trod on velvet. I know that one misfortune after another has swept over us until we really are poor. But some way I cannot realize it. I want many things that only money could bring and I want them so fine and in such countless numbers that I never could hope to have my hopes and dreams realized. But there are joys that are mine that have naught to do with banknotes and real estate and they stand between me and poverty like a vision of paradise. And they lighten the burden of life like the touch of a hand celestial.

Scott brought me a huge book to copy my old letters in.[2] I cannot think of attempting it for some time. Just the sorting them over and destroying the bulk of them will be a task. My love to Lou and Birdie and Carrie, to all who love and remember me. I owe letters everywhere but each minute of my life seems to have one hundred uses. Your Barbara.

❦   ❦   ❦

31. Julia Daniels Moseley in her garden togs, ready to give full vent to her work: raking, hoeing, and keeping the grounds of The Nest in order. Ca. 1905–1909.

32. Julia Daniels Moseley in her afternoon dress, reading some letters from Scott. Ca. 1905–1909.

To E.S.

Little Hal says, "Turn your head, darling, while I give you a kiss." He grows in strength, in knowledge, in height and in mischief day by day. And with his wonderful amount of character and energy, he is as quick as a flash and so brave over his falls and whacks for he fears nothing and is, of course, constantly getting little bumps and bruises. But underneath all that is such a warm, little heart and such a love of all things sweet and beautiful.

The other day he was weeping in a most pitiful fashion over some disappointment and I took him in my arms, saying, "Don't feel so bad, darling." And he looked up through tears and laying his head on my breast, said through a sob, "Oh, Mama, I must feel."

When his Papa found him playing with the saw yesterday and told him to put it down, Hal paid no more attention to him than to the cry of a hawk that was at that moment flying over the house. Scott took the saw from him, saying in a very gentle, loving voice, "Don't you want to be Papa's good boy?" And Hal said, "No." And pointing to Carl who stood near said, "There's your good boy." And laying his little, baby hands across his breast gave a little low bow, exclaiming, "I'm your bad boy," looking the while like a cherub from out those lovely eyes and his hair like a cloud of gold. And in another moment the rogue had given a shout and rushed into his Papa's arms and had forgotten to be bad.

He loves to help. His feet are willing ones and joyfully carry him to and fro about the house on little errands. When I am at work in the garden he runs to me, saying, "Me help. Me help. I can pull roots." And it is fun to see his little hand fly from one to another and his quick glance so readily discover the weeds from among the young plants.

"Mama," Carl says, taking my hand, "let us go look at Hal while he is asleep. He is so beautiful when he is asleep." And if you could go softly to that little bed whereon he lies and lift the curtains of blue and see the vision of living innocence and rest with the Sistine Madonna, you, too, would say with little Carl of Lancaster, "He is so beautiful when he is asleep."

Not long ago Frindy gave him a bath by lamplight on the back porch and just when she was through and had turned to unfold his gown, he gave a cry and plunged into the darkness and such a chase as the children had for him. It was perfectly black outside and they could only follow him by his laughs.

He is very fond of the butterflies and he is so deft in handling them. He never breaks a wing and often sits and rocks one, holding it against his cheek, saying, "Rock-a-by, butterfly. Rock-a-by, butterfly."

We have arranged the Whist for my especial use this summer. It is a perfect haven to me for rest and quiet. I can come out here alone or with Scott and not hear the noise and confusion and no one enters without a permit from the queen herself. I can write here and a letter can lie undisturbed for a week if I choose. There is a large lounge with plenty of pillows, a rug, a large, strong table, a shelf two and a half feet wide running across the entire west end of the room, a case of drawers for drawing boards and traps, pictures and trinkets, palms and wild things, five windows and a door with a passion vine to wreath it. Who shall say it isn't wealth?

          🌿   🌿   🌿

May 15, 1885

This morning Claude brought me an armful of water lilies. The dew was still on them and they, too, looked glad. How many things a flower will say! I've had flowers sometimes, as I pass them on a walk, look up at me from out some moss-lined crevice and say, "Do not take me from this dear little home of mine." And if I've had to go back flowerless I could not have torn it from the spot it loved. And, then again, one will seem to lift its head and cry, "Oh, gather me, gather me." And when I've fastened it in my belt it will nestle down as if full of content and seem to murmur, "It was here I longed to die."

And it was so with the water lilies. When they were on the table in the Little Heart among the palms where vines clambered down the walls and wild, ragged daisies stand in such careless beauty under the face of St. Cecilia, where the broad mantle looked like a terrace of flowers, and the swallow corner blushed pink with its little sea of oleander blossoms. The creamy lilies with their trembling hearts of gold looked as if they were amid loving companions.

While I was arranging them Hal came in. You should have seen the eagerness in his face, the wild, ecstatic delight. Up went both of his little arms. "Just hold them, just hold them a minute." And I laid them all on his little arms. Then he stood perfectly still. He seemed hushed by their beauty and what a picture was that. He had on a pale blue dress, a deep lace ruffle in his neck. The lilies came almost to his chin and as he bent in speechless worship over them a more perfect little vision of humanity one could hardly imagine.

Few mortals have known greater happiness than I know or have known. But there are some hard knots in my life and this thousand miles that is soon to be put between me and my love again is something so cruel. I never feel as if I could write or talk of it to anyone. We cannot all go. The older children's health demands this climate and they are too young to be left alone.

33. Carl drew profusely from an early age. This montage of drawings, made when he was five, was pasted into the big book in which Julia copied her letters. Especially attracted to boats, wood-burning locomotives, machinery, houses, and street scenes, Carl also drew caricatures of people.

34. The first of Carl's drawings to be published was one for David C. Cook and Company of Elgin. Immediately after seeing some of Carl's drawings, Martin Beck, the company's art manager, placed an order for his illustrations to accompany an article on old-time bread making.

This time Carl goes, too. No one knows the pride and hope we have in that young life. His companionship is more to us than the friendship of kings. His voice, his sweet intonation, his love that speaks in kisses and caresses many times each day, his bright quick imagination, and the wonderful work of that little left hand that makes for us a picture every hour.

35. Sunnyside Bungalow, the large, two-story log home of John and Susan Browne, was built about 1907 to replace an earlier frame structure that had burned. The Brownes used old logs from their first cabin to supplement new ones, creating a spacious home—the largest twentieth-century log cabin in Hillsborough County. John Browne had homesteaded in the 1860s. His daughter Lena, who married Oscar Windhorst, lived in the home with her family until the 1960s.

There is nothing great enough to purchase from me the companionship of my boy, save the love that allows him to go beyond my sight for the sake of the comfort he will be to his lonely Papa and for the welfare of the blessed child.

I've just finished a book of his drawings to keep while we live and to be saved for his children. The book is ten inches wide, a little over twelve inches long and contains ninety-one pages of drawings, five hundred and ninety-one illustrations.[3] A large portion of them are what have been made in the last year to send in his Papa's letters, although I have begun with some of his first baby tracings to show how he gradually developed from shapeless lines to interiors in the city of Babylon. He was only six little years in February. Should heaven be kind to him and to us, we hope someday to see the dreams of our youth fulfilled in our son.

I've much work planned for the summer. Among other things, I've concluded to try and copy what I think best to glean from the old letters. I've no lace or jewels or sous to be left for my boys, but Scott wants me so much to do this work for them so that they may have a little shadow of our lives in the years to come when we can speak to them only from the past.

Our piano is coming soon and then we shall have music.

❦ ❦ ❦

Date unknown.

Scott and I spent a day in Browne's Hammock, a hammock where, even after they had cut down and demolished enough for large fields of sugar cane, there is still over sixty acres of magnificent southern growth left un-

36. Some of the best pines in the area grew opposite John and Susan Browne's house.

spoiled.[4] I hardly think any other woman has penetrated so far within its wild tangles as did I that day. I fairly crawled on my hands and knees through many a snarl of roots and undergrowth.

I'll only stop to tell you of one thing. We heard a rather strange cry from above and two clouds swept over our heads. We followed as fast as falling trees would permit and were just in time to see two huge cranes alight upon the crest of a tall pine and feed their young. To see them up there, between sixty and seventy feet above our heads, in that strange nest was something to be long remembered. When that long, uncanny neck was thrust up and the mother dropped that choice snake or some other rare dainty within was enough to make a goblin stare. While you lie in your hammock under the maples watching a robin or a bluebird or perhaps a brown thrush now and then, think of me gazing up among crane's nests with redbirds in my own oaks. Flocks of curlew winging their flight over my cabin roof. The grim, old buzzard floating round and round among the clouds. The larks to call me with the first smile of the sun. And, even in the nighttime, a mocking bird often sings to me of all the beautiful things I love. And remember that there are joys pouring in upon me, though the hours are often lengthened by care and hang heavy with the burden of endless work and worry.

Scott has built us a little bathhouse and we call it the Deluge. You know we never have just common names for things. We get tired of them. On the back porch are long, tight places like a lounge that open with hinges. One holds certain things that are used in washing and we call that one Purgatory. The other one is to toss things in that are lying about and to keep the place tidy, and we call that Hades. If Mr. Osborne should survey our plantation I think he would think I had fulfilled my mission, for he used to say I had a talent for naming people and things. The fun of it is that we never speak of any of these things by any other name than their own.

37. The little Deluge, built in 1885 for bathing with a bucket of water, is shown in a 1909 watercolor by Julia's niece. The old logging cart-wheel had come from one of the ox-drawn carts used in the area.

chapter 9

The Binding Ties
of Sickness, Sorrow,
and Trouble

July 6, 1885

Hal is two years old.

July 9, 1885

To Scott

In The Nest. My dearest heart, "we do but part to meet and meet to part."[1] Yesterday I painted several hours. I kept busy that I might not have one moment of time to weep.

Just as the sky began to grow lovely with the sunset colors, who should come like a sweet comfort to me but our dear Mrs. Coe. Her hands were full of crimson roses and she was the only person within hundreds of miles that I could have endured to have seen that first hard day of our farewell. We had our supper in the glory of the beautiful sky in the open hall with the roses on the table.

She would not allow any of them to come with her. She knew that to me it was a sad and sacred hour. But Mr. Coe was coming to take her home later. But when she found that I would love to have her spend the night, she sent a note home telling them they must do without her. It was a little cool after the shower and we had an open fire. We sat in the Little Heart and talked and Frindy played for us in the east room. And before I realized it, morning had dawned and the terror of the first night had fled.

❧ ❧ ❧

July 9, 1885

To Carl

My darling, my darling, already Mama has missed your good-morning kiss, your clasp about my neck, your sweet voice, your step all over the house, and even your gay touch on the piano. But well I know how eager you are over every new and delightful change and incident and what a comfort you are to as dear a Papa as a little child ever had. Oh, Carl, remember all your promises to Mama and be good to Papa. Cheer him, love him, and be so quick to do his bidding. And remember always that Mama is following in her thoughts and loving you beyond all words.

❧ ❧ ❧

July 12, 1885

I've painted a little stream of flowers round the curtain of my bed and the deep frill that runs around the canopy. The effect is lovely on the sheer material. They're mostly in shades of yellow and browns. It is Hal's delight and often he looks up and claps his hands, saying, "Mama's pretty bed, pretty, pretty bed."

Mrs. Coe said our home was such an ideal one in so many ways. Mrs. Omey sent me such beautiful flowers.[2] No matter how many I might have, I always love to have people bring them to me. There is nothing else that I like to have hardly anyone give me but flowers.

I've made Hal a little white flannel affair we call his "Noah." It is just for him to play in the showers. A low neck and short sleeves and two tiny legs an inch or so below his waist. As soon as it begins to thunder, he runs in calling, "My Noah, my Noah." And on it goes and he and the showers have the place to themselves.

I asked him this morning where he thought Carl was. And he laughed and shook his head and said, "Oh, sitting on Papa's knees." And every little while I hear him say, "Papa loves me, Papa loves me—cover with kisses my Carl for me."

I was up before 5 o'clock, painting away at the panels for the east room. I painted until dark and when I counted them over I found that I'd painted twenty-one. The effect is lovely, too. The colors are so soft and rich.

Hal fell out of the hammock today and gave his head a fearful bang but he did not shed a tear. He put his little hands up and held onto his head, saying, "Oh, my. I do not want to break my head all to pieces. I'm a nice little boy." I was going to write just as I gave him his good-night kisses for you and Carl and I asked him what I should say to you for him. He gave me a sweet little smile, saying, "I say sweet dreams."

I have such lovely dreams of you and Carl. My anxieties some way do not poison my sleep and I am so glad, for love and anxiety are near of kin and I dare not think of the dangers that lie all about you, and our little child, but I strive to banish fear and think only of brighter things.

Be sure and show Carl a picture in the August St. Nicholas, called "The King Drinks." The artist's name is not given. Explain to him the meaning of the word "majesty" and tell him that is what Mama thinks that picture portrays.

I'd gone to bed but I could not sleep. The night was too beautiful for closed eyes and I went out among the trees. The night is brilliant. I've been standing under the bananas. Five of them are in bloom. You know all that I saw. Why should I try to describe it? No one can do that. Then I came in and read over your long letter of today. I'm worried over Carl. I think from what you write he is as he was last year. He will outgrow it, the doctor says, if we can keep him well, but he would not have strength to battle against a severe illness. "Mama," he said one day, "by and by I will make for you the most beautiful home a mother ever had."

I've painted days and days since you left me. I've swung those brushes back and forth out on the back porch, which is turned into the jolliest little studio. I work as if a life was at stake.

I think perhaps in spite of my joys I mingle a hint of despair all through my work. This separation is so terrible and haunts each hour. When Mrs. L. was here she said I had done enough just in this house to have filled a lifetime and that she believed I really created time.

But you know my "tricks and my manners" and not to all the world do I disclose my "dodges and shortcuts." They think the forty-eight panels in the east room the work of many weeks. We will never tell them it was only the dashing swing of two or three days of those old brushes. They wouldn't admire them perhaps. And the mingling of countless tones in the painted window looks like the work of tedious days. Do you suppose I'd rob it of one word of praise or one admiring glance and tell them it was but the work of a few hours?

What could I ever do, where could I ever find time for one fanciful stroke if I could not work, as sis says, like one inspired? There is neither form or method, only madness in my work. It is done for the eyes I love, not the

38. (left) Humorous self-caricature of Julia Daniels Moseley, who after a financial reverse blithely promised Scott she would do all of the household cooking and cleaning. 1877.
39. (right) Another of Julia's drawings, showing her after months of the promised "scrubbing and grubbing." 1877.

world. But if others enjoy it, I am delighted. But I'll never reveal to them secrets of my wild brush and crazy fingers. I love to hear them think I can "make it." It is a gift I've often longed to possess. I'd never let old age lay a finger on us. We should be forever young and forever given over to sweet follies. Time is a splendid fellow if one's sweetheart hasn't left one to entertain him alone. Then sometimes even he grows wearisome.

Often when Hal is very tired or is in some trouble, I say, "Poor little thing." Tonight I held him until I thought he was asleep, and as I laid him down said, "My little darling." Without opening his eyes or without making the least effort to move, he said, "Yes, I'm a poor little thing."

Good-night, up hill or down, I'm always your Juliet.

☙ ☙ ☙

August 3, 1885

Dearest.

Shall I describe to you a picture breathing of homelife and youth and innocence and music and a breath of the tropics? You know over the piano in the east room is the "painted window." It is just the length of the piano and now that the eight-inch panels are finished and go entirely around it, the effect is lovely. The bottom of the lower panels comes just to the top of the instrument and the rich, yellow tones of the window are so beautiful. The piano was open. A great bowl of flowers stood on it. Frindy sat playing "The Harmony of the Angels." On the broad window sill over her head lay a banana leaf, freshly opened. On it lay the bud from a banana with its deep crimson cups and strange blossoms with tiny pink bags of honey, a crest from a pineapple, a brilliant pomegranate fruit of the most vivid scarlet, and a passion vine with its fringed blossoms of pale lavender. I had arranged it a little while before to see the marvelous effect. Hal lay along the sill in the attitude of a graceful Italian boy in ____'s picture of "The Poet."[3] One cheek rested on the palm of his hand, his hair fell over his shoulders, blending with the yellows and old gold of the window. Not a sound did he utter as Frindy sat playing over and over the exquisite harmony. They did not see me. Tears dimmed my eyes. I so longed for you to see it. Perhaps now and then you will steal an hour or two to wander with Carl into some lovely gallery or perhaps see some rare picture in a studio, but you will find nothing more beautiful than that, for sweeping from the east and the south was the soft sweet air and such a sky as not canvas ever held.

In the night Hal awoke. He crept over to me, saying and only half awake, "Does Papa love me? Does little Carl love me, too?" When I told him yes he fell asleep without another word.

You often laugh at me over my overflow of qualifying adjectives. I think you would think that Hal has inherited it if you could have heard him today when we were in the garden. A little rabbit was frisking about, the aroused Dutch dog was nearby, and a hen with one chick strolled in. Hal shouted to me, "Isn't that a nice hen, mama? Do you see that cute little chicken and isn't it a cute rabbit? And, have you seen my precious dog?" All of it as fast as his little tongue could wag.

He knows all the varieties of our cactus and nettles and the palms and every plant and flower about the place and he calls them by their names. It is fun to hear his little tongue trip along over thunbergia and hibiscus and periwinkle. He knows all the birds and he watches the ants at work and is somewhat fond of the different families of worms. But the butterflies are his chief love.

The little garden, the dear little garden. What a magic thought it is and how it grows and blossoms. There have been countless passion flowers and the fence is almost buried in vines. The ferns have hidden the north end and they hold up their delicate heads and say, "We are growing for the eyes you love." The wild plant that blossoms like fire has put out long shoots and their tiny forms clutch me as I pass and tell me they, too, are growing for him. The vine that has clambered across the gate and clutched the swaying branches of the mulberry tree, as I look up, nods down upon me and says, "Tell him not to wait too long. I am making a bower of green to cover him as he stands at your garden gate." And the little geranium vine looks up in a flutter as it scrabbles across the path and says, "I'm hurrying every sunny hour and I sup up every drop of rain and dew I can get. For I, too, work to surprise him when he comes." And the poor little balloon vine at the east window, who was such a beauty in her prime, clings with a paint-faded tendril or two to her daily lover, the morning glory, and tries to climb with him to the rooftop. Her little balloons prattle to me hopefully, saying, "We know she will be too late, poor old mama balloon, but we are ripening fast and our little black heads will soon be under the rich earth and when he comes we shall greet him with the daintiest green of all." The old bean vine has lost all of its pure white blossoms. It coughs and mutters hoarsely, "I'm too yellow and big for a little garden. I'll climb the fence and run clear out of sight before he comes." The sensitive plant draws aside her delicate verdure as I approach and dares not speak, but day by day her beauty grows. And do I not know for whom? But they know it, even from my finger tips even as I pull from their roots the choking weeds or set them laughing with a shower bath from the green sprinkler. And they hear me tell little Hal as he stands near or dances at my side, "For Papa? Yes, for Papa, all for Papa." Your Juliet.

❦ ❦ ❦

August 6, 1885

Little Hal sits at my feet in a white gown, all ready for his long night's sleep. I should go mad with grief and loneliness at times were it not for that beautiful young face and those arms that often lie about my neck in loving caresses. The Russian was here today. He said Hal was the most beautiful, perfect specimen of a child he ever saw and so old and wise for his two little years. Such splendid health, such a fine physique, very beautiful, and is already an honor to me.

He had never seen Carl's book before. He thought it wonderful and as he turned the pages would constantly exclaim, "Carl, Carl, and you but six years old." He did not require much entertainment as he wrote a letter of over twenty pages while here.

We have something new. We call it the "Tuffit" [*sic*] in honor of Hal's beloved Miss Muffit [*sic*] and her little spider. It is a cushion, five feet long and a yard wide and a quarter of a yard deep, stuffed and fat with palm leaves. Piled high with scarlet cushions, it lies on the floor of the open hall and it is just jolly and adds greatly to the inland air that pervades that old hall with its big rug and huge chair.

❦ ❦ ❦

August 8, 1885.

I am sitting on the stairs at Valrico, Professor Tausey's home.[4] Miss Averill's 70th birthday is being celebrated here. I did not think I could go but the

Coes urged me and here I am. Everyone is here and how glad they all seem to see me. I did not suppose they did imagine they liked me so well. All asked for you and Carl and those who had not seen Hallock said they had heard of his beauty. Not one has spoken of him today but has spoken of that.

I must write but a line as I have stolen away and hidden on the stairs. I want you to know I am never forgetting you. However great the number that surrounds me, it is your face I see plainest, your voice I hear above all others.

The Professor took me out to dinner. His conversation is charming, his language so choice, and his voice so low and clear. This is a lovely spot, full of beautiful possibilities. The nursery already contains some thirty thousand young trees.

I've had several invitations but have refused. If I accept one, I must accept all. Both home and Hal need me and then it is just as well, people shouldn't know me too well. They may think me more choice. You know many worthless weeds are held in high esteem simply because they are scarce.

Later. Hal was so tired from his day of constant play that when I laid him on the bed he looked up, saying, "Oh, I'm so tired I can't say goodnight, Papa. I can't say goodnight, little Carl. I can't say, sweet dreams."

You know he has never worn stockings, but always these little white socks. The last you sent were blue and when he saw them he exclaimed, "Oh, I'll be a nice little gentleman now." If ever there ever was a little joy giver, it is this bairn of thine and mine.

❦ ❦ ❦

August 11, 1885

Mrs. O. and Jennie and Harry spent the day. It was a very pleasant one. Frindy played and they sang "The Watch On the Rhine" and many other German songs. In the evening the "ridiculous philanderer" came over with his old fiddle and played for an hour or two. A "Cracker" dance he does very well, but he is not the embodiment of harmonious sound.

Tell my glorious little son I cherish each picture that is the work of his precious hand.

❦ ❦ ❦

August 21, 1885

Darling Carl.

Tonight Hal was so tired and sleepy he did not want any supper, just a glass of milk and to go to bed. And I very cheerfully said, "All right, darling, just let Mama wash you a little." He looked about as if he wished all water and sponges were in Greenland, but he gave a little nod and a sigh. I washed his face and hands, but when I began with his back and he feared his bath was coming he gave a wild yell of rage and disgust and screeched out, "Oh, you are washing me big, big. I want my milk." He does not believe in any variety of false representation and will never countenance it on any occasion. But he is a pearl, this little sunland brother of yours and he talks of you and misses you every day of his life.

❧ ❧ ❧

August 26, 1885

Dearest.

In the Little Heart. I've been out walking alone in the moonlight and thinking of being with the blessed child that bears thee such sweet company. The clouds, the room, the shadows, the stars, the moving of a great bird all try to prove themselves the sweetest. I cannot wonder but they love me. They love me, they do. But must not I be eyes for two and it seems as if the very skies must miss thee and all things long for the hour when you shall come and walk among them again. I know no bird ever sings to me when thou art gone but there is a touch of sadness in each long rondelet.

There are no less than a thousand flowers tonight in the Little Heart. The old chimney is banked high with flowers and palms and is fit for the wedding of a fairy queen. And under the white honeysuckle is a new fungus I found the other day that is large enough for a banquet table for a dozen gnomes. The top looks like ivory. As I look through the door I can see the palms waving in the hall. How quiet is the house. How still seems all the world. Oh, do come in. Oh, when can I hear that step of thine?

❧ ❧ ❧

September 4, 1885

My beloved.

I am sitting on the Coe's piazza. They've brought me up here for a rest so I can get away from the noise and confusion and already I feel better. I do not know how long it will be before I feel that I am myself again. It is hard enough to live with all these weary miles between us when I am well. But, oh, when I am ill and in pain and must lie still, it is torture. I feel at home here. I could not have gone anywhere but here. They came and carried me off bodily.

❧ ❧ ❧

September 5, 1885

It was my first night away from Hallock and about midnight he awoke and said, "I cannot find Mama." Frindy ran to him and sang to him and soon he was quiet. But in a few moments he called out again, "I cannot find Mama." Then Frindy explained about my being gone and he seemed satisfied and fell asleep and soon after in a happy voice he shouted joyfully, "Hello, Mama." He had found me in his dream.

How I need you. But all my days are your days. Your Juliet.

❧ ❧ ❧

September 10, 1885

Today I prepared the skin of one of those huge rattlesnakes we have wanted so long.[5] It is nailed with over one hundred tacks to a smooth plank. It is over five feet long and eleven and one-fourth inches wide. It is magnificent. Its beauty is to me a marvelous thing.

We have had a dozen calls today. I like to have people come to The Nest but I like our quiet days best. I hardly find an hour to read and soon I will steal some time for I am hungry for my books. I almost enjoyed the work on that old snake. There are such countless tints among his scales. Such delicacy. Such strength. And he was so supple. It seems as if nature must have had some fine purpose in view when she produced such a mechanism as this fellow.

While I was at work a lady came out to the tree under which I sat and, after looking at me with considerable disgust, remarked, "I could never do a thing like that." She is quite given over to the most hideous crocheted impossibilities to adorn chairs and tables and bureau tops and, with a rather wicked smile, I observed that I thought it on the whole almost as elevating as making "tidies." I think a great many mean things but I try not to say them often. Now and then they have flown from off my tongue before I can curb that unruly member.

🌿 🌿 🌿

September 20, 1885

Everyone tells me how well I look. And I am well, only tired and nervous. The doctor says all I need is rest and quiet. I live too hard and feel things too much. I must be calm and live up to my philosophies. He says I think reasonably but I live unreasonably. I do enough for half a dozen people and have only the strength for one. But you see I really am all right and all your worry

Grassy Pond - behind Limona Clubhouse

40. Claude Moseley, self-described "Indian," fishing for shiner bait on a sinkhole lake behind the Limona Improvement Association building, ca. 1907–1910. He had built the light, flat-bottomed boat.

41. Claude Moseley during the Spanish-American War. He was the only Moseley boy old enough to serve. 1898.

is in vain and I must keep busy or I'll go mad. I cannot live calmly. I dare not even try.

Tell Carl not to forget that his brother Claude shot an alligator ten feet long on his fifteenth birthday.[6]

It is raining hard, coming down in torrents. Hal is out in his Noah. I'm sitting on the "Tuffit" [*sic*] here in the hall and every little while he comes up the steps, turns a somersault on the back porch, walks over to me and gives me a dripping kiss, and then off shouting and laughing, rolling over and over in the little pools of water. You never saw such a set-up. He seems more like a sprite than a child.

🍂   🍂   🍂

September 23, 1885

To Carl in the Whist at home.

Do I often think of Papa and thee, my little bairn? Yes, darling, I'm always thinking of thee—all day long when I sit and sew in the Little Cheer or among the palms and flowers in the Little Heart, when we are at table in the open hall, or when Frindy is making music for me in the paneled room, or when I am at work in the kitchen, or busy in the garden, and when I steal out alone in the dead of night and walk alone under the oaks, or stay in and watch the bananas whose leaves are like sheets of silver these bright nights. I lift my eyes and watch the clouds. Sometimes a bird, pitying my loneliness, sings me a song.

There is not a human sound to be heard. The old cabin looks deserted. There is a great peace upon the earth. It seems as if I was alone in the world. I whisper your names. I put out my hands to touch you. When I lie down the soft glory of the night sweeps in through the wide windows and doors and floods the room and I fall asleep, only to find you again in my dreams. And when the morning breaks, it repeats your names in every sunbeam. Always I am thinking of thee. Every thought and glance repeats thy names, my absent ones.

*   *   *

October 8, 1885

Dearest.

It is against all orders and commands and entreaties that I write you a few words, although I am lying flat and could not for my life sit up to hold my pen. But I must say something to you myself. I cannot lie here any more days and keep silent. The doctor sent you a line yesterday and you have had word from someone daily. How I have longed for you these awful days of pain I can never tell you. The doctor has been so good to me. He has been here eight days and nights in these two weeks. No other doctor in the world would have done for me what he has. Yesterday I said to him, "You could not do for all your patients what you have done for me, could you, doctor?" And he said, "No, not for one." His devotion and kindness have saved my life and however much we may differ with him in some things we must never forget what he has been to me in this illness. A thousand miles from you and so helpless.

Later. I could say no more and hid my letter under my pillow for I will write. I'm homesick for you. If I cannot write, I'll die. I know what I want. No one else does.

I could not take medicine often at times and I've had it injected in my back and arms seventeen times.

The doctor is very busy. So many are ill.[7] During my worst two days when I spoke of his going he said, "I dare not leave you." And when I reminded him of the families on the Alafia, he said, "I shall stay here. Your life is worth all the rest." Perhaps they would want to shoot him but you may be thankful that he stayed to fight for my life. When he was nearly wild one day with a terrible headache I said, when he came into my room at night, that I feared he hadn't had everything to make him comfortable that he should have had. But he said, "Yes, everything." All that troubled him was when I was so sick and needed such cheerful faces about me he should have had to look so gaunt.

He is a strange man but in many ways his nature is a beautiful one. So patient at a time like this, so unselfish and so unforgetful. I want to write now and tell you how good he has been. I may forget it bye and bye. We are so apt to forget our kindnesses when they are past.

Mr. Coe and Percy have brought me fresh milk every day. They are going to take me up there the first day I can be moved.

Later. I am up at the Coe's. Came Wednesday. Mrs. P. came over the same day for a call. I was so tired and her slow, dull conversation made me so nervous but soon, to our surprise and my delight, Mr. Chamberlain walked in. His brilliant, dashing repartee and chat, after Mrs. P.'s wailing, was like the flash of a meteor after a long drizzle.

When they told him I had been so ill and so long he said he did not believe it. I was lying with my head on one of my scarlet pillows from the lounge at home. I had on a scarlet skirt and that pretty jacket, trimmed with that lovely old velvet brocade, and a pair of the prettiest Indian moccasins. Mr. Chamberlain laughed and, after surveying me, said, "An invalid! Look at her. She looks more like an East Indian princess." He spent the night and decanted my wine for me for I have to drink something exhilarating three or four times a day. He was in splendid humor and it did me a world of good. He made me feel so bright and as if a part of the world had come back to me.

The doctor is delighted with my progress and he says all I need is patience and courage and time. Mrs. Coe is reading a book aloud to me. I cannot read yet as my head is not strong enough. Mrs. Coe said, "It's as good as a show to have you and Mr. Chamberlain here. I wish you would stay a month, both of you." Do you remember what fun he and I used to have, rattling on together, and you used to so cruelly take me down, though not for long?

I must tell you when I see you of such a funny story he told us about his father when they all came from Philadelphia to spend a season in Tampa. Just after supper he came to me saying, "Run in the other room now and lie on the lounge and have a nice little rest while I go out on the piazza and have a smoke, for bye and bye I want to tell you a lovely story and I don't want you too tired to enjoy it." Doesn't that sound like old times for do you not remember his orderly way of arranging for everything, no matter what?

I'm at home again. While at the Coes I sent Frindy a note one day and a little, laughing face that was for Hal's kiss. He would kiss it over and over and kept it with him nearly all day and at night brought it to her saying, "I want to send my Mama's kiss to Papa." When I came he put his arms around my neck, laid his head against my shoulder, and said not to go away any more.

Hal gets a funny kink in some of his words. He often hears us say "Springfield, Massachusetts" and the other day when someone asked him where you were he said, "In Pringwheel, Massafia."

᙭᙭᙭

October 17, 1885

I grow strong so slowly. Ill health in no way belongs to me. I was made for action. I love strength and I love to live every breath I draw and not crawl on the way. These days are torture to me.

I was so glad of the olives and do you know that little rogue of a Hal loves them, too. I can walk without trembling and that is quite a gain.

Never speak as if you dislike the doctor. You do not know him if you feel like that. When I sent for him for Hal that day we were so alarmed about him, he was far from well but came in spite of the storm. And when I said it seemed too much for him, he said, "No, you know it is one of my ambitions to see what your boys are going to make of themselves." It was sometime before Hal was out of danger or really conscious, and as he bent over him he said, "Oh, the world has need of such. See how splendid he is."

I know in some things he is a strange being and I readily understand how so many dislike and even ridicule him and yet in many things they might take off their hats to him. But were he more complete he would be a great physician in Russia today, a wife at the head of his table and serfs to comb his curly head and do his bidding. He would bow down to the Czar and keep his lips closed on political matters and smile upon slavery and oppression, instead of being an exile in southern Florida, living in a house little better than a hut and saving your wife from an untimely death.

I cannot tell you of all the loving attention I've had. Your heart might well be stirred with gratitude toward the whole countryside.

I love the painted window more and more. I believe it is the prettiest thing I ever made. And to think of the wall I plan to make for you. And not one inch of it can I accomplish. Still it lives in my mind, a thing of beauty, and some day if I live it shall delight your eyes beyond any work I've ever done.

The children cannot get used to my being among them again. It is not that I was ill so long but that I was so very ill. There was one night that I lost all hope and I had Frindy open the picture window that I might see the sunset once more. And I told her to tell you I saw it the last time through that window you had made with loving thought for me and through which we had watched the evening sky so many times. That was a sad night. They all cried.

Hope for a time seemed to have departed from us all and soon I was out of my mind and weeping because you had come home to find the palms all dead and Carl would insist the scarlet poppies were stars and I thought his brain was gone. By and by the doctor came and gave me something to put me to sleep and the next day I was better and my spirits revived. Such agonizing days. I feel as if I could endure anything if only we could all be well once more.

I'm reading an Irish novel and at table I tell the children the story as I read. It makes no difference if we have much to put on our table or not. It is always a merry meal for it is in here by the open fire, on the south porch in the sunlight, or in the hall under the palms. The table is always so pretty. The flowers are never forgotten. While the palmetto chair of sweet Hal's holds a sunbeam whether the weather is fair or not. We feel let out of prison. Frindy ends up every meal with a bit of music on the dear old piano and she plays for me in the moonlight. We have such pleasures from the sweet toned old instrument. It is worth more than gold to us.

I'm so glad Mr. Grivi is so full of interest. It is so nice for Carl as well as you. How satisfying and ever fresh real knowledge is. I wish there was someone I could meet often of whom I could learn. It is a sort of struggling on in the dark and alone with overwhelming forces against me. I cannot endure the thought of growing less as I grow older. I want to climb higher. There is no beauty in age if we do not. I often feel as if I must fly back to the world and have a taste of a different life but I fear I would gladly turn my face toward my own wilderness. My deficiencies would loom up more plainly than ever for a little world is often very flattering. I know how mine is for it is scarcely outside my own domain and those that love me are blind to my faults and treat me as if I had none until I, too, will become blind to them and content even with my own shortcomings.

Mr. Chamberlain said even southern Florida couldn't spoil me or vanquish me. You know he loves the climate and hates the rest. I never see him but think it is such a pity that he should waste his years down here. How arrogant he could be if he chose. He is a mixture of good and bad qualities. You know I always said he was the most entertaining guest we had at The Nest and yet I never had much faith in him as a real, true man. I often think how unjust we are to people. How I like him because he has fine manners when he is with one to whom he chooses to display them and because he is so entertaining. Had he not a gift of speech I would not care for him. And yet good, truly great dull people I often snub just a little. That is, I wish they would let me enjoy the sweets of solitude in unbroken peace. And does it not seem a little unfair that a gift that is some brilliant freak of nature in one's makeup should have greater weight than positive virtue or genuine goodness that often is the result of patient endeavor, noble self-sacrifice and many other fine qualities?

It takes away so much of the sting in this cruel separation from Carl to know he is where he is, growing in the way I long to see him grow, in an atmosphere that is pure and where he can learn what is fine and good. I can see his eager little face and his very attitude as he begs you to stop in your walk that he may hear a little clearer the mystery of the formation of the mountains.

Did I tell you of the lovely panel I've made of the lichens you sent? It is of birch bark nearly a yard long and half a yard wide, covered with the mosses and lichens and under it is written, "From the woods in which three generations of Moseleys have played as boys—Carl of Lancaster, his father and his grandfather." The colors are so varied, some so pale and delicate, others so rich and warm.

❧   ❧   ❧

Gretchen is here. When she found I would not go to her she came to me. After they had left the Carolina mountains and started for home, she said to the colonel, "I want Jule. No one can comfort me but Jule." And he said I should go to her at once but I was not able. They buried their little boy on a little island up there in some stream among the Carolinas. She is like the gay Gretchen of old at times and then again she is overcome with sorrow.

I had a long talk with the doctor today and he said he had always realized how great was my love of nature but never before as he had during my illness. He said when I talked or wrote of it, it charmed those that loved it and awoke the heart of those that did not.

I was talking to Hallock of your going and asked him if he remembered and he said, "Oh, yes, but I didn't went away and left Mama all alone. Oh, no." And you said only the other day that as long as you lived you would remember him as he stood among the wild flowers and grasses, his delicate white dress and deep lace about his neck, his little socks and slippers, his hair all about like yellow sunshine, the little hands upraised and waving a good-bye. Alone he stood, the tall pines above, the matchless moving sky. Ah, just that Hal can stand at that gate for you nevermore. The childhood of our children with all its flush of joy and radiant promise holds ever the note of a farewell in each new unfolding.

I want to tell you something I need sadly. I long to read the Idylls of the King in this beautiful October weather. The fates only know when our poets will be brought down from Lancaster. Buy me a simple copy. I need it above anything else just now. I know our wants for common everyday things are many, like Christ's poor they are always with us. If we waited for the necessities and the wise purchases our poets would never come. But who would not make way for a poet? Surely, not you or me.

❦   ❦   ❦

June 1891

Note—Dear boys.

Papa sent me the book at once. I read from it the very last morning I ever sat in the Little Heart. It lay beside my breakfast tray when the first sound of the fire reached us. Mama.[8]

I so wanted you to see the beautiful effect of the little hanging garden in the open hall that I tried to paint it for you. But it is nothing. I cannot catch it. Oh, poor, helpless hands. Why art thou not able to make a reality of what my heart so longs to send to bless the eyes of those I love? Why can I never put that rare cunning into thee that shall make me able once in my life to look upon thy work and say I am satisfied? That is what I have tried to accomplish. But still whatever we may be able to do, always we must dream of finer things than we can do. Always strive for a higher peak than we can reach.

When I read a fine poem or see a wondrous picture, it is not the poem or picture that I envy the poet or artist for. What great difference does it make who does it? We who love it, possess it. That finer poem that revels in his brain that never was put into words, that marvelous picture that lived only in his mind—they are what we should envy for they never can belong to us. It is so with everything beautiful and fine that a human mind is capable of and is my first thought when viewing it. If they can create this, what must that ideal be that they never can attain?

But the living picture in the old hall is so lovely, clinging to the wall in its rich brown covering, the palms bending over its sides, a banana waving its broad, cool leaves, the oleander and delicate ferns and vines caressing everything with their tendrils, and in the midst the largest pineapple I ever saw with a lovely crest of deep rich reds and greens.

Colonel Mayo is here. Came this noon. He calls me Mrs. Jule. His manner is charming. He came just after our lunch was over and while I was arranging his Gretchen led him from spot to spot. So many of the things that people admire the most and that they often think are the result of tedious hours are the things I do in a flash. Almost the first words the colonel said were, "I'm perfectly astonished. So much originality and beauty in the same length of time I never saw in my life." Gretchen could not wait but had brought forth this and that in her eagerness to have him see it and after dinner took him out to the Whist to show him Carl's book. He says he never saw a child that seemed to be such a perfect mingling of both parents as Carl's book proves him to be. Hal always calls Gretchen "dadmudder" and he is very fond of her. He often says, "Dadmudder, I think you are sweet. I love you."

Mrs. Wilder this morning sent me a basket full of flowers and under them lay an orange, a lemon, a citron, and two hot baked sweet potatoes for Hal's dinner.[9] Who shall say that even a Cracker does not know to mingle the beauty with their neighborly acts. She often does. I send her things to read and share a dessert with her or some fresh fish or vegetables and I take pains to send it in some pretty fashion, knowing she is never well and thinking it might tempt her. And she says, "If I didn't like it, I couldn't help but eat it. It always looks so pretty." And now if nothing but a geranium leaf is at hand, she lays one on the plate on which she sends me a fresh tomato, a few guavas, or even a slice of "hoe cake" to show she thinks of me. And it always pleases me for it shows someone is thinking of me kindly and remembers that even with my "hoe cake" I like beauty.

🌿 🌿 🌿

November 6, 1885

I do not know which is most to me, Hal or Hal's beauty. I hold him close to my heart and wonder that I can ever repine when such wealth is mine. But, my thoughts wander to that other boy of boys in his pretty jacket and his unbuttoned overcoat, cap in hand, walking down the aisle of the beautiful church and as the sweet strains of the music fall upon his ears, his thoughts fly southward until they reach the old cabin underneath the palms and the pines where his mother is starving for him. And if I starve for Carl, what must my hunger be for you, my love, who are more precious than my sons, more to me than my own youth?

Do not worry that I have to work. I have to work. Ease is for idiots and lovers of idleness. I often wished I had more time for the things I love and for more quiet hours with my books. But just to rest I never think of. When I am too tired I paint, or read, or walk in the woods, or write to you or work out some fancy. I return to the routine refreshed and stimulated.

🌿 🌿 🌿

In the Little Heart. A mad fire in the old chimney, a young moon outside, the house asleep. My beloved. Tell Carl the rose is from Hal's shoulder and that Hal kissed it for him just before he went to sleep. After he had had his bath and his gown on tonight, I let him play on the rug before the fire. I was standing near the table, singing a little song. He climbed in a chair and then on the table and, putting his arms around my neck, said, "I love you Mama." I took his little face in my hands and looked for a moment in his eyes, thinking how heavenly sweet his manner, his beauty, his vivid sparkling nature was to me. And then I said, "I love you, Mama's baby." He smiled and with his face still in my hands, said, "And your eyes say they love Mama's baby." Do you wonder that I couldn't let him out of my arms until he went to sleep? Do you wonder that when all else seems gone from me and there is nothing to turn to and my very heart seems dead within me, that he brings the joy to my life and lights up all the dark way of these lonely days with his bright, sweet presence. I can never tell you what he is to me these days of dreary waiting—a little rock wherever I lean but a rock so enhanced with the blossoms of innocence and beauty, so bright with the perpetual sunshine of his joyous, radiant nature that it illumines while it rests.

Today I heard him saying to himself, "Papa will come home again. Papa will come again. Papa will come home to me. Papa loves me. I love Papa. Oh, yes, I love Papa." Never was there more of the very essence of life in two little years and three short months than in his young life.

Today I made a bag of the beautiful fur of the palm and the skin of the huge snake.[10] It is so handsome. There is joy beyond words in creating something beautiful. As it grows beneath your touch you are scarcely conscious of your body and when it is finished a feeling of such exaltation sweeps over you and life seems such a splendid thing.

It is the same I've felt among new flowers or even some new and especially pretty arrangement. I've felt it often when I've set the table. Not long ago I arranged it with everything especially delicate and in a pure, white shell laid passion flowers, letting the leaves and tendrils trail here and there along the cloth. When it was complete it made a picture so lovely I could feel my cheeks grow warm.

I shall never forget the first time I ever saw cardinal flowers, save perhaps a stem or two. I had gone with my grandfather and some acquaintances to look at some woodland of his beyond the city. I was playing about and found

42. Rattlesnake bag incorporating the palmetto fiber that Julia made in 1885. Fortunately, the bag escaped the fire that destroyed the log cabin and is now part of the Moseley Collection.

a new butterfly and in trying to catch it, wandered away from them and running wildly forward, forgetful of everything, felt the earth moist and soft beneath my feet. Stopping, I found I was surrounded by cardinal flowers. I began gathering them and then when my arms were full stood looking down upon them. Never shall I forget how the vivid color affected me. The tears rolled down my cheeks. They seemed to hold me spellbound with their very intensity and I thought, "That is the color of my heart when I am so happy

I cannot tell it." I've never seen one of these flowers since without recalling it and I could not have been more than eight years old at the time.

There is so much in color, often more than words. When I was a young girl I once saw some very lovely watercolors from some Italian painter of the rare purple hills and sky of Italy. I rarely look at my picture of St. Cecilia without seeing those pictures, long ago as it was that I saw them. Something in the sad, sweet expression of her face recalls the exquisite quiet and peace and twilight beauty of the tones that belong to the purple glory of the Italian landscape.

I'm reading the Friendships of Mary Russell Mitford.[11] I like it much this far but, oh, what pleasure is half a pleasure unless shared by you.

In one of your letters not long ago you wrote, "My Julie, my darling, God knows how I love you. It is beyond my own describing. You are in every thought and even lie imprinted and upon my work and must always continue in life and in the hereafter. My Julie, I am nothing but yours." Such words almost make the thousand miles of little moment and when we have lived together for ten long years what a blessed thing to be lovers still. Good-night, life of my life. The fire has burned low. The moon has disappeared. I think of Carl asleep in your arms, perhaps. I see a smile upon your lips. I'm sure in some happy dreams you are with me.

᭝ ᭝ ᭝

November 12, 1885

Mrs. Coe says whenever I feel I would like a rest or a change to fly up there and stay for a few days. It is always a comfort to them, she says, to have me there. Mr. Coe said I looked as fresh as the morning itself. Now to look as fresh as a summer morning even in Massachusetts is a good deal. But when you can look as fresh as a Florida morning, who can ask for more?

I went to the bed to see if Hal was awake and when I drew the curtains aside, he looked up saying, "I'm all here, Mama." As he turned the pages of Mother Goose, he said, "Little Miss Muffet sat on a log, eating a Christmas pie."

᭝ ᭝ ᭝

My love and my soul, the very foundations of me. Do not worry over me so much. I cannot rest. I must keep busy. Why should I promise to do otherwise? I could never keep it. I love my home. We three are so glad to be alone with our music, our flowers, our little jokes, snatches of a book as often as time will permit, our wonderful climate that glorifies and pervades everything like a joy in one's heart, making even unpleasant tasks radiant, and our marvelous little Hal. We get on very well. There are times when the agony of the separation is so overpowering that I know not of anything else and life is a torture. I've begun Idylls of the King and am reading Charles Lamb. I miss you on every page.

❧   ❧   ❧

To E.S.

I want to tell you a few things of Carl that Scott has written me and that I have never told you. In Springfield is one especially beautiful church with elaborately carved doors and massive hinges. You know Carl went North with Scott before he was but four and remained some four months and has not been since until this time. So that his remembrance of architecture is very faint and I do not know that he has ever heard church music before in his life. One evening Scott took him for a walk and they went by this church. The light came through the rich stained glass and the music floated through the open windows and doors. Carl was in an ecstasy of delight. He stopped and listened, went up to the beautiful doors, laid his cheek against the carving, kissed the hinges, and then said, "Papa, take me home and let me think about it." Scott took him home in silence. Carl lay down on the rug and when Scott asked him if he wanted him to read to him, he said, "No, Papa, I do not even want to talk. I just want to lie still and think of the beautiful church and the music." At nine o'clock he said that he wanted to go to bed. And in the morning his first words were, "Oh, I've had such a beautiful dream of a church, Papa."

Later in the season they were out for a walk and sat on those same steps. The church was empty and the organist was playing for his own pleasure. Scott said that it was so beautiful that it almost brought tears to his old eyes and Carl listened, scarcely breathing. Scott says nothing seems to fill Carl with the intense admiration that massive architecture does. His favorite walks are among the churches and a few striking buildings. One pair of doors on a bank building he would carry away bodily had he the strength of Samson. He loves nature but not in the way Scott and I do. A beautiful building is more to him than a beautiful tree. He loves the elegances of life. A lovely room adds grace and ease to every motion for him. The more refined and exquisite his surroundings, the happier and more contented he grows. It has always been so with him.

❦ ❦ ❦

December 7, 1885

To Scott

In the Whist.[12] Dearest. I love you. I never loved you as now. I am all yours. Be brave and trust me. I am happy, brave and full of courage. The dear, old Nest is quite gone. It was burned to the ground this morning. Do not despair. Do not let it spoil your happiness for one little hour. It is not a sorrow, my darling, my love, my life. It is only the house we lived in. We are safe and well and full of hope. I covered this sheet thick with wild olive blossoms and fastened the wild grasses you liked best among it this very hour that you might know I was still myself. Write that you, too, are not despairing. Cover with kisses my boy. All yours, Juliet.

❦ ❦ ❦

December 8, 1885

In the Whist. Evening. Little Hal asleep on the floor. I wonder if it is possible to go back and tell you all about it. Oh, darling, it was only yesterday and it seems months ago. Let me try.

It was a very heavy frost that morning and we were just finishing our breakfast and such a merry meal was that last one in the beloved home. Frindy and Hal sat on the rug before the fireplace. The table was drawn up close and I sat in the Dutch rocker. We would have heard the fire sooner but were laughing and talking and our chimney roaring. All at once the sound seemed deafening. We flew to the wide hall door and flung it open but it was a mass of seething flames. The little bridge was already blazing and brands had fallen, burning the rugs and furniture below. I said to Frindy, "Our home is gone. Water will do no good. Fly with Hal and come back quickly and keep your wits about you and let us save what we can." Frindy said fear left her then. She said that she felt I knew what I was about and she would obey me and think of nothing else. And she did, as if she was an old, trained soldier.

The first thing I took down was Carl's gun and cap. Everyone came but we had but a few moments. The fat pine rose like an explosion almost. To think of that east room, full of our work together, and all the panels I've made for you and the countless trifles here and there that you will never see. "But she can never show him, never that swan's nest among the reeds."[13] And the window that I painted for you while you sat outside and planned the little witch of stairs. No wonder the glass caught the glory of those happy hours. It was not just paint but your love for me and mine for you—a dream, a fancy, a glad laugh, like all work in which love dwells. How Frindy loved that window as she sat and played. She said it made her touch softer. And as I used to lie and listen, looking up among its rich tones, the music used to seem to stop there and now it is only a drop of melted glass left.

Frindy saved my old letters and the large book.[14] They were her first thought. The flames fairly licked her face as she ran from the room. After everyone had left the house and were screaming to me to fly for my life I still stood in the Little Heart in which we shall sleep never more, the room in which our glorious Hallock was born, the room in which I have lain at the door of death since last we looked in each other's faces. Can anyone ever know save you what that old cabin was to me? I stepped on the lounge and sprang through the broad south window, the very bed in flames, the yards upon yards of airy frills I had painted for you kissed lightly into nothingness in one hot breath. Think of the bright frieze with its countless flowers that the winds have tossed so many times, "The Vintage Festival," the swallow corner and the old brocade, the jars and bowls for flowers, the books upon the shelves, the lovely curtains, the old mirror wreathed in lace. The kitchen was not entered. All my lovely old china and the cups and saucers of past generations—every precious dish gone forever.

Mrs. Coe said, "We have all lost so much in that house. It belonged to us all. We all had pride in it." And Mrs. D. sent word that we were not the only ones who had lost in the fire. "Everyone that ever went in the rooms had lost. It was all the beauty that was and it was gone." I cannot tell you how kind people are and the tears that are shed. It seems just a little strange and to me so sweet that everyone that has them sends or brings me flowers. No one has yet said a word about our loss as if it were in dollars or cents, but the beauty of it. And even when speaking of you they seem to understand that it is what money cannot replace that will be the real grief to you.

As soon as they left us alone yesterday we arranged everything and although nearly everyone has offered to share their home with us we shall settle down alone here and live as best we may. We went down to the hammock and gathered palms and wild things and raised them in the Whist and I nailed boughs over the doors. You would be surprised to see the air of home it already wears. Some of them shed tears when they came in this morning and saw it and wondered at such a time I could think of such things. But it is when it is darkest I need it most. I cannot keep up if I do not first gather some beauty and brightness about me.

It is cold though and has rained but I cannot go for a day or two to Tampa to get a stove. I have already ordered some lumber and before I slept I planned the new addition and will tell you of it in a few days. I did not close my eyes until daylight but tonight I hope to sleep. It is hard. God only knows how hard. We have struggled so hard and now in many ways it all has to be done over and the hard part is yet to come. When the excitement is over and it is an old story to all save us and we must sacrifice and economize to make up for the loss, then comes the real anguish of sorrow and trouble. When the dull days are here in which no one cares to hear. When other things have come to make your trouble of small moment, but to you it still lives and throbs and must be endured as best you may. But we are still happy in what fire cannot touch.

I've written this letter with an old quill from a buzzard's wing and from a bottle of discarded red ink that happened to be here. But you can read it and soon all these things can be arranged.

It was a beautiful sight that morning. Frost stood on the wild fields and on the trees over our heads. The sky was so blue, the air so sweet and clear, the sunlight bursting upon the new day. The flames overspread the entire roof and were running wild through the hall, darting up the old post and beams, crash after crash. I stood back near the grapefruit tree that directly faces the hall. I was proud of the old Nest and thought, "Even in death it is beautiful." I was so glad there were so many flowers within, glad of all the fresh palms and new wild beauty I had hung there only last week. I wonder if ever I shall have a home I love as I've loved that. It is gone. Never save in memory can we cross its threshold more.

❦   ❦   ❦

December 11, 1885

In Tampa. I just bought such a jolly stove. You can open the front and see the fire burning through a little grate. Mr. Chamberlain is so kind. He has been with me nearly every minute today and helped me in so many ways. He says I do not look as if I had been through a fire or as if trouble or misfortune could ever touch me. He will see that all my things are packed safe and shipped at once. He says he will write you tonight.

❦   ❦   ❦

December 17, 1885

The Russian was at Col. Mayo's when the word reached them of our loss. He said Gretchen nearly fainted. He came at once out here. When he came in he looked about and the tears sprang to his eyes. "Nothing can harm you," he exclaimed, "nothing can make you poor. Mr. Moseley will always be a rich man while he has you." I am very nervous but I feel that I must never allow myself to give up once. Mr. D. will begin work next week on the new room.[15] We are to have an open hall on the west, ten by twelve, a porch on the south ten by twenty-four, and a room across from the open hall twelve by twenty-four. My plans for windows and various little things I'll tell you later. All on one floor and no steps. We shall call the new room The Cuckoo for it is not the real Nest. That will come later on the dear, old spot. I am going up to the Coe's to paint. They have given me the middle room upstairs and they call it the Studio. I shall paint a frieze and some more curtains. I am full of plans and am too busy to mourn. I have not yet had time to weep and besides I cannot spare my eyes. The other morning I was look- ing for something near the old house and looked up and saw Hal not far off looking so pitifully at the dead ashes. I knelt down beside him and laid his head against my shoulder. He gave a little sob, exclaiming, "Oh, Mama, comfort me." My eternal sunbeam has come the nearest to getting under a cloud that he ever has before. He misses so many things and he still says so often, "And, will I never go into Mama's pretty room again?" Yesterday he surveyed the Whist just after it was put in order for the day and exclaimed, "Isn't it a nice little home, Mama?" And when I didn't reply, he said, "Say yes, darling." And so I said, "Yes, darling."

᭤ ᭤ ᭤

Mr. Weeks came with a load of lumber this morning and, stepping up to the door, took off his hat and surveyed the room. "Well," he said, "but you do look nice. I tell you, Mrs. Moseley, to take it brave like you is a heap the best, I reckon. You've got your palms yet, haven't you?" And do I take it brave? I wonder. Who knows how hard I find it, how almost beyond my power to control, how I miss the music, the beauty of the rooms, the comfort we had begun to gather about us and all that was so dear and held so much. And you are so far, so far, and I need you so.

᭤ ᭤ ᭤

Dearest, the moonlight is beautiful. Frindy and Hal lie asleep on the floor—not a hard bed for it is stuffed thick with palms and the sheets are so white. How happy and restful they look. "Care keeps his watch in every old man's eye and where care lodges sleep will never lie. But where unbruised youth with unstuffed brain doth couch his limbs there golden sleep doth reign."[16]

In the mail tonight came a square box and I thought of course that it held some Christmas trinket for Hal. And when I unwrapped fold after fold of soft paper and beheld my lovely cup I clasped my hands in delight. And you should have seen Hal. "The dear little balls. Are they legs, Mama? And the little handle, so lovely." And he bent and kissed it over and over. His pet playthings are an old adz and a hammer but he does love delicate and dainty things and he brings me so many little things that are so pretty and he handles them so tenderly. The other day he was walking with Frindy and he stooped and laid his hand on a crisp, dried-up stalk, and exclaimed, "By and by there will be sweet flowers on it, Frindy." You see how far-reaching is his beautiful bump of hope. I can hardly wait for morning that I may have coffee from my new cup. Who but you would think of such things in the midst of such discomfort. It will make all my days easier during this confusion of building. I finished fourteen yards of the frieze so you see my hand has not lost its cunning. Miss Alma said today the flowers had such a careless air, as if someone had tossed them on the canvas. We are all going up there for Christmas. "The dear old cabin," Hal says, "we loved it, didn't we, Mama?"

🌿   🌿   🌿

I'm too tired tonight. I couldn't go up and paint tomorrow and wanted my frieze drying before Christmas so worked all day today and it is finished—twenty-five yards. The little velvet fly we found yesterday and it has been admired by us all. Hal has said "Oh" to the red spots under his wings and "Oh" to his blackness and "Oh" to the rows of gold buttons along the edge of his wondrous mantle.

🌿   🌿   🌿

December 26, 1885

We had a happy Christmas. I was homesick and sad, of course, but I couldn't show it by word or look. The children must be kept happy and then everyone was so kind to us. Even the "Crackers" remembered us. I [*sic*] had sent me all sorts of wild things they thought would please me, from curious pine knots to the plumage of birds and roses until the little room looked like a bower. The beams we had buried in mistletoe and scarlet berries. Letters and loving messages came almost without number. But, oh, so hungry was I for you and Carl. I longed to run away and hide from everyone and cry my heart out.

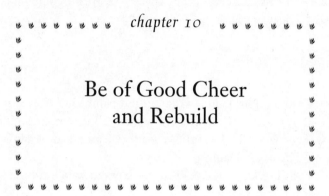

chapter 10

Be of Good Cheer
and Rebuild

January 31, 1886

Well, sweetheart, I'll begin with the Whist for we have so little room we cannot use it just for a kitchen. And then where we work it must look pretty or the work seems too dull. I have shelves here and there and they are arranged in such a quaint fashion. The Cuckoo is finished and I sat down to tell you all about it. It is so simple it seems almost silly to try to describe it. And yet it is very sweet and cozy and is as odd as it can be. A frieze runs around it on a blue and scarlet background. In the west peak is a lovely face, an engraving from a painting of Frederic Dielman's.[1] It happened to be left among some other treasures in the drawers in the Whist.

We keep fresh palms in one corner and everything looks so bright and clean. The effect of the long, narrow Cuckoo with its pretty frieze and long windows that slide back and forth, the high peak among the beams, the long lounge twenty-four feet in length that runs down one side and half across one end, the painted window, the screen, the large table, and the huge bowl from which the palms bend over you as you walk beneath—all make the room in spite of its roughness almost bewitching. I've only basted or over-cast or stitched twenty-five times around this room. So you see aside from the painting it is choice, being handwork. On a panel of the mirror I painted my old motto from Goethe: "We must read a poem, listen to music, and see a picture every day."

The lower the tide ebbs the more need have I to remember these things. "Be of good cheer" is painted across the top of the screen. I abominate mottoes as a rule but there are places I like one now and then and "Good cheer" seems to be the keynote everywhere. It is a surprise to me as I look about. Everything has a contented air as if joy inspired each thought and touch. And yet they have been hours of pain to me.

I've been so homesick for you and Carl. I've so mourned for that lost home. I've worked in desperation and slept only to see it burning before my eyes. I seldom speak of it. I know that our sorrows are soon tiresome subjects to acquaintances and the world at large and they all have their own ills. There is not a planed board in the Cuckoo save the floor. Even the window sills are just as they were sawed at the mill. But I must have a room at least as large as this. You know I scorn small rooms. And I must not bring debts upon you. I came in the room and I found Hal standing by the table and I said, "Who is Mama's darling?" He crossed his little hands across his breast and made a little bow, saying, "This it is that is Mama's darling."

No one knows into what perplexities I get and I have to get out of them alone as best I may and I make blunders great and small. But you never imagine I am going to disclose them, even to you, my love. Do I not want you to think me as wise as possible? In March we are coming to you. Oh, heavenly thought!

         ᾧ   ᾧ   ᾧ

February 5, 1886

To Carl of Lancaster on his seventh birthday.

I'll tell you about Hal. Perhaps that will please you as much as anything. He had quite a time over a sandspur and when I asked him if it was still there, he said, "No, I felt round and there it wasn't." One of our cold days he ran out to play, dressed to play as usual, but soon came running in, shouting, "It is cold, awful cold, I want on my little shawl and my petticoat and my sleeves."

I send you a scrap from Howard Pyle.[2] I think he would please you. To me he is one of our most ingenious writers and artists. Everything is so quaint and droll. Some day I hope you can have more from his pen. I'm sure you would think his drawings charming. Were you here today what a birthday cake we should have and seven little candles burning. Mama has had fresh flowers and palms everywhere in honor of her dear boy's birthday and every thought is a loving wish for your happiness.

I must tell you one sweet thing of Hal. The other day he had a fearful fall and was so badly hurt he could do nothing but sob. To try and take his mind from the pain I went for a little walk with him but he kept saying he was cold, he was tired. I stopped and took him up on my back like a little papoose. He laid his head on my shoulder, gave a little sigh, and in a low, sweet voice murmured, "I'm not cold now." We walked on and soon he said again in the same low voice, "I'm not tired anymore." It was so sweet. Such peace and content was in the voice.

🐾 🐾 🐾

February 14, 1886

Tonight there was a sunset all in pink. Everything seemed covered with blushes and the moonlight followed. I've stolen part of the day to read. The Russian was here for the first time since the first lumber came. He was perfectly surprised. I was sitting sewing in the Cuckoo. He was in ecstasies. "You have done the work of years," he said, "and yet in such sorrow. And yet you sit here with such a happy face. I never saw such beautiful bravery. I knew you would be brave but not like this, not hold out like this."

🐾 🐾 🐾

March 6, 1886

Only eight days before we start. We have a little garden started on the south and east. Morning glories, passion vines, ferns, lilies and other things, pomegranate and crepe myrtle set out for it couldn't seem a home until it has a garden.

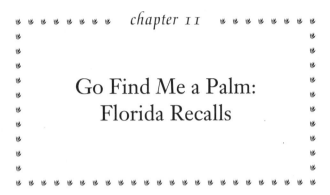

chapter 11

Go Find Me a Palm:
Florida Recalls

July, 1886

To Frindy at home in the Cuckoo.

Springfield, Mass. We think Carl is safe now but the illness has left him very frail. It may be months before he is as strong as he was before. They have been terrible hours to us. The fire was nothing to what it was to see our beloved little child lying at the very door of death. One day I sat watching him lying very still, just looking so very old and thin. He unclosed his eyes and seeing me said, "Mama, I do not want to die now. You know I have never made a real picture yet." He was brave and patient, never complaining, but always so still. But now that he is better he is very irritable and is a constant care.

Hallock goes everywhere with me and is greatly admired. I never take him out but I hear someone say, "What a beautiful child." Carl said yesterday, "Mama, Hal looks like a beautiful little prince out of a fairy tale." He is a little rogue, though, and loves mischief as the birds love fair weather. When he wanted the hammer yesterday I told him I was afraid he wouldn't be good with it but when I asked him how long, he vowed, "Two miles." I wish you could see him this moment, sound asleep in his little bed with his Chinese doll beside him. Everyone has been very kind to us during Carl's illness but I am too busy to think of much but Papa and the boys and if a quiet hour comes to me I drop down with a book rather than go out as I ought and return my calls. I'm afraid I should never become a model society woman.

☙ ☙ ☙

Florida Street, Springfield, Mass. Hallock to Frindy—My darling sister, you remember, dear, that Mama slipped a postal in the letter box saying we were all going to Westfield Sunday and soon she would tell you all about the visit. But Mama has some barberries to put up and some juices and my new aprons to make so she has left the story of that rare day to me, your little Hal, who was "in it" from first to last and in everyone's arms. We started early in the morning.

It was a glorious October morning and the woods had been kissed by the frosty, brilliant lips of autumn until they are bright and beautiful with her loveliness. We went over the same old wooden bridge that Papa went over when he was as little as me, wrapped warm and cozy in his mother's arms. Or a little older, sitting like a proud little gentleman beside his father. And so it was one recollection succeeding another from that time on until we came home beneath the light of the veritable old moon that bewitched the mountains and hills and streams and beautiful Connecticut River for his young eyes and which was making for his little boys a world of beauty all these long years after.

We watched for the little windows in the bridge and laughed with delight just as he did and loved the rumble of the wheels on the old boards and all along the way in the same houses or on the same spots where new ones now stand, he told us of the people who once occupied them and of places he had often been with his dear parents. Then we came to the stream where he learned to swim and at last to the old home, the home our great-grandfather built and where our grandfather, Seth Moseley, was born.

It is a charming old place. It seems to me anyone would like and enjoy that old home. Just think, Frindolin, I warmed my hands by the same fireplace where our great-grandmother has sat and held up our grandfather's little pink toes more than eighty years ago. We went up the old staircase, and such a pretty staircase, and, oh!, the old Franklin stove where a fire was burning in a room upstairs. I laughed at that. I think anyone would. It has a sort of look as if it were holding onto its sides with merriment.

I could never begin to tell you of all the precious old things we saw. The house is alive with memories and you must come and see it with your own, sweet eyes. We went into the old garden and down the very walk that was laid out in our great-grandmother's day and Mama gathered a bit of sage and one or two little things from the very spots where hers used to grow and blossoms to send to you, her great-granddaughter, whose roses bloom all the year around. We ran on the grass under the mighty elms that were planted when our grandfather was a little boy and we all sat down at table with such a quantity of Moseleys in the same room where they have sat so many years—a hundred next summer. And although a hundred isn't much to an old chap like Claude's Homer or Professor Newman's beloved Greeks, it seems quite a long time to a baby of three little eager years. How does it seem to you, my beautiful, wise sister of twenty?

Then we went with Cousin Mariah and Cousin Edward to ride about the town and especially above all else to see the house on the bank of the river where our own Papa was born. Carl said to me last week, "Just think, Hal, perhaps we will see the very door through which they carried Papa when he was a little baby." And, we did! Mama could see grandmama so young and full of joy, looking out upon the river with such a new and sweet significance to all her life as nothing else had ever been able to bring to her. She could hear the little, fluttering cry and feel the helpless little clutch of the baby fingers but we have not yet reached that height, sister dear, and we are willing to wait for they tell us the sublime heights are reached only through the darkest waters, the most rugged climbing.

We went to see Great-aunt Mary and I kissed her for grandmother and hugged her just as tight as I could and when Mama said, "Hal, it is grandmama's sister. They used to be little girls together and play as you and Carl do." I couldn't realize it. I looked my wisest that day. I tried to be an honor to my family. But, Frindy, it was all as incomprehensible to me as "Jack in the Beanstalk."

We walked over among the bogs and gathered some Indian pitchers where they have grown for generations and we climbed the hill back of the house to see the beautiful view from the top and the woods and ravines. We found a chestnut or two and will send Claude one to keep from the tree Papa gathered them from when he was a boy. Mama found a bird's nest in an alder bush on the edge of the lane down which Papa used to go for the cows when he was little. She wouldn't take fine gold for that nest.

Cousin Mariah gave Mama a little wheel on which our great-grand-mother used to spin flax. And I said, "Mama, do give it to me for my little bicycle." But you should have seen the scorn with which she refused me.

While we are talking of old houses, let me tell you of one that is grand-father to the other. It is a house that our great-great-grandfather built and we went into the parlor out of which fourteen brides have walked, each bearing the name of Moseley and representing five generations. Everyone was so nice and kind. It was such a happy time. There was only one thing to mar the day—it was the absence of the girl we love best and dear old Claude.

I woke up singing out of my own little Mother Goose book "Sing a song of sixpence, pocket full of rye, merry little hoptoads baked in a pie," and when Mama ran up to see me the first thing I said was, "Where is my great grandfather's house?" Now I had not really believed one-half of what I had seen and heard. I had not comprehended one-tenth. I would not vouch for any of it, Frindy. I tell the tale as it was told to me. But do you suppose I dreamed it, dear? There is the little wheel and there is the little nest. It must be true. But, who am I? Am I my great-grandson or am I me? Whoever I am and wherever I am, I am your little Hal who loves you and needs you.—Hal Preston Moseley.

❧ ❧ ❧

October 15, 1886

To Florence

One morning Papa went to Hartford and as he was starting he said, "What shall I bring you?" and I said, "I don't care just so it is some darling old thing." And he looked in a lovely crockery store and found an old, blue dish that they said had stood somewhere about the establishment for twenty-five years and he brought me that. It is an old darling, cover and all, and while he was gone I painted all day and Papa seemed as much pleased with his surprise as I was with mine. I'm afraid Papa and I are going to be very foolish to the end.

I wish you could see our little sitting room as it was yesterday morning. We went into the woods and came home loaded with lovely things. I found another print of "The Vintage Festival" by Tadema and a lovely interior by

Coomans. They are framed in oak and are very pretty. Then there is one lovely bit of statuary and Rosa Bonheur's lion's head and one or two others that I put here and there without frames.[1] Everything is pretty on the cream walls. And some of our wild Florida things—the palms and long banana leaves are beautiful among the others. A lady was here on an errand the other day and Mrs. C. told me she asked her if it was not the home of an artist next door. She said it seemed the sweetest little room she almost ever saw and every trifle looked so artistic. Everyone seems to admire it and the mantel they "rave" over.

            ✹   ✹   ✹

October 17, 1886

When Hal put on Papa's glasses and sailed about the room, I said, "Well, who are you?" And he said, "Oh, some old thing." He is so full of life. He flew at Carl who sat quietly drawing at the table and gave him such vigorous hugs and caresses as nearly to drag him from his chair. Carl laughed and hugged him, saying, "He is such a jolly little thing. He doesn't mean any harm, Mama. It is just Hal's way. He might crush a person but it is just his manner."

I went upstairs yesterday and found Fannie, the Chinese doll, tucked carefully away in Hal's bed with a cloth wound round and round her neck, just one yard long. When I asked what was the matter, he said, "She had an awful sore throat and I had to give her Acconite and be so good to her."

            ✹   ✹   ✹

October 19, 1886

Last evening Hal was asleep and Papa had gone to some errands and to the library and Carl and I were alone when Mrs. C. and Maude and Leothe came. We were in the little dining room. It was so pretty, too cold in the sitting room. So I brought some things in from there and closed the doors. On the buffet is a large, yellow English jar full of golden rod and beech leaves. On the table with its soft cover of warm, subdued shades is a deep red Midain jar and in it a huge mullein plant with broad, pale leaves of thickest plush. We found it in a hollow hidden from frost and sun. Such a one as we never saw before. The lamp is a fine burner and lighted up the room until every eye in the peacock feathers on the Japanese background back of the buffet seemed to be looking at us. And the flowers in the Japanese frieze above seemed to have blossomed anew.

The three guests looked so rosy and fresh after their brisk walk that I told them they should help decorate the room. Mrs. C. wore an Indian shawl and I spread it over the dull, old sofa with its high back and made her sit on it and her soft brown silk and a hint of glimmering trimming here and there looked so rich and pretty. Maude wore a long fur-lined mantle. I spread that with the fur up over Papa's armchair. She wore a witch of a red dress and her hair is wavy, willful and golden—all in a fluff and a tumble. What a picture she made, laughing and talking nonsense. Indeed, we were all in a "lark" from first to last. Leothe's broad-brimmed red felt was lovely on the cherry stand with a Kate Greenaway volume opened beside it. And her velvet jacket with an olive lining lay across the back of a chair while she, in a scarlet jacket, a dark skirt full of broad folds, her black hair and large dark eyes, sitting in one of my antique yellow chairs made such a bewitching contrast to Maude with her golden head sitting on her fur throne. They laughed at my audacity in using even my guests to enhance the effect of my room and we had such a merry time. When Papa came he, too, was delighted. And he and I sat up long after they were gone to talk over many things.

❦ ❦ ❦

November 20, 1886

Dear ones at home in The Nest.

The boys are sleeping and the dear lord of this house is in New York. How can I stop to go so far back as a week ago and tell you of Aunt Jennie Clark's visit?[2] Yesterday Papa packed fifty-seven jars of fruit that I put up to send south. And among them are some cranberries I was preserving that very day when the dispatch came saying that she would be here in two hours. She had not come from home rested and well but quite tired out and from some distant place where she had been to help settle some estate in the Clark family. She said it seemed just like getting home to be with us and nothing pleases you more than to have a beloved guest feel like that. Every-thing was in order when she arrived. Papa went to the train and supper was ready. The table looked lovely. I have a lovely square I often use for the center. It is of Dutch linen with morning glories in color. Aunt Jenny says Hal is the most beautiful boy she ever saw. Carl, she thinks exquisite. And

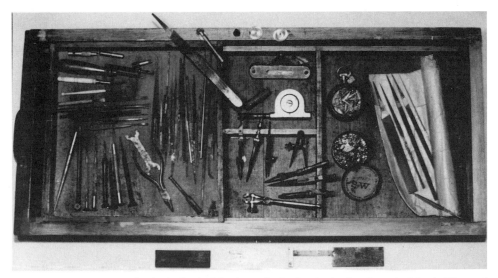

43. Scott Moseley was indeed "the lord of this house" whether in the South or the North. Pictured is a drawer of the tools he left to his son Hallock.

she loves to describe lovely pictures and places and statues to him. And he is such a charming listener.

While here she had a letter from Uncle George saying the great glass for the Lick Conservatory was pronounced perfect and beyond their highest hopes and accepted. I happened to be at their house when the great Russian glass was just completed, and last fall when they were just packing the Lick glass. So I have seen the two great telescopic lenses of the world just as they were ready to begin their marvelous careers. Monday Aunt Jennie went to Westfield but returned Wednesday with Aunt Mary and Cousin Mary, who spent the day with us. And what think you she brought me? A piece of flooring from the loft in the old house where Papa was born, a custard pie plate of Grandmother Noble's, a lovely cup and saucer, part of a wine decanter that was given your great-grandfather on his wedding day, and the old spice mortar that belonged to them. Aunt Jennie says they are in love with me and told me many things I am too modest to write but I will whisper some of them to you some day for I am very glad to have Papa's New England relatives like me and I'll never care very much for being liked even for Papa's sake. A love that isn't given for one's own sake is very thin and of little value. Papa will soon go to Dubuque, Iowa to be gone perhaps two months.

44. A Moseley Lathe Company advertisement, ca. 1900, showing the tools arrayed like guns to underscore the copy's assertion that these lathes were more effective than Admiral Dewey's guns in repelling the invasion of the handmade Swiss watch.

I was telling Aunt Jennie while here two or three things of Hal and the journey and it reminds me that I have never told you of them. My illness so soon after my arrival put everything out of my mind. At Hartford the most startling dandy entered the car, spotlessly dressed, delicate gloves and linen, waxed mustache, and an air of "don't come within a thousand feet of me" that made a little ripple of a smile run all down the car. Hal was standing up with his arm around my neck. The young man sat down just back of us. Hal surveyed him in that calm way of his from under those gold locks and in his clear voice and in the most solemn manner said, "Have you a family?" The laugh that followed from some gentlemen and even ladies who sat near enough to hear was refreshing, for the entire car had been a little amused over the young man's appearance and manner. But neither Hal nor the immaculate young man saw any cause for laughter and remained silent and apparently unmoved.

All along the way Hal was interested in everything but he made a practical application of his constant study of pictures and illustrations and our explanation of them. He had never seen three houses together before nor a train of cars. But the moment we entered a sleeper he said, "This is a palace-car, isn't it, Mama?" He knew it at once from the illustrations. When we came to a large lake where a variety of watercraft was moving here and there he seemed to know them all. He had never at that time seen any kind of a boat outside of a printed page save the one, old disused rowboat on the shore of the lake. But he called out, "See the steamer, Mama, and the little tug. And there is a sailboat. It's a sloop, isn't it?" A lady and gentleman directly back of us had been much amused and she remarked, "Just hear that baby talk!" And the gentleman replied, "Yes, these children that live at one end of the globe one-half of the year and at the other end one-half are wonderfully precocious."

But my little Hal was as much a child of the desert as one could find and no child on earth had seen much less of the actual world as he who had never been two miles from home before that trip. He had never seen grass but how lovely he thought it, though he supposed the lawns a variety of sand at first and said, "See, Mama, how beautiful is the sand in the north." And he had never seen brick chimneys, only the old mud ones of his own Florida. But he realized at once that it was similar and exclaimed, "See how beautiful is the clay in the north." Everything is either north or home and Florida to him. One day when he was first let out of doors to play he came in perfectly breathless, calling me to come and look. I supposed it was some machine passing for he seems bewitched over machinery of every description. I ran to the windows and he pointed up to an uncommonly clear, blue sky above and with tears streaming down his lovely face, he exclaimed, "See, Mama, see, Florida. Oh, Florida." He has missed and mourned for his beloved sunshine, his warm sand, his trees and flowers, his dear, dear Frindy from first to last. And he often says, "Oh, do go somewhere and find a palm."

※ ※ ※

November 26, 1886

To Scott in Dubuque, Iowa.

My beloved, if only you could look in and see how lovely is the room. I cannot keep the sitting room and dining room both heated. It is too much trouble and I thought we would just nestle down here as cozy as we could. So I stole some of the prettiest and best loved things from there and have made a little, soft warm bower for us here. The large yellow rug I've thrown over the tall, great sofa and it looks superb now and so inviting with its pillows. The pictures and the old table with its cover of skins stands in the corner for me to write on. Everything we wanted is here and we are so complete. I do not know why it is but always people say of my rooms that they look like some quaint studio.

The day has been bright and sunny although my best and brightest sunbeams were your two postals of the morning and two letters that came in the afternoon. Hal has asked so many questions concerning your absence and his little lips quiver as he talks of you. Ah, how young we begin to feel the pangs of love. Joy and sorrow are twins, for a heart capable of deep affection must be capable of anguish. I keep busy that I may not be so lonely. I was not afraid when night came and it was a mad night, too. The blinds blew open and slammed until morning. And the windows rattled as if they had an ague fit and the wind moaned all night long. But I held Carl's hand in mine and fear did not dare approach. When I put Hal in his crib, I said, "Hal, don't you need Papa?" and he replied, "Yes, I need Papa but Papa is away and I need you, too, and you are here." Isn't he a sweet little philosopher?

❧ ❧ ❧

November 30, 1886

Dearest, I'd give all my ribs to see you this day. It has been an uncommonly happy one too. Mrs. C. has talked of taking me over to the Goldswaith's some day. And it being a very bright one she drove over early and Hal and I ran away with her, Carl being invited out to lunch with Leoth. We left the breakfast dishes, the unmade beds, and the dust and commotion to pout it out among themselves and followed our own sweet will. It was as you well know a most beautiful drive, the broad river, the hills everywhere, the lovely old homes. Mrs. Goldwaithe had a face that was to me so uncommonly lovely in its expression that I felt I would like to take her cheeks in my hands as I used to do my angelic voiced old grandmother's and kiss her many times. She seemed full of an undemonstrative, unconscious goodness and as if her mind had always dwelt on the sweet side of life. The house is full of antique things and a few fine family portraits. Everything seemed to belong to the past, even the flowers in some pots on a windowsill though freshly bloomed were of an old fashioned kind. They were lovely to me though I was a stranger. The dear old lady held my hand at parting and the daughter said when I was talking to them of Florida, "You seem to take us there as you talk. You make it so real." The goldenrod in the letter came from there. I ran down the hill to get it for you.

How many, many faces we meet just to see and long to see again and must be torn away from perhaps never to know ought of in all our lives. I never saw them before. I probably never shall again and yet I felt a real pang at parting. Their welcome, their refinement, their conversation, the old unspoken memories that breathed in everything about me, the old mansion itself sitting quietly apart in this lovely spot, seemed some way to belong to me as if we had a drop of the same blood somewhere and I had a right to break their solitude with my younger life, to waken the forgotten voices with a breath of my living self. It is strange how some people and some places affect us and others never stir a tremor.

You know that well-reared children are often taught that if they follow their own sweet will as I did this morning they are sure to come to grief. Well, so came I before the day was done for when we turned the corner at just 12 o'clock our steps were flooded with Westfield cousins, five in all. They wanted me to see Harry and he is a splendid appearing fellow, large and handsome, a fine address and laughing eyes. Well, the way those disorderly rooms of mine rushed into my poor little mind was terrific for half a moment. Mrs. C. said, "Is there anything I can do?" I smiled in their faces, gave them the very gladdest welcome I could, and as I turned to gather up their wraps, murmured to Mrs. C., "Fly to the little bakeshop and smuggle a loaf of bread and a lovely pie into the kitchen some way." And she did. The room was out of order but it was a sort of pretty disorder and they seemed to enjoy it. I put on the loveliest dishes, made a cup of delicious coffee. The bread and the pie being homemade was very nice and they thought I had made it and never shall I undeceive them. They just think I'm a cook whether I'm anything close or not and I must have some reward for the pangs of fear I endured for fear they would get their eyes on my kitchen or discover that I had to send out and buy their dinner. Indeed, I did put up the fruit and I had made the cream cake but some way the pie and bread had the most praise. But I enjoyed the whole affair very much. You know I always scorned the smooth well-beaten paths. I always liked the ones that brought us into the very worst places and that took a deal of climbing to get out.

How they admired Hal. He had on the new suit from New York that fits him like a prince. The dark rich brown is lovely with his hair. His ride had left such color in his cheeks and I was very proud of him. Carl did not return until they had gone. They seemed to claim me as their very own. I feel very much at home with them and love to have them feel as if they could really love me.

Oh, I want you. So many things I want to hear and so many I want to say. What is there like talking over things with each other? Oh, there is no one, no one, like us for love and joy in each other. Why are we ever apart?

✺ ✺ ✺

December 3, 1886

Dearest. There are six inches of snow and it is snowing fast. Winter is really here. I do not really like him but I am not afraid of the old wretch. Such a great cold nose that he has to go poking into all the chinks and crevices of this rattle-bang of a house. But I build roaring fires and treat him with the contempt that he deserves. So many come to see us—not an evening to ourselves. Every evening is quite a little reception of merry souls and those that come often declare that it is the brightest room in Springfield. Carl says, "When they come to see us and we are happy, it will make the time seem shorter until Papa comes." Always Papa with that Carl of yours. Oh, life of my life, I, too, think first and always of thee. Your Juliet.

✺ ✺ ✺

December 5, 1886

Dearest. Hal dashes through the room with the speed of a shooting star shouting, "Make way for the fastest monkey in the world." Yesterday he played he was a mad whale. Last night when Carl said his prayers I asked him why he was so long and he said, "Oh, I had so much to say to him. I asked him to save Papa and not let the cars run off from the track when he was on and not to let his tooth ache and not to let him be too cold and just everything I could think of. I do so want him to take care of Papa." I told him he was a darling son to his Papa and asked him if he did not pray for anyone else. "No," he replied, "I forgot to and I'm too sleepy. But I'll try and remember to pray for you tomorrow night, Mama."

When we were talking of going home Carl said, "I want to see them all but you know, Mama, we leave the sweetest and the best behind when we go away from Papa." Ah, how well indeed I know it and how I shall starve until

45. Julia's 1892 painting "Dawn" hangs high near the peak of the lofty, beamed ceiling in the south end of the Palm. Julia always described the painting as a representation of dawn lifting the veil of night from the world.

I find it again. Little Hal pipes up in that voice so clear and sweet, "Mama, I'm waiting for Papa. Will he come pretty soon?"

☙ ☙ ☙

December 7, 1886

Just one year ago this morning that the dear old home was burned. I cannot write or talk of it. I went down in the snow storm and just enjoyed it, the first walk I've had in snow for five years. I felt just as I used to when I was a girl.

Mrs. C. brought me a great bunch of flowers. Everyone is so lovely to us and seemed really sorry to have us go. My life has been half made up of partings.

☙ ☙ ☙

Christmas night, 1886

Dearest. We are just home from Westfield. Cousin Tom met us at the train and brought us at night. Such a delightful day it has been. The house was full. We did not have a regular Christmas dinner, but a sumptuous lunch. The large table in the long lovely old dining room was loaded and then half a dozen little tables were scattered here and there. We had such a charming, informal time. I enjoyed every moment. I was almost ashamed to be so happy on Christmas Day away from you. The boys behaved beautifully and were an honor to us all day. It seemed to me our beautiful Hal sat on someone's shoulder half of the time. I was a trifle too gay I'm afraid. I feel as much at home in that delightful house as if I were a real Moseley and everyone that came was so cordial. We had so many calls and some came, they said, just to see me. It is just as well I should hie me to the South before I get to the second round of my fabulous yarns. I'd give a good deal had I that truly wonderful collection of Florida flowers that were burned, for everyone so admired the stray bits I have and they are nothing beside that. They had a beautiful box of presents from the cousins in Savannah and they read a letter from Aunt Silenee's sister, a delightful letter, and she is eighty years old. It reminded me of the memories of some of the old French dames.

The Lost Enchanted
Log Cabin Remembered

The Old Nest, January 11, 1894

Dear Harriet

It was a log house in a Florida wilderness.[1] But it was built by a Southerner, who came to Florida with more means than most people who came to that portion of the state in those days, for it was before our railroads and when the city of Tampa with its two million dollar hotel, its electric cars and lights, was a sleeply [*sic*] dead little village. Our forests were as nature and the Indians had left them, and the choice of the pines were at one's disposal. The house was built of logs large enough for a fort, every one straight and sound of heart.

There were two large, square rooms, a broad open hall running between, wide porches the entire length of the buildings. The front faced the south. On the north was a kitchen, long and narrow.

When we bought the place the house had been sold by the original owner and the building was used as a church or "meeting house" by the "Crackers" and was called "The Old Hope."

There was but one window in the entire establishment, no floor save in the north and east rooms. Daylight swept through on every side, and the porches and open hall were entirely without floors save a few rough planks.

The building was like an array of immense corn cribs made of magnificent logs. No tools save an adz, a drawing knife, auger and hammer were used. The shingles were made by hand on the place. The corners of the house were beautiful in a rough fashion. The huge logs were notched and laid one on another, the ends protruding, with their rich hearts formed of rings of transparent pitch and yellow pine. In the distance was a lake and near its shore a small hammock of palm, live oak, yuccas, vines, brakes, white and blue violets and other wild life that grows in the heart of these little oases in the wilderness. The grounds held a grove of young pines on the north and a grove of grim old pines on the south, oaks of many varieties, and such a wealth of weeds as would make a lover of respectable gardens faint with despair.

Such was the place when we went over to look at it with the thought of trying to make of it a home. It was forlorn enough. We waded through sand and sandspurs, the weeds nodding against our shoulders, the house the abode of bats and owls, a dilapidated log fence over which the lizards and chameleons played from morning until night. But we knew what beautiful things would grow in this rare climate and what doors, windows, rugs and books and pictures could make of a home. In our minds we swept the weeds away and planted green grass. Roses and vines and flowers held full sway. Trees threw shadows on the lawn and we read books and dined and supped in sight of the lake, while the sky held sunsets that we had already learned to know were of exquisite beauty in that soft and tropical climate. And we bought the place and loved it from the first for the promise that it held.

For nearly four years we lived there working and planning and sacrificing, trying to fulfill the dreams we had woven out of its wilderness. I'll not tell you of that slow, and often discouraging process, but of the home as it was when the flames swept it from us.

The grounds held young orange, lime and lemon trees, plum, peach and persimmon, palm and magnolia, umbrella and bay. Roses, vines and flowers grew in beauty and sweet content on all sides. Castor beans grew to such a size the children climbed them and sat among the branches, whistling answering strains to the mocking birds in the oaks.

We dug a well whose waters were so cool and sweet for a Florida well that it won a name clear across our state. Long caravans, often numbering ten pairs of oxen, on their way to and from Tampa used to fill their water jugs at our well. There were no railroads then and everything was carried by ox and mule teams, and, as we lived on the old "Indian Trail" that was blazed from the Gulf of Mexico to the Atlantic coast, all these caravans passed our gates.

The United States troops were stationed at Tampa then and the sunset gun echoed nightly among our pines. But all this is over now, and they seem to belong to a much longer past than they really did, so rapidly have the changes grown in the last few years, and so much like the rest of the world has much of the life become.

From the northeast we built another open hall and put up a room with windows on all sides, for it is the heavenly climate that holds the charm of Florida and to give that full sway is to lend to a spot the breath of Paradise.

Every room and every thing about the place had a name of its own. This room was intended for a maid, and as help would bring good cheer, we called it the Cheer. It never held a maid (the country seemed devoid of them), but it served as a sort of sewing room and Carl had it for his drawings, which sometimes were almost knee deep within. The rafters were uncovered and below was a frieze made of wild things. The room was a little treasure of a room and stood alone and reserved like a little watch tower. Nestled beside it and hemmed in by the open hall of the Cheer and the east room, was the fern garden. Such a spot as that was! It was always cool and dewey [sic] with ferns. Morning glories blossomed in the shade there, lasting so long that often in the moonlight I have gathered hands full of the delicate pink and blue and white cups, and they have brought the dewey [sic] freshness of the morning into the bright lamplight of the evening.

There was not a thing in that garden that I did not love. From a seed or tiny slip I had watched and nursed it with such hope and care. Morning and evening I walked among the growing things and they whispered to me of each new leaf and tendril, each shoot and bud, and I confided to them what I could tell to no one about me. We had no secrets between us. We confided to each other every thing. My love for them taught me their needs and desires. Their gratitude and beauty gave me the comfort and companionship that kept my heart light in dark hours.

Human sympathy, I well know, is perhaps the dearest thing life holds. It is, I sometimes think, the soul of human happiness. Yet human sympathy often pretends; it is not always genuine. It deceives us and itself in the belief that it is for us it feels, when it is but pouring out solace for its own sorrow or the effulgence of its own joy. When it is pure and simple and without alloy, no jewel of the human heart is more to be desired, but that unalloyed variety is so rare one cannot hope to receive it often; and when there is a dearth of it, we that love her, turn to nature and she answers our longing, never with falsehoods or pretenses. The more we give her the more she gives us in return. All she asks is love. And while she scorns deception, she can never be deceived. Nature in those years was my closest friend.

Our table was set in the open hall nine or ten months in the year and our dining room held sunsets and morning skies and noonday clouds that were beyond the power of monarchs to have wrought in any canopy of man's device. The days held a thousand beauties and the night held almost as many in her hushed splendor.

Day was like a happy child awake, shouting, laughing, dancing, full of variety and sparkle. Night was like a sleeping child in whose little limbs at rest, whose motionless hands, whose closed lids, the pink on whose cheek, in whose very hair, peace seems slumbering. The innocence, the unconscious beauty of attitude, all hold and charm you until you say, "Was ever my child so lovely before?" And so it is with night. The dancing light is gone, the birds and the bees are stilled, the flowers are sleeping. Everything is in shadow, the moon looks down, the stars seem trembling in the night blues above and you think, "Was the world ever so beautiful as this?"

It is not the proper way, I well know, to fly from the main road up every little by-path that offers, but nature was the goddess of that home, and if I should leave her out, dear Sis, it would be like painting a picture of a brook whose bed was dry. It was the atmosphere, the nameless charm in sky and lake and air that was the secret of its life. Aside from those it was a desert. They permeated everything and with the power of magic bewitched the world for you.

Perhaps you would be in great haste over some task and wholly absorbed in its completion and walk through the open hall. A cloud would be hanging off there in the south that would hold you for a moment by its beauty and it seemed to envelope [sic] you until you were a part of it and the task lost half its dullness. Some morning you might not feel like breakfast. Your night had held some worry that had stolen your best hours of sleep, but when you sat down before the table and a great creamy pitcher of water lilies seemed almost to speak to you, the very dew still in their yellow hearts and on their white petals, how speedily the day changed and all the future looked brighter!

Let a storm come flying toward you as you stand on the steps, and see it fly along the tree tops like some fantastic fury, come with a rush across the lake, its very footfalls beating on its dark bosom, the angry clouds all striving to outdo each other in speed, the water coming down in streams from off these stiff crests of the tall pines until each tree looks like a waterfall. Then as suddenly everything is changed, and the sun bursts forth, and the rainbow down by the "bayhead" is changing the greens of the foliage to purple and crimson and orange.

Sit alone in the house some sweet spring morning and let a mocking bird light on a tree or trellis near by and sing as it only can sing when free and in its own clime. Ah! Does it seem as if there could be a spot on earth that those clear notes did not fill? Care vanishes, joy is flooding all your being.

And at sunset when the sky changes to pinks within pinks and the lake blushes and a pink mist fills all the world far as your eyes can reach and the color in the sky spreads until all the heavenly dome above is a rosy glow, you sit entranced. You neither care to speak or be spoken to. The world seems to be in a dream of beauty and a voice might waken it. Night falls rapidly. She drops down like a flower tossed upward, and the trees and all the tropical foliage begin to darken until it is black like ebony, and the young moon hangs low down in the sky, where the pink glow still lies. As long as your eyes can find the light it is a rosy light. You are not the creature you were. Nothing seems commonplace. The bloom has stolen into your fancy and thoughts. Life seems easier and brighter than it did when first the day began to close.

Ah! but who can tell of the nights? They are not like the joys of ecstatic forgetfulness. They are like hearts that have known sorrow and disappointments and overcome them. There is the solemnity of small things passed into nothingness, of temptations overcome. A nameless peace enfolds you. You walk among its shadows, and the everyday things about you that were so familiar are clothed in an incomprehensible beauty. The moon in the blue vault of heaven—how far off it seems—how large the stars! Everything is quiet. The world is at rest. All life seems sleeping. Then a bird breaks the hush and the song he sings is a new song and thrills you through and through. The restlessness of the world seems beyond space, and peace seems to have laid her wand on everything, even your heart.

We will begin with the open hall as everything centered there. It was the dining and reception room and where we spent more hours perhaps than in any other portion of the house. It was twelve feet in width and twenty feet long, but the porches being added made a sitting room some forty feet in length. A large thick rug was on the floor. The table was covered with a cloth of pale brown, with a border of wild sunflowers and scarlet poppies. Low chairs and ottomans were scattered about. A large divan-like cushion in scarlet and blue lay on the floor, where you could take a noonday nap if you chose. It was piled high with cushions and always invited repose.

On one side, supported by palmetto logs, was a "hanging garden" that held palms and vines and ferns, forming a canopy of green. One huge chair, which we called the Trix, always sat in the hall. It was made so you could sit outside in high winds and still be comfortable. It was low with a seat a yard square and the back on two sides ran up a yard in height. It was upholstered in blue and scarlet, with a huge pocket to hold books and papers. There was great comfort in that roomy Trix that defied wind and dew. Indeed I've sat curled up there with a lamp perched beside me and read many a page after the house was asleep, so snug and cozy the hours stole by unheeded.

Above the main rooms we had a floor laid, forming low but roomy chambers. The open hall ran to the roof, and to connect the rooms we made a tiny bridge with a railing of oleander wood and broad palm stems. It was when the Brooklyn Bridge was being built and a great deal was being illustrated and written about it. So Carl called our little passage way by that name and it is always spoken of as the Brooklyn Bridge to this day.

The effect of the hall from beams to floor was most inviting. We often hung boughs of oak or oleander on the dark, rich, rugged walls, or stood tall cabbage palms along the side and wreathed the ropes of the hammock with vines and flowers. It was always cool there, no matter how warm the day, and every little playful breeze stole in and out freshening the air and frolicking with the leaves and flowers within.

I want to tell you of my dear and lovely dishes, and while we still linger in the open hall where our table was universally set is just the place to do so. Everything of that kind was left in Lancaster and stored in such a way we could not get them very well. The summer we spent at Lake Erie we kept house in a doll's house of a cottage on a cliff, but before going there we met in Fredonia the loveliest old gentleman. His family were all dead and gone. Not one near relative was left. He had the same home he had lived in for many years. It was full of things that were to him most sacred. He had always had an especial fondness for delicate china, not as a collector, but because there was to him a great delight in the daily use of delicate and pretty things.

He had kept everything of that kind he had from the first years of his marriage, and among his treasures was some lovely, fragile, old china. It was torture to him to think it might some time fall into the hands of someone who would not only have no feeling for his beloved dead, but would not even value the dishes for their own beauty and worth. He grew to love us and, one by one, he gave me many of those beloved dishes, and some we bought, until my table was almost entirely set with china that had seen more than half a century. Among it was some of my own and a few pieces that had belonged to three great-grandmothers. No matter how simple the meal, the table was always a "thing of beauty," always flowers, morning glories for breakfast, roses and wild passion vines with their violet fringes among the beautiful leaves and curling tendrils. And the hall was such a cool and restful spot with the lake in the distance and the sky that always held some marvel of color or form.

The kitchen was a droll place, long and narrow, sloping out at the bottom until on the outside it bore a likeness to some Egyptian habitation. Back of the dishes it was pale blue, but the edges of all the shelves were scarlet and every ugly thing hidden, when the work was done, by scarlet curtains. Even in the kitchen there was always a bowl of flowers, and, with a door at each end and windows on the side, it was a cheery little spot.

I must tell you of the back porch, for it was there we picked over fruit and did all sorts of things. Along one end and side ran broad, low seats that opened with hinged covers. In one, certain things were kept in place, and we called it Purgatory, but the other was where scattered things could be flung in a hurry and we called that Hades. They were never spoken of by any other names. Wide shelves ran along the other side out there too. And the whole was a delightful place to work, shaded by trees and vines.

The front porch had quaint, pretty seats the entire length, hammocks always swung there and vines clambered to the roof and broad steps led down to the drive.

The paneled room was the large one on the east. A wainscot, some three or four feet high, of a dark warm red, ran round the room, and was headed by moldings that held in place panels eight inches wide and all lengths, from five feet to five inches. This band of panels ran up the sides and capped the door and window casings, each painted to suit the place it held. The effect was more quaintly pretty than I can describe. The walls were cream with a broad frieze. A bewitching little staircase ran up on one side with a landing and then crossed over, stopping at the bridge. In the corner was a niche built in the wall, arranged to hold palms, which bent over you as you climbed the stairs. A window looked into the fern garden on the east. The logs of the house were so large the window ledges were broad like those in a stone house, and in one, a cushioned seat made a pretty nook to sit and read and enjoy the sweets of the garden.

On the south side one broad window ran up and down the center nearly from floor to ceiling. Then one on each side met this about half way and ran lengthwise to the ends of the room. The effect of this odd window, encircled by panels, and its deep casings, was beautiful. You could not see the road or garden from the high ones, but such a sweep of sky and tree tops came in there and the ledges were such lovely places to set jars or bowls of flowers, with their background of sky against which every color seemed enhanced. Often I would lay just a broad, cool banana leaf in one of these windows and lay on it some crests from the pineapple, whose beauty when cut at certain seasons of the year is most exquisite, often a silvery green so pale and crisp at the tips and ending in a vivid scarlet at the base. And then I would add fruit from the pomegranate whose color seems almost like a living thing, so like a flame it is. Beside it a stem would hold the bloom of the banana. There is a large, deep, rich, soft crimson cup that holds these strange flowers and when it falls away the blossoms lie at its base in shades of brown with slender pink bells that drip with honey. The final touch to this bit of tropical "still life" was a great crest from a certain variety of castor bean. Rubies were not more enchanting to the eye than were its many shades of crimson. Sometimes, to give an air of poesy, we would trail a long branch from a passion vine, whose beauty trembled down the wall and swept the floor.

The upper half of one of these windows was painted, mostly in rich, yellow tones, and under it stood the piano. I cannot tell all the room held. There were pictures and books. A broad shelf was fitted in cornerwise and edged about with panels, a large square table with a shelf at the bottom to hold engravings and art journals. It was a room you would have loved and I can never get over the sorrow it is to me that not one near friend ever saw our old home after it was in any way a satisfaction to us.

About a hundred yards from the house under a group of oaks was a room some thirteen feet square. It was put up for me when I was very ill and could not endure the noise and confusion of a household. We called it the Whist, for people had to keep still there or be banished. We had that fitted up as a sort of study and studio. It escaped the flames and is the kitchen of our present house.

Near it is a little bath house which we named the Deluge. And now I come to the last but dearest room in the house, the Little Heart. We named it so because it was my room and the mother's room is the heart of the home. A wide door opened into the hall on the east, heavily curtained in olive. The bed was cream with scarlet trimmings, curtained in cream with a deep valance at top and bottom, bordered with a painted wreath of flowers and grasses in colors. Near to the bed was the "Dutch door," which looked as if it came from some Holland interior, when the upper half was swung back and you leaned on the shelf that ran across the lower part and looked out under the trees of the back garden. In the southeast corner was a large wash stand and on it was the loveliest wash bowl and ewer, with Venetian scenes in blue, that came with the old china, while over the stand hung a mirror that for half a hundred years and more had reflected faces sad and gay. On the south side ran a low divan, with a large double window over it. The book shelves were in this room and were finished with large palm stems, rugs on the floors, a white frieze strewn with scarlet poppies.

In this room the flowers ran riot. It was always a bower of them, and the pictures and trinkets we loved best were gathered here. The old chimney was on the west side of the room. And such a fireplace as it was! It would hold great logs and huge piles of the fantastic pineknots and when the brilliant fire was burning the hot pitch would roll out and lie like balls of amber along the hearth. Over it was a wide mantel and above it hung a print of Sir Frederick Leighton's "Vintage Festival."[2] High up, beside the chimney, was what we called the picture window. When I said to Scott that there was nothing we could ever hang on the wall that would hold the beauty that the western sky held, he said he would make the frame and nature could hang the picture. The delight that window brought I never can tell you, no two hours ever the same. It was where I looked first in the morning and last at night. It only held the sky and the faint line of a forest in the distance. When they thought once that I might not live the night through, I called Frindy and told her to tell Scott I saw my last sunset through the picture window he made for me. But I lived to see the window in ashes before another summer came, but not the pictures it held.

Thank God for memory! What an empty and black thing life would be without it! All through my life will sunsets come and go through that window, storms of surpassing beauty, birds floating by whose warm tinted plumage no more haunts that then wild spot. Long since the hunter has frightened them to the Sea Islands and the Everglades. But my birds fly through my waking moments and ever in my dreams the picture window for an instant holds a vision of a flock of paroquets like winged emeralds or pink curlews whose wings seem made of sunset clouds.

The day before the fire, almost as if I had known it was to be the last time I could ever hang wreaths or palms on those dear walls again, I had filled it as it was never filled before. Over the door of the Little Heart, a wreath of wild things hung encircling the bridge and falling down like a shower of blossoms. Fresh palms were everywhere. It was cold, the frost that came was in the air and I cut down things that I knew its breath must kill and brought them in, little dreaming it was a farewell to every loving touch. I thought of those flowers when I saw the flames licking roof and beams and was glad that we could always remember it a bower of sweets, a house of palms and roses and fresh wild life.

To others the spot is a barren waste of weeds and stunted shrubbery that tried to grow from burned roots. But I see the old house, full of memories of firelight and moonlight, fragrant with flowers, voices I have loved, music that can never be stilled. There are but three things that have braved the flames and spring into beautiful life: a wild trumpet and yellow jessamine that grow in a tangle together and whose vines would nearly run round Florida if woven in a wreath. The third is a magnolia that burned even with the hot sand but is now a tall and stately tree. Its flowers are fit for the "Garden of Hesperides." You can never get used to them and gather them as you do many things that have grown familiar with the seasons. It is a flower apart. With its fragrance, its unspeakable beauty when you hold it in a cluster of its rich foliage heavy with dew it seems almost a sacred thing. It has the care one gives to beloved friends who have kept close beside you in dark hours. And yet I have stood alone in the moonlight with my arm around it and superb and real as its beauty was, it was not more real to me than that vanished house. So marvelous a thing is memory and love.

46. Ten Mile Lake, ca. 1884, fringed by longleaf pines and oaks. The Moseleys' dock and bathhouse are shown at the left. The paddle-wheel boat in the center was an innovation of Julia Daniels Moseley's brother Pet.

47. The new Nest, 1886. The Cuckoo is shown at the left, with the open hall and the Whist beyond, joined by the porch to the Palm, the east porch, and the Snug. The decorative fence was put up to keep roaming animals away from the plants (Florida had a "no-fence" law until 1948).

48. The Moseley family, minus Charles Scott, on the front porch of The Nest. Left to right: Charles Scott Moseley, Jr., later known as Karl; Julia Daniels Moseley; Claude Moseley; Florence Moseley; and Hallock Preston Moseley. 1886.

49. Moseley family members in the Whist. Left to right: Carl Moseley, his mother, his father, and Florence. The sign Cup and Bucket Inn suggested by the well, not shown in this picture, designated the part of The Nest containing the Whist, the Cuckoo, and the porch. The sign expressed the family's fondness for English novels featuring highway inns. Drawn by Carl during a brief visit home from New York City in 1898, it has now been replaced by a more permanent sign.

50. South part of The Nest, showing the Moseleys' living quarters after the fire in 1885. The Whist, which survived the fire, is shown at the left. A hall lay between it and the long Cuckoo, which extended its roof to the Whist. At the extreme left is the family well used by many "commuters" traveling on the old Indian trail from Fort Meade to Tampa. 1896.

51. Looking southeast at the Whist. The Cuckoo is behind, with the wrap-around porch and well in front. The family lived in the Whist after the 1885 fire, until the new Nest was completed around its core. In the right foreground was a specimen yucca, set on a slight rise created by Scott for Julia, who longed for a hill. 1897.

52. Julia Daniels Moseley at the family well. 1897.

53. The open porch of The Nest. This part of the house, which included the Cuckoo, kitchen, and dining room, was called the Cup and Bucket Inn, after the indispensable well (shown in the background) that had gained a reputation for sweet water among travelers. The effective overhanging eaves and low sun screens, right, enhanced the natural cooling arrangement of the porch, open on four sides with three units of rooms around it. The balustrade in the extreme lower right encloses an area that functioned as an earthen vase when filled with palm fronds, ferns, and other wild plants. 1897.

54. After the turn of the century Julia enjoyed the serenity of this spot and entertained here. Scott designed the tables and chairs and Julia designed and embroidered the tablecloth. Hallock built the pool in 1909, before entering the navy. 1909.

55. Julia Daniels Moseley at her writing table in the Palm. This room was named for her unique wall covering, made from native palmetto fiber and decorated with a rich flower-and-vine motif. Behind her, at the windows, and on the lounge and table are hangings and coverings she designed and made. Her painting on the wall at the right is of a walkway in the Tampa Bay Hotel gardens. 1907.

56. One of Julia Daniels Moseley's favorite customs was writing letters in natural surroundings. This table and chair are immediately east of The Nest. Julia planted the large oleander bush and the camphor tree shown at the right. Part of the path to the east gate is visible in the white sandy area at the right. 1899.

57. East end of the long Cuckoo, one of two rooms in which the Moseley family lived after the first Nest burned. Examples of Julia Daniels Moseley's work include a frieze that decorated three walls of the room, lounge covers, a tablecover, hanging bags for shoes and clothing, and flower and plant arrangements. 1886.

58. (left) A corner of the Palm showing sand boxes. These held wet sand for palms, air plants, and flower arrangements and were decorated with ruddy brown palmetto bark. The little Dutch rocking chair in the foreground was saved during the fire. A Persian rug covers the floor. 1887.

59. (below) North end of the Palm. 1897.

60. South end of the Palm. 1897.

61. Lounge in the Palm. 1897.

62. Northwest corner of the Snug, where the books "lived" in the new home. The "tuffit" cushion Julia made can be seen in the foreground. 1897.

63. The four-poster bed in the Snug, built by Scott with hangings decorated by Julia. 1898.

64. Some members of the family gathered around the bamboo Julia planted. Left to right: Hal with bicycle, Frindy, Carl, and Julia. 1898.

65. Professional photographers Mr. Morast and Leon Cannova of the well-known Morast Studio, relaxing outside The Nest and admiring their work. 1898.

66. The second Nest, rebuilt after the fire in 1885. Note the tops of the windowpanes, painted for decorative effect as well as to screen the sun. Julia Daniels Moseley designed and made the tablecloth. 1897.

67. This live oak in the western part of the hammock near the lake was estimated to be one hundred years old in 1898 when this picture was taken. It lived until 1990, when it was struck by a tremendous bolt of lightning in a fierce summer storm. Magnolias, oaks, pines, and vines now surround the spot.

68. The white sand path north of The Nest led to the lake through a grove of young longleaf pines. Julia raked this path herself and often strolled along it with guests by moonlight. The pines were lost in a severe drought in 1898.

Notes

Chapter 1. Florida, Here We Come

1. E.S. was Eliza Slade of Elgin, Illinois, a musician and Julia's lifelong friend. Julia always enjoyed the company of those older than herself—like Eliza, who was five years her senior. With the exception of several letters written to her children from Massachusetts in 1886, the letters Julia copied in the large, leather-bound book had been written either to her husband Scott or to Eliza. The first letter Julia copied in her book was written on the Moseleys' marriage day, May 18, 1876, but the unedited letters in this book begin sixty-eight pages later with the family's trip to Florida.

2. The author of this poem is unknown. It is almost certainly not Julia since she was not known to have written poetry.

   The poem obviously appealed to Julia because she used it to begin an article published in 1889 in a northern newspaper, a clipping of which is in her papers. The untitled article read:

   > Come to my sunland, come with me
   > To the land I love, where sun and sea
   >   Are wed forever, where palm and pine
   >   Are filled with singers, where tree and vine
   > Are voiced with prophets.

   You ask for a breath from the south to mingle with Xmas greetings from the east and west.

   Laugh not too scornfully at thought of the gentle winds of our sun-kissed land, trying to hold their own amid the icy blasts of a northern Xmas tide.

   If once you could walk beneath her brilliant skies, feel the velvet touch of her slumberous air, breathe the fragrant balsam of her matchless climate and revel in the witchery of her entrancing nights, you too would feel that the wooing of her gentle spells was more potent than ice cliffs or snow clad hills.

   It is not the "sweet gum" or the bay we shall bring in for the "yule log," but the fat pine knots that will burn with such fantastic life and sparkle as shall put all other fires to shame and the doors and windows will be flung wide open and the sunlight will dance along the floors and leave a smile on every glistening orange leaf and on the blue wave of each rippling lake.

We shall wreathe our doors in mistletoe from our own oaks.

Pray doff your furs and enter; for beneath it every northern friend will find a "merry Xmas" and a "southern welcome."

The clipping illustrates how difficult Julia's script is to read. On the copy she saved she had written in three corrections where the newspaper's editor had failed to decipher her handwritten submission. As a little girl Julia had watched her grandfather Preston doing his business accounts at the end of each day, admiring his distinctive sprawling penmanship as his hand flew rapidly across the pages. She vowed to write as he did and always retained a similar handwriting style that defies casual reading.

See untitled clipping in Moseley Collection.

3. Julia's mother never forgot the pages read and reread in Hampshire, Illinois (then called Henpeck) that first winter.

Julia's parents were Carlos M. Daniels and Elizabeth Preston. Daniels studied medicine in the East and finished his training in St. Louis. He practiced in Hampshire, Joliet, Mackinaw, and Elgin, Illinois, as well as in Pattonsburg, Missouri. In his later years he owned an Elgin insurance business with his son George.

The eight Daniels children were Frances, Edward, George H., Charles, Preston or Pet, Julia, John, and Bess.

See Florence Moseley Notes; Alft correspondence.

4. In this paragraph Julia uses two terms that reflect the culture of her time: *darkies*, which she always capitalized and enclosed in quotation marks, and *mud chimney*, an old term for fireplace. Mud chimneys were literally made out of mud or clay and stabilized by pliable boughs, wood, stones, or metal bands.

5. The Moseley family and other Union sympathizers used the term *secesh* to refer to people and things connected with secession. Apparently Julia's brother Charlie had acquired an account book during his service in the South and used its blank pages to write a letter.

See Florence Moseley Notes and standard references on colloquial English.

6. Daniels became ill while practicing in Joliet, Illinois, during a malaria epidemic. His granddaughter Florence believed that he had malaria in addition to dyspepsia (a catchall term often used to describe common digestive disorders). He later told the family how helpless he and his partner, Dr. Daggett, had felt in the face of the available treatments for malaria. During this stressful time Daniels' brother Norman visited, urging that Daniels return to New Orleans with him to regain his health under the care of an elderly French doctor. That doctor not only cured Daniels but also shared his recipe for *tanta miraculus*, the tonic responsible for the recovery. Later Daniels manufactured this remedy in Elgin, advertising and selling it throughout that part of the state. Unlike other patent-medicine purveyors, Daniels was ethical about his tonic's efficacy, stating in his

advertisements that the vegetable tonic was "not good for any other class of diseases" except dyspepsia.

See Florence Moseley Notes; Alft correspondence; Alft, *Elgin Days*, 77.

7. When Carl was an adult and a professional artist, he changed the spelling of his name to Karl on the advice of his uncle George, whose marketing skills were much admired by the family. Daniels had been instrumental in helping his nephew enter the Art Students League in New York City.

George Daniels, who became general superintendent of the New York Central Railroad, introduced and named the attendants known as "red caps," initiated baggage checkrooms, and made speed synonymous with luxury passenger service. Through his efforts, the U.S. Postal Service pictured the Empire State Express on a two-cent stamp and the Express's Fast Engine 999 was exhibited at the 1893 Chicago World's Fair.

Daniels' contacts with the Fair were helpful to Julia, who was hopeful that her wall covering could be displayed in the Women's Building there. Finally her work was exhibited instead in the Agricultural Building, Florida Space.

Daniels as a devoted elder brother supplied Julia and Scott with railroad passes and books and magazines. Julia treasured the memorabilia he shared from his many contacts and enterprises for the glimpses these gave her of the sophisticated northern circles in which he moved.

See Florence Moseley Notes; Alft correspondence.

8. Frindy and Frindolin were the pet names of Florence, Scott's daughter from his first marriage, who was born in 1866. Florence's mother died when she was five; she was sent East to live with relatives, remaining there until her father remarried five years later. As an adult Florence remained in The Nest and became the first custodian of the Moseley Collection.

9. The unpublished maritime research of Tampa historian Julius Gordon shows no *Mary Morgan* docking during these years, an indication that the ship continued directly from Cedar Key to Havana and that the Moseleys took another boat on to Tampa. During this period the Miller-Henderson line made regular overnight trips between Cedar Key and Tampa. Its steamers were described as roomy and well equipped. However, a contemporary writer's comment that one could take them "without the prospect of a dive beneath the briny waves" indicates that the voyage Julia found delightful could also prove daunting.

See Julius Gordon research; Barbour, *Florida for Tourists*, 63–64; Brooks, *Petals Plucked*, 271.

10. Although Julia could understand why the plantation owners, who lived like kings, would fight to preserve their investments, both she and her family strongly disapproved of slavery. Her grandfather Preston, an abolitionist leader in his town, contributed funds to buy slaves their freedom.

The family's position on slavery had been strengthened by frightening events they had experienced in Pattonsburg, Missouri, a border area with many Confederate sympathizers. Daniels, who had practiced there since Julia was seven years of age, was an outspoken opponent of slavery. As tensions grew, relatives in Illinois became concerned for the Daniels family's safety, sending Daniels' eighteen-year-old son George to persuade them to leave and return to Illinois.

George's experiences on the trip to Missouri convinced him that there was no time to lose. He urged his mother to pack a few belongings, then rushed her and his younger siblings to a train. Later they learned that this train had been the last to accept passengers leaving the region.

Dr. Daniels had intended to leave Pattonsburg after closing his practice and packing the rest of the family's belongings. But that night, close friends came on horseback to warn him that agitators were planning to form a posse to capture and hang him. Concealing Daniels within their group of riders, they got him safely from Pattonsburg to another railroad line fourteen miles away. It was some time before he was able to reach Elgin and his family. Missouri friends packed three trunks of the Daniels' belongings, including Daniels' medicines, and brought them to the family after the war.

Julia was reminded of these Missouri events later when she witnessed discrimination against an African-American woman riding on a train near Jacksonville, Florida. This event inspired her to publish an article entitled "What Slavery Was" in a Chicago newspaper. In it she described her experiences with slavery during her Missouri girlhood.

In Missouri, close family friends opposed to owning slaves nevertheless hired slaves belonging to others. One of these slaves, a girl of eighteen named America, was assigned to watch the friends' daughter, one of Julia's companions. America soon took responsibility for Julia as well, and Julia became quite fond of her. Then America's owner died, and while the estate was being settled plans were made for the sale of some slaves, including America and her siblings.

Julia thought the sale would be exciting, so she persuaded her friend to leave school and attend with her. When they arrived Julia's father was there, looking as she'd "seen him when he came home with the word that someone was dead." He fixed her with a pained expression but allowed her to stay.

Julia watched as America and her siblings were brought to the block. Up to that point America had feigned an indifferent attitude, but suddenly she let out a wild cry and ran to the father of Julia's friend, clinging to him and begging him to buy her. But the man was opposed to slavery and refused to do so. The siblings were not sold as a group, and a harrowing scene ensued as the young people said their good-byes. Julia ran away alone, threw herself on the grass, and wept as she "had never had the power to weep before."

See Florence Moseley Notes; Moseley, "What Slavery Was."

11. Cedar Key is located about one hundred miles north of Tampa on the Gulf of Mexico. Florida Senator David Yulee used his political influence to alter plans

for the railroad that was to connect Tampa with Jacksonville, diverting it to Cedar Key instead. Owing to this railroad and the area's abundance of cedar trees, used in pencil manufacturing, Cedar Key had become a thriving port by the time the Moseleys arrived. In his 1875 travel book, Sidney Lanier says there were five hundred residents when he visited. Like Julia, he pointed out the beauty of the wide expanse of water, which he called "great level enchantments-that-shine."

See Lanier, *Florida*, 99.

12. The Cedar Key Historical Society has in its collection Eliza Harn's handwritten diary dated 1867–1877. A typescript was prepared as part of a Works Progress Administration historical records survey in 1937. The entries in the diary, which recount Harn's pathetically unhappy life and her impressions of Cedar Key, contrast sharply in tone and style with Julia's letters and offer a valuable picture of the difficulties an unmarried woman could face on the frontier.

Several of Eliza Harn's qualities would have appealed to Julia. A genteel woman, she found joy in the beauty of her garden and the coastal surroundings. She also was an amateur writer, commenting in the diary that she was writing for posterity and including a number of her poems. Although Miss Harn's minimal knowledge of spelling and punctuation was evident in the diary, it probably was not apparent in conversation.

Eliza and her sister Amelia were the daughters of Captain Thomas Harn, an early settler of Alachua County, Florida. During Indian conflicts there in the 1830s Harn built Fort Crum, named for his wife's family, and raised a company of men to defend area settlers.

In financial difficulty and poor health and a widower, Harn moved in 1863 with his unmarried daughters to Cedar Key, then blockaded by Northern forces. Eliza wrote that only she and Amelia and one or two other women did not flee but remained to help tend the wounded.

Harn died in 1866, leaving his daughters without a means of income. Eliza opened a school but students' parents refused to pay, and later federally sponsored teachers set up a competing school. Although Amelia's health was poor, both women tried to make money from dress and quilt making. But again people refused to pay for the work. The sisters had a flourishing vegetable garden, but other settlers stole their produce. By 1870 Eliza and Amelia were making the palmetto-frond tablemats and hats to which Julia referred.

Eliza felt very isolated and persecuted in Cedar Key, which she described as a "sink of pollution" without religion. She wrote that other residents attempted to burn down their house and that their land was homesteaded by African-American settlers, who built a meeting house on it. She reported that some people used the sisters' plight to beg money, keeping the funds they had raised.

Eliza hoped to become a missionary and took comfort in the reward she expected to gain in heaven. If the missionary life proved unattainable, she hoped to move to Cuba or Mexico with other former Confederates to escape the injustices she attributed to abolition.

See Harn Diary, Cedar Key Historical Society.

13. The wide Manatee River that flows into Tampa Bay was also an active port during this period, with passenger boats frequently crisscrossing the Bay. Many researchers also consider it among the most likely sites for the 1539 landing of Hernando de Soto.

14. Fort Brooke had been decommissioned but was temporarily reactivated in May 1880 to house soldiers evacuated from Key West because of a yellow fever epidemic. That year Tampa had only 772 residents, and when Abbie Brooks visited she remarked, "The place looks discouraged from sheer weariness in trying to be a town." But by 1882 Tampa was booming, and by 1885 its population had swelled to 2,376. This was confirmed by traveler and author Harry A. Peeples, who wrote that when he arrived in the central Florida town of Eustis in 1882, the citizens there "All bear the smile of prosperity from a few years living in Tampa."

See Robinson, *History of Hillsborough*, 73; Peeples, *Twenty-four Years*, 89–91; Brooks, *Petals Plucked*, 288.

Chapter 2. Northern Newcomers, Drawn to Health or Wealth

1. This is a continuation of the letter describing events after the arrival in Tampa.

2. The Moseleys had learned of Limona through business associates and friends and knew of the Elgin Watch Company's plans for a Florida winter colony. The company already had established a summer colony at Lake Geneva, Wisconsin. In 1877 the company had sent foreman Edwin E. Pratt to survey possible Florida sites. While staying at Tampa's Orange Grove Hotel, he met Judge Joseph Gillette Knapp of Wisconsin, who had purchased land east of Tampa. Knapp gave that area the name Limona because of the citrus already growing there, adapting the Spanish word for lemon. He established a school, a church, and a cemetery and soon secured a post office. Pratt was attracted to Limona and settled there in 1877.

When Knapp arrived he found that many of the early settlers had no clear titles to the properties they were occupying; nevertheless, they felt entitled to the land. Knapp repeatedly advised them to homestead or to purchase the properties, but the settlers asserted that anyone who claimed their land would find himself occupying a "spot two by six feet north." They wrote to Knapp, warning him that if he didn't leave in ten days he would "hear the pine trees crack and the jack asses bray." The settlers signed the letter "many sitizens [*sic*] of many counties." But Knapp's experience as a territorial judge and his earlier work as a missionary to Wisconsin Indians had made him resolute; he remained, continuing to advise his neighbors about property law and courting their good will.

The Elgin group formed the Limona Park Association and purchased eighty acres, subdividing these into four hundred lots. The Association listed Charles Scott Moseley, one of his brothers, and his father as investors, although Scott and Julia Moseley had bought land outside the Association's tract. While the Association expected most visitors to buy and build, plans were also made for a park, a hotel, rental units, and even temporary tent camping. Charles Carte, an early land purchaser, even built a cottage on his lot for invalids needing to escape the severe Illinois winters. The two sinkhole lakes on the park property, then known as Euclaire and Beau Lac, are now unnamed small lakes within a county park.

The relative attractiveness of Limona is revealed in the Association's promotional brochure, which offered travel alternatives for those making the forty-nine-hour railroad trip from Chicago. For example, visitors could elect to be met at the Mango stop a short distance north. Cautioned not to be put off by the "low and uninviting" lake area around Mango, they were assured they would find a higher elevation and a much more attractive setting in Limona. This was important information for visitors to subtropical Florida, who had been amply warned of the dangers of malaria.

The colony continued to attract interest in Elgin, first through newspaper articles and later through shop-window displays of citrus grown by early Limona residents. The flourishing colony lost some residents after the great freezes of 1894 and 1895, but many other settlers remained.

Clementine Averill, one of Julia's neighbors, vividly described the road from Tampa to Limona in an article published in a New England paper. Averill wrote that the roads were no more than paths. "Coming out from Tampa, the first few miles, the roads are very sandy, then come the cypress swamps, where we have to tread through water sometimes for nearly half a mile in the wet season." She commented that these numerous sandy paths were "full of 'Konfederate Kross-roads' and no guideboard to tell the weary traveler where to go."

Julia refers to E. E. Pratt as "Dr. Pratt" because he also practiced as a homeo-pathic doctor. His children were Mary Elizabeth, Hattie, and Eddie. A widower then about fifty, he married Hannah Smith in 1885.

See Alft correspondence and Alft, *Elgin*, 107; Warner, *Home Life*, 158; Averill, Our Florida Letter series, *Milford Enterprise*, March 19, 1878, and October 8, 1878; Limona Park pamphlet; "An Elgin Colony," *Elgin Weekly Courier*, March 15, 1890; and the notes of Knapp's niece Georgia K. Mead (the latter three items are in the Moseley Collection).

3. Lyman Joel Coe, another Illinois resident originally from New England, married Pratt's sister Alice Emily. They settled on Lake Whittington (now Lake Chapman) in Limona with their sons Burton and Percy in 1877, the same year Pratt settled in Limona. Coe and his sons operated some of the first sawmills in the area and also had citrus interests. Because land had to be cleared for agricul-

ture and ties supplied for the railroads under construction, mills were popular and profitable. An acre of pines could produce 5,000 square feet of timber, which in turn could sell for up to $1,500 because Florida pine was considered superior to the yellow pine of North and South Carolina. A further inducement for Florida newcomers to strip their land of pines was the belief that this practice would prevent lightning strikes.

The mule teams these settlers used may have been part of the hack line that traveled into Florida's interior three times a week.

The distance to the spring mentioned in Julia's letter suggests that it was either Sulphur or Lithia Springs, two of the many springs in the region. The early settlers of the community near Lithia Springs, also briefly called Pelot during this period, are fairly well identified and Captain Smith was not among them. It is more likely that the Moseleys' destination was Sulphur Springs; careful documentation of the residents near that spring began later.

Perhaps it was on this excursion that Julia first became intrigued with the possibility of using saw-palmetto fiber for some artistic creation. The air plants she refers to were the native bromeliads.

Here and later in her letters Julia speaks of *hammocks*. In Florida usage, the word describes a dense growth on comparatively dry soil with shrubs such as saw palmetto and trees including oak, holly, cypress, magnolia, red bay, cabbage palm, and sometimes pine. Hammocks are characterized topographically as high or low; the hammock where the Moseleys settled is a high hammock.

See Lithia and Sulphur Springs files, Tampa-Hillsborough Library Special Collections; Lanier, *Florida*, 102; Hawes, *Tampa Tribune*, June 13, 1993.

4. Julia inserted this note in 1891 at the bottom of the page she had inscribed earlier.

5. Author unknown.

6. The log cabin Julia described was not the one on Ten Mile Lake in which she and Scott later made their home. It was one of the Limona Park Association cabins, located on Lake Whittington, a short distance north, in which they stayed temporarily.

The ubiquitous moss was the bromeliad *Tillandsia usneoides*.

7. The common name of this pale blue flower, described in wildflower books as ephemeral, is dayflower; the botanical name is *Commelina erecta*.

8. The name Thonotosassa is thought to have been derived from *thlonoto-sassa*, a Seminole-Creek word meaning "flint is there." Records indicate that between 1812 and 1820 a village had been established near the southeastern side of the lake by Seminole-Creek Indians driven south under the leadership of Charles Cavallo (Stout Chief). In 1878 the lake became the site of one of the first planned citrus groves in eastern Hillsborough County.

The oval-shaped lake is one and one-half miles in length and nearly as wide. Its unusually high shore inspired one developer of the period to brag that "for beauty and grandeur [it] has not a rival sheet of water this side of Niagara."

See Hillsborough County Real Estate Agency pamphlet, 34; Grismer, *History of Tampa*, 312; Covington, *Southwestern Florida*, 48–58; K. Porter, "Thlonoto-Sassa," 115; Wharton, personal communication.

9. Native Floridians and Georgians now embrace the term *cracker*, but in Julia's time it was still being used pejoratively. Travelers commonly used the term to describe the self-reliant white plain-folk they found in Florida, whose different lifestyle they failed to understand or appreciate. These so-called crackers, who had moved to Florida from adjacent states between 1821 (when Spanish ownership of Florida ended) and the beginning of the Civil War, soon made up a significant portion of the population. Perhaps buffered by Florida's semitropical abundance, many crackers seemed willing to lead a migratory hand-to-mouth existence. Certainly they placed a low value on what would now be called community standards and authority. They reacted to Indians, African Americans, and other outsiders with prejudice if not outright hostility. Historian James Denham suggests that crackers responded hospitably to travelers who treated them with respect, while giving as good as they got to other, more disapproving newcomers.

The origin of the term cracker is uncertain. The word may derive from the sound of the whips these people used as they drove their livestock. Or it may have been associated with corn milling. More common than wheat as a flour source at that time, corn was milled in a process called cracking. Although the crackers' jocular way of speaking is sometimes offered as a third etymological possibility, it is almost certain that the word *crack*, meaning "joke," became part of American parlance more recently.

For a description of crackers similar to Julia's, see DeLand, *Florida Days*, 176–85. See also Denham, *Florida Historical Quarterly*.

10. Julia probably camped at what later became known as DeSoto Beach, at that time a beautiful pristine estuary on McKay Bay southeast of Tampa.

11. Efforts to identify this family using state and federal censuses, Hillsborough County property records, and the published and unpublished research of Julius Gordon have been unsuccessful. Isaac Berry was an African American who owned a farm not far from the Moseleys, but no record has been found of a son named Andrew to support the identification of this family as the one to which Julia referred.

See Gordon, *Afro-Americans of Hillsborough*.

12. Although the Moseleys cultivated extensive citrus and other fruit trees and undoubtedly had some vegetables among their dooryard plants, they did not

initially raise livestock. Julia's letters refer to the purchase of foodstuffs, including milk. When she mentions her garden in later letters, the plants she lists indicate a flower garden close to The Nest.

13. Julia gave no salutation for many of the letters she copied. While the identity of many recipients can be inferred, this is not true for all. Consequently, the editors have chosen not to alter Julia's text by suggesting probable salutations. Julia wrote that she was copying the letters to form a history for her children, so the content was more important than to whom the letter had been written.

14. Olive was a dear girlhood friend in Elgin.

15. Clementine Averill, the daughter of a prominent pioneer Milford, New Hampshire, family, was born in 1815. She settled in Valrico, about four miles east of Limona, during the Christmas season of 1878. She and two companions, Victor Woods and Mr. Gaskin(s), hoped to establish what Averill called a "reformers industrial cooperative home." She had lived in several Utopian communities but had found them unsatisfactory. As a younger woman she had worked in the mills in Lowell, Massachusetts. The mills provided dormitories and after-work activities that would have afforded Averill ample opportunity to develop her philosophy through discussions with coworkers.

Averill, who insisted that the Valrico home have a spiritual orientation, found her coworkers to be overly influenced by material considerations. Although she was a Socialist, she specified in her diary that she was not a Communist, as she believed Gaskin(s) and others to be.

Averill lived first in a tent and then in a cabin on the plot she had homesteaded. She wrote that the land had been cultivated for twenty-five years before her arrival. A portion of the plot must have remained wild, however, for in her diary Averill wrote of clearing it and doing much of the grubbing herself—very strenuous work for a woman her age. Within three months she and her partners were building a proper home.

Averill's diary reveals how the settlers routinely shared tools and plants and how they often bartered for foodstuffs and services. The diary also provides a fairly complete inventory of native plant and animal foods available and of what the settlers planted.

Once she had a semblance of a house, Averill supported herself by taking in boarders and overnight guests. When she managed to get paid, it was usually in bartered goods. She also sewed and quilted for the settlers, even tailoring men's suits. Her diary reveals a woman of prodigious energy and will.

Julia wrote that Averill wore bloomers. Pictures of women in the Oneida Colony, a group identified in the Moseleys' oral history with one of Averill's Utopian adventures, show that women's bloomers were not the full, gathered pants often associated with that term. Rather, the pants had a narrow cut and were worn with a tunic that reached the midcalf. The pants also had adherents outside the Utopian communities. Judge Magbee, the editor of the *Tampa*

Guardian and a neighbor of Averill, may have become convinced of their practicality by observing Averill. In his paper he urged the wider use of bloomers, even calling on the Women's Christian Temperance Union to add the pants to their agenda. Although Julia did not wear bloomers, she did wear shortened skirts.

Averill kept up a voluminous correspondence related to her industrial home, cataloging it in her diary. She also wrote articles and editorials about her plans for New England newspapers, including the *Milford Enterprise*, the Manchester, Massachusetts, *Union*, and the *Socialist*, the magazine published by the Oneida Colony.

See Clementine Averill diary; Milford, New Hampshire, Library collections; *Milford Enterprise*, June 25, 1878; *Tampa Guardian*, September 22, 1886; Klaw, *Without Sin*, various photographs.

16. George T. Chamberlain became a prominent Tampan, coming to Clearwater in 1877 and then moving first to Limona and later to Tampa. There he served on the Tampa City Council and the Board of Public Works. He bought and sold land as the owner of the Hillsborough Real Estate Company. He became known as the "Champion of Ybor City" because of his efforts as an officer of the Ybor City Land and Improvement Company. In 1901 in his Ybor City office he was murdered by an unknown assailant. A photograph of Chamberlain in the records of Tampa's Oaklawn Cemetery reflects style and urbanity and confirms Julia's descriptions of this young man, who was only two years her senior. Unmarried when Julia writes of him, he later married Julietta Harvey Casket.

See Clementine Averill diary; records of the Hillsborough County Clerk of the Court; Oaklawn Cemetery records in Tampa-Hillsborough Public Library Special Collections room.

17. The Russian was Theodore Frederic Nicholas Leontrieff-Weightnovel, at that time one of the Tampa area's most flamboyant residents. His origins are obscure. He claimed to have escaped from prison in Siberia, where he said he had been held for protesting against the czar. When he petitioned for citizenship in Tampa in 1886, he stated that he had resided in this country for thirteen years. Advertising his services as a physician on the front page of the *Tampa Guardian* (October 6, 1886), Weightnovel said he had lived in Hillsborough County, Florida, for seven years as well as in the "Northern States of America."

Clementine Averill recorded in her diary on July 13, 1878, that Weightnovel came to her home looking for a homestead, telling her he had walked to Valrico from Mellonville. That settlement in Seminole County, Florida, had been established around Fort Mellon at the southern end of the river-lake system on which steamboats transported passengers who had disembarked from ocean liners at Fernandina on the Florida-Georgia border. It was adjacent to the community that would be incorporated as Sanford. Travelers used the roadbed cleared for the railroad then under construction between that area and Tampa as a convenient pathway.

E. M. Rehbinder, who identified himself as a fellow Russian immigrant, was living in Fort Meade when he contributed to a 1957 article in the *Tampa Tribune* confirming that Weightnovel was part of a Russian colony in the Sanford area. Rehbinder asserted that Weightnovel's real name was Leontien and disputed Weightnovel's claim that he was a trained physician. Although the Sanford County Historical Museum has no records of a specific Russian colony, there may have been a number of Russian exiles among the three groups of Swedish workers contracted to work for Henry Sanford, who began to develop the area in 1870. Sanford advertised his planned city all over Europe, attracting both workers and settlers.

Weightnovel homesteaded in Valrico and purchased additional acreage in 1886 from Joseph Brooker, a well-known early settler in the Brandon area. The *Tampa Guardian* reported that Weightnovel had fenced many acres, removed tree stumps, and planted five acres of watermelon. He was quoted as saying that reports of a complete citrus kill following the 1885 freeze were exaggerated because he still had citrus alive and in bloom.

By all accounts, Weightnovel's appearance was impressive. He had a large stature, a massive chest, and commanding blue eyes. But his most striking features were his thick, shoulder-length, curly black hair and beard, to which Averill referred in her diary. A cultured man, he was said to have taken a front-row seat at every concert at the Tampa Bay Casino. Both Julia and Averill noted that he sang well and often. Julia was able to judge his mood as he approached through the woods by whether he was singing in a major or a minor key.

In his 1886 ad Weightnovel appended M.D. to his name, stating that he had received his degree in 1863 from the Russian Imperial Moscow University. He advertised that he had twenty-five years of practice in "general medicine in Russia, England, France, Germany," and the United States. His medical skills apparently enabled him to quickly build a practice in Tampa and its outskirts, and according to Averill he made his rounds on a large, gray mule. He told her of his plans to establish a hygienic home, which might work in concert with her reformers industrial home. In his ad he offered treatment "in his own place and residence—Homestead Humanity 'Felicity Home'." The ad went on to offer: "Obstetrics and Diseases of the Genital Organs, and Nervous System, of both Sexes, Special attention. Treatment personally or by correspondence. Uses all kinds of Chemical, Physical and Mechanical agents. Scientifically proved to be beneficial for restoration health, or prevention of disease."

Certainly Julia and her friends had confidence in Weightnovel's skills. During her illnesses and those of her children he remained at their bedsides, and Julia and Scott credited him with their recoveries. Later, others in the Tampa area raised questions about Weightnovel's credentials; however, the Florida

Board of Medical Examiners apparently discounted these questions, granting him a license in 1892.

Weightnovel made and sold patent remedies, drawing crowds to his presentations while floating on his back in the bay. He was so adept at floating that he could simultaneously read a newspaper, smoke, and even eat a meal.

Weightnovel organized the Free Love Society in Tampa. In 1885 he led a parade of members, on horseback and wearing emblematic sashes, through Tampa's Ybor City to a banquet at the Hotel de la Habana, which burned in 1905. The dining-room windows were open to passersby, who saw naked African-American waitresses presumably serving tea containing aphrodisiacs. The police were called to break up the meeting and the Society apparently disbanded shortly thereafter.

Averill wrote that Weightnovel tended to defend Communism in his discussions. It seems apparent that he had liberal beliefs, and he acted on them when Fort Brooke was deactivated. Squatters moved onto the property before other speculators, trying to gain control of the land that had been allocated to Dr. E. S. Carew. Weightnovel became one of their leaders, claiming homestead rights. He suggested that the group incorporate as the town of Moscow and apparently was either chosen or self-appointed as its mayor. The squatters then attempted to defend their municipality by forming a militia. Armed mainly with clubs, they were no match for the local authorities and soon abandoned the land where the fort had stood.

Although Julia and Scott and their friends safely relied on Weightnovel for medical care, others may not have been so fortunate. He apparently performed abortions and in 1902 one of his patients died, causing authorities to charge him with manslaughter. Convicted of this crime, Weightnovel was sentenced to six years of hard labor. He died in jail in 1906, either suffering what has been described as a stroke or committing suicide. He was buried at Tampa's Woodlawn Cemetery, with few mourners and without a religious service. The local paper commented, "It is said that with this old man died many secrets, which, made known, would shake the social fabric of Tampa." In both the 1905 and 1906 Tampa city directories he is listed as living in rooms at 809 Tampa Street, although he was almost certainly confined to jail at that time.

In her letters Julia chose to speak primarily of Weightnovel's positive attributes, crediting him with having cured family illnesses. But although she appreciated his colorful, vibrant personality, she also was aware of Weightnovel's less attractive qualities. A letter from Julia to Scott in October 1885 suggests that Scott may not have been as tolerant of the Russian as she.

As far as is known, Weightnovel had no family in Tampa, although he told Clementine Averill on his initial visit that he had three children.

See Hillsborough County Chancery Degrees, Book A, 144; Grismer, *History of Tampa*, 218; Clemmons, "Tampa's Free Love Apostle Was Ahead of His

Times," "Dr. Weightnovel, Who Claimed to Have Escaped from Siberia, Had Lurid Career;" Clementine Averill diary; Mormino, "Rasputin," 21–22; telephone interviews, Sanford County Historical Museum; Tampa city directories for 1905, 1906; *Tampa Guardian*, May 5, 1886, October 6, 1886; records of the Hillsborough County Clerk of the Court.

18. Julia probably did not intend for her words to be taken literally. However, health benefits due to the state's climate were being widely reported at the time. Lanier wrote that people took to undeveloped Florida's open air for the "rude life cure." The climate's efficacy for aiding recovery from respiratory illnesses was highlighted: Tampa was favored by consumptives. When Mrs. Henry Ward Beecher, wife of the famous American clergyman, visited Florida in the 1870s, she wrote that the great numbers of ill people there made her feel like she was in a "vast lazaretto." The Limona Park Association's promotional brochure emphasized Limona's curative powers by printing testimonials from formerly ill residents. Among them was Scott Moseley, to whom the brochure attributed "immediate and permanent relief" from his asthma.

See Limona Park Association brochure; Beecher, *Letters*, 71; Lanier, *Florida*, 100.

19. The area east of Tampa, including Limona, has a karst topography with many limestone sinkholes. These features produced a number of small lakes, including Ten Mile Lake where the Moseleys lived. The lakes made the area attractive to early citrus growers, who knew these bodies of water would help ameliorate temperature extremes.

20. This widely known hammock was Six Mile Creek Hammock, located along an unspoiled tidal river. The creek, which had a good sulphur spring near the railroad bridge, was favored as an excellent fishing and swimming spot well into this century. Its location six miles from the center of Tampa also made it a favorite campsite for caravans traveling inland.

21. The paroquets Julia saw were by then almost extinct, having been killed indiscriminately for their plumage. As recently as 1874 they had been distributed across the state and in many places were abundant. But by the early 1880s a sighting of six to twenty birds was rare enough that such a report immediately sent ornithologists off on a search. Unfortunately, one of the paroquets' behavior patterns contributed to their extermination. An injured bird would make loud outcries to recall its flock; when the other birds returned to surround the wounded member, they became easy targets for hunters.

See Austin, *Chapman in Florida*, 74; Howell, *Florida Bird Life*, 283.

22. Julia obviously spelled this word as she heard it. There is a similar-sounding, mildly impolite Russian word that refers to a woman of questionable character.

Chapter 3. Reaching Out to Cracker Neighbors

1. The two-room log cabin had once been used as a church before a new church structure was built on another site. That new church building became known as

New Hope and the log cabin was differentiated as Old Hope. New Hope lent its name to the community that would be formally named Brandon in 1890. A more complete description of the log cabin home, written a few years after the first home was destroyed by fire, is given in chapter 12.

Julia said the cabin stood on five acres. In fact, the Moseleys later were given an adjoining ten-acre plot owned by Julia's brother Pet, who had moved near the family while Scott was in the North. Pet's small house was surrounded by citrus he had planted. A hunchback, Pet devised ingenious ways of getting around that were much admired by family and friends. He left behind a paddle-wheel boat and a handcart on a wooden track leading from his house to the lake, both operated from a central seat.

See Moseley Collection; Dinnis, *The Early Days of New Hope Church*.

2. The sunsets the Moseleys saw during this period had been made more spectacular than usual by volcanic eruptions on the Indonesian island of Krakatoa in 1883. Volcanic clouds from Krakatoa circled the globe, producing an unusually vivid glow in the sky after sunset. This phenomenon continued well into 1884.

See Ley, *Dragons*, 295.

3. Edward Everett Hale's popularity began with his story of the man without a country in an 1863 issue of *Atlantic Monthly*. Many of Hale's pieces in that magazine were based on his letters. Julia also may have read one of his three travel books, in which he told of his journeys to experience art directly rather than relying on the descriptions and opinions of others.

Julia had a special fondness for the *Atlantic Monthly*. The Prestons, the grandparents in Aurora, Illinois, with whom she lived for two years (from age seven to age nine) to get a proper education, were charter subscribers to the magazine. Julia remembered being driven on long summer rides along the Fox River in her grandparents' carriage, her grandmother reading aloud from the magazine whenever the path was smooth. Since the first issue of the magazine was published while Julia was living with her grandparents, it is likely that her grandmother brought it to her attention.

See Florence Moseley Notes.

4. Julia referred to Weightnovel as both "the Russian" and "the doctor," but it is evident she is talking here about E. E. Pratt, who also practiced as a homeopathic physician.

5. W. H. Parker was a Methodist minister responsible for the Alafia Circuit, which probably included New Hope Church. In his letter, published in the June 8, 1882, edition of the *Sunland Tribune*, he described a church service attended by a crowd of three hundred people. This suggests that participants had been drawn from a wide area.

See Dinnis, 24–25.

6. McDonald (1824–1905) wrote *Castle Warlock*, which he called a homely romance. First published in England in 1881, the story was published in this

country soon thereafter under the title Julia uses. This is just one of many indications that she was able to keep up with the most current literature while relatively isolated in Limona.

7. Julia and Scott named each room of their home and called the whole The Nest. Earlier they had also called it Goose Nest. They called the home, including the property on which it stood, The Land of Timberly for its abundant trees— particularly the longleaf pines.

8. The boiling spring they could not find, to which Averill also referred, may have been Lithia Springs. Contemporary records describe it as having a 75-foot diameter and an average flow of 25 million gallons a day.

9. Julia notes that the Coes were generous with their books. The Moseleys also made their growing library available to friends and later to the community. Before a formal library existed in that part of the county, portions of the Moseleys' collection were transferred first to the United Brethren Church in Limona and later to the Woman's Club Building in Brandon.

10. *Century Magazine* absorbed *Scribner's Monthly* in 1881 and published many se- rials, short stories, and essays.

11. Because both *Harper's New Monthly Magazine* and *Harper's Weekly* were being published in the 1880s, it is impossible to know to which Julia referred.

12. Bella Wilfer, a character in Charles Dickens' *Our Mutual Friend*, was a spoiled beauty described as giddy and capricious. Lacking purpose, Bella was always fluttering from one thing to another. Allusions to her would have been logical when the girls were thinking of themselves as "such limited little beasts."

13. Scott's children by his first marriage were Florence, known as Frindy, and Claude. When the Moseleys first moved to Limona, these children remained behind with relatives until the family home was established.

Schooling was undoubtedly a serious consideration. Once Frindy and Claude were settled in Limona, Julia directed their studies by reading aloud to them and having them read to her. Both parents provided as many educational oppor- tunities as possible in Florida, and when Scott traveled north on extended busi- ness trips the younger boys accompanied him to attend regular classes there. Scott also was one of the founding shareholders of the Limona Academy of Arts, Letters and Sciences, established in 1882 by Judge Knapp, who donated the land. Two volunteer teachers served the academy's pupils: Georgia Mead, a niece of Judge Knapp, and Hettie Legate, the wife of Wilbur A. Legate, who first visited Limona in 1879. Hal and probably Claude attended their classes.

See *Tampa Tribune*, February 21, 1960, a clipping in the Limona file, Special Collections, Tampa-Hillsborough Public Library; records of the Hillsborough County Clerk of the Court's offices; Moseley Collection.

14. In their letters to each other, Julia and Eliza Slade often used pet names. "Your Barbara" is one of these.

15. Julia had good reason to worry about teamsters and other passersby when she

was alone, for the dirt road alongside the Moseleys' property was heavily traveled. Formerly an Indian trail, it was later used as a route for mail, troops, and supplies between Tampa's Fort Brooke and Fort Meade in the state's interior. For this reason it was sometimes called Government Road. Freight expresses—broad-wheeled, tarpaulin-covered wagons drawn by three or four yoked oxen—were used for this commerce. The road was also used for recreation. A prominent Tampa pioneer, Capt. John T. Lesley, described a high-stakes horse race in 1859. Race participants stopped to water their horses at the lake, even then called Ten Mile Lake because it was ten miles from Fort Brooke.

See Peeples, *Twenty-four Years*, 103.

16. Screech owls, among the smaller Florida owls, were prevalent around the lake; their distinctive cry is often described as mournful and almost human. John Muir, in his trek across Florida, called them the "noisiest of the unseen witnesses . . . who pronounced their gloomy speeches with profound emphasis."

See Muir, *Walk to Gulf*, 94.

17. Julia was now pregnant with her second child. Perhaps she was not ready to tell E.S. about the pregnancy. More likely, she had written to her friend already but did not choose to copy that letter.

18. Scott's father was Seth Moseley, a surveyor; Will was Scott's brother. The family had lived in Massachusetts since 1629, when John Moseley arrived from Lancashire, England, on the famous ship the *Mary & John*. The family settled in Dorchester, Massachusetts, but moved to Windsor, Connecticut, in the 1660s. The Moseleys then moved to Westfield, Massachusetts, in about 1677, becoming some of the town's founders. Most of the family still lived in Westfield in the 1880s; Julia writes later about her visits there.

See records of Westfield Historical Society.

19. Beginning in the seventeenth century the word *whist*, probably of Irish derivation, was used as a command for silence or as a noun meaning "silence." It also became the name of a popular card game. The room called the Whist played a key role in the Moseleys' life. Built during Julia's difficult second pregnancy, it was her refuge from the noise and confusion of the main household, which often swelled to as many as eight people when relatives were there. The Whist is depicted on the bookplate Carl later made for his mother and was the only room to escape the fire that destroyed the adjacent main house in 1885. It became the core of the rebuilt Nest.

Later Scott had his own retreat and workroom south of The Nest, called Old Shady for its overhanging trees. The Scrap, a small building west of Scott's workroom, was used for storage and for visiting relatives. When Claude entered his teens he was allowed to move into it. Later, as an adult Claude married New Englander Clara Burr Lake and built homes adjacent to Judge Knapp's and later The Nest. The couple were quite active in the Limona community's affairs, and Clara was a well-known music teacher in the area.

20. At one point the Limona Post Office was faced with closure. Florence Moseley remembered being told an official mail count for one month was done and showed that Julia was responsible for over two hundred of the letters handled. On the basis of this volume the Post Office survived. Upon learning this Julia said, "If I had known they were counting I would have written more."

Chapter 4. Rest and Quiet Save the Day

1. William Black's book, first published in 1883, was very popular and reprinted a number of times. Once again it is evident that Julia had access to the books and magazines cultured people were talking about.
2. Julia is in her Whist retreat.
3. Julia copied here the special birthday-party invitation Carl gave his father.
4. This is an obvious allusion to the coming baby.
5. The Moseley men rode with Mr. Chamberlain in some type of drawn vehicle. Settlers used horses and mules for transportation as well as for work on the land. The Moseleys never owned such animals and were inveterate walkers, both from necessity and for the sheer joy of tramping through the countryside.
6. At eighteen Scott Moseley began working as a machinist for George H. Fox in Boston. His first contact with the watch-making industry was in 1852, when he became a machinist with the Denison, Howard and Davis Watch Company in Roxbury, Massachusetts. Moseley moved with the company to Waltham, Massachusetts, later becoming shop foreman and master mechanic. From 1859 to 1864 he worked for the Nashua Watch Company in New Hampshire, designing and building the machinery that produced watch movements.

   After the Nashua Watch Company stopped production, Moseley moved to Elgin, Illinois, where a small group of entrepreneurs were establishing the Elgin Watch Company. He became the superintendent and developed the machinery and assembly procedures this company and most of the watch-making industry were to employ for the next forty years. Moseley remained in Elgin as plant manager until 1877, when he left to pursue other interests. He continued to serve the watch-making industry as a consultant for many years.

   Moseley and his brothers opened their own tool-manufacturing company in Elgin, producing machinery for precision work. Although particularly well suited to the watch-making industry, their tools had other applications as well. Moseley's most influential invention was the split-chuck lathe, an important development in the machine-tool industry. He later devised a smaller bench version known as the hollow-spindle lathe, which he put on the market in 1859. Not only was this new lathe lighter and easier to use, its tool bits could be changed more rapidly and its chucks were self-centering, reducing set-up time. Some of Moseley's other innovations included an interchangeable wind-stem mechanism and a dust excluder. In addition to watch-making inventions he devised a patent regulator, a time-stamp machine, and a machine that stamped out a variety of metal products such as globe valves from raw metal stock.

See *Elgin Daily Times*, November 16, 1904; *Dubuque Weekly Telegraph*, October 10, 1890; Abbott, *Watch Factories*, 127–28; Shiver, National Register nomination submission papers, 1984; and Moseley and Company's promotional brochures in the Moseley Collection.

7. "Vintage Festival" was painted by Laurenz Alma-Tadema (1836–1912). Born in Brussels, Tadema had gone to London in 1870, the year he painted the picture Julia loved. His wife and daughter were also well-known British watercolorists. When Julia described her visit to Lake Thonotosassa in one of the articles about Florida she wrote for the Elgin newspaper, she said that at the lake "all that was wanting was a marble seat with a high back and faultless curves" to make her think she was "living and breathing in one of Alma-Tadema's Italian pictures."

See "Florida in March" clipping, Moseley Collection.

8. Stained-glass windows by Edward Burne-Jones were sometimes placed high on interior home walls and called picture windows, as was done at Wightwick Manor near Wolverhampton, England. Julia was particularly attracted to Burne-Jones' art and may have been influenced by his high windows. Her painted window in the paneled room of The Nest may have been a simulation of the Burne-Jones stained glass she so admired.

The view through the first clear window by the chimney in the Little Heart was enough like a picture to have inspired Julia and Scott's name for it. In the 1950s similar large windows, also called picture windows but placed lower on the wall, became a popular feature of Florida homes. Scott and Julia were ahead of their time in this and other architectural innovations.

Julia's work was patterned after the pre-Raphaelites, who designed from nature only. Out of this short-lived movement grew the Arts and Crafts movement, influenced by pre-Raphaelites Edward Burne-Jones and William Morris in particular. In the mid-1800s Burne-Jones and Morris, both newly married and preoccupied with furniture and interior decoration, came to feel that artists such as themselves should be involved also in these "lesser" arts. Julia's saw-palmetto wall covering, her fiber arts, and her designs on wood are very reminiscent of the fabrics and wallpapers designed by these men and their disciples.

See Clark, *Arts and Crafts*, particularly plates 17, 24, and 43; also Naylor, *Arts and Crafts Movement*, 96–99.

Chapter 5. A Wild Story of a Wildcat

1. Sonnet VI of Elizabeth Barrett Browning's *Sonnets from the Portuguese*.
2. Scott and Julia named their new son, born July 6, 1883, Hallock Preston. Scott had waited until little Hal was a month old before leaving on business, taking Carl with him.

Later Hal joined the navy, becoming a chief petty officer. He was fortunate to be on the USS *New Yorker* when the fleet was sent around the world to showcase U.S. strength. During World War I he served in the merchant marine and later as an engineer on freighters in the Caribbean and off the west coast of Africa. In 1917 he married Ruby Winifred Davis.

3. Julia and Scott called each other by pet names, including Trix or Juliet for her and Jax for him.

4. This note is included where Julia later inserted it, at the bottom of a page of her copied letters. When Scott received the wildcat letter he failed to recognize the story as fantasy, although "Trix" makes the distinction clear in her last line. Concerned for his family's safety, he was about to abandon his business in the North to return to Limona; fortunately, fact was separated from fiction before he could depart.

    The wildcat Julia writes of is also called bobcat or *Lynx rufus;* it is common and well distributed throughout Florida and many other states.

5. John Bentley Dopp and his wife Martha were pioneer settlers who homesteaded land to the west and south of the Moseleys before the Limona Park Association bought land for development to the east. In those days, the Dopps' uncleared land held a hammock of significant size.

6. John and Mary Weeks were another pioneer couple living near the Moseleys. The Weeks and Dopp families were related.

7. Judge Henry Crane and his wife Mirabel lived in Tampa but also owned land near Limona.

8. Perhaps Julia became familiar with this French word meaning "God given" through its popular use as a sobriquet for Louis XV. The term was also a favorite of medieval poets.

9. Unfortunately, Julia destroyed all but a few of Scott's letters, preventing others from seeing either his intimate thoughts to her or his descriptions of his inventions. The few words she quoted in her letter of November 10, 1885, hint at the depth of feeling Scott expressed to her when they were apart.

10. The Moseley property, located ten miles from the center of Tampa, was a convenient rest stop for mule or ox teams. The teamsters drank from the well on the property, which gained a reputation not only for its convenient location but also for its fine water. The wagon teams were watered at the south end of the lake.

    See Florence Moseley Notes.

11. The South Florida Railroad, constructed between Tampa and Plant City in 1883, was the first to have stops close to The Nest (at Mango and Seffner). When the Florida Central and Peninsula Railroad was built in 1890, Limona, Brandon, and Valrico were among its regular stops. However, residents were also able to arrange for convenient individual stops between stations.

12. Author unknown.